T0248420

THE FRANCHISE

SAN FRANCISCO 49ERS

A Curated History of the Faithful

CAM INMAN

Library of Congress Cataloging-in-Publication Data

Names: Inman, Cam, author.
Title: The franchise San Francisco 49ers: a curated history of the faithful / Cam Inman.
Other titles: San Francisco 49ers
Description: Chicago: Triumph Books, 2024.
Identifiers: LCCN 2024020839 | ISBN 9781637276228 (hardcover)
Subjects: LCSH: San Francisco 49ers (Football team)—History. | BISAC: SPORTS & RECREATION / Football | TRAVEL / United States / West / Pacific (AK, CA, HI, OR, WA)
Classification: LCC GV956.S3 I66 2024 | DDC 796.332/640979461—dc23/eng/20240506
LC record available at https://lccn.loc.gov/2024020839

This book is available in quantity at special discounts for your group or organization. For further information, contact:

Triumph Books LLC
814 North Franklin Street
Chicago, Illinois 60610
(312) 337-0747
www.triumphbooks.com

Printed in U.S.A.
ISBN: 978-1-63727-622-8
Design by Preston Pisellini
Page production by Nord Compo

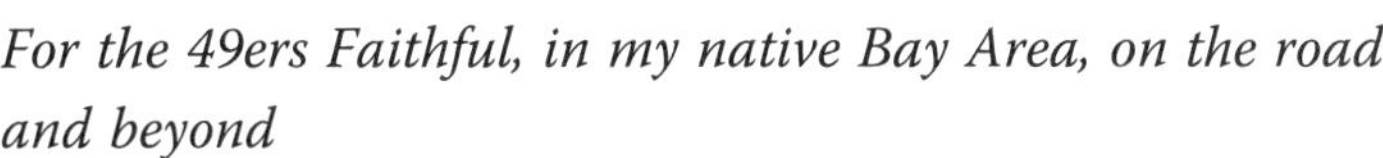

For the 49ers Faithful, in my native Bay Area, on the road and beyond

In memory of my mother, Irene Inman. Veni, vidi, vici

CONTENTS

Foreword

The San Francisco 49ers mean so much to me because they gave me an opportunity to do something I always wanted to do since I was a kid. The crazy thing about it, a lot of teams took me off their draft board just because of my injuries to my knees and shoulders. People were saying I wouldn't be in the league more than two or three years. Scot McCloughan talked to Dr. York and the family, and they gave the go-ahead to take me in the third round in 2005. That was big, man. For them to give me an opportunity when other people were taking me off the board and even the team doctor at the time gave me a red flag, that was everything.

I came here and took care of my business. They gave me a second contract and a third contract to be able to take care of my family. Every time I had a game in San Fran, Ms. York made sure she was at the locker room to see me. Jed and his mom, they still checked on me and made sure I was okay when I went to Indianapolis in 2015. When I played them in Indy, guess who came to the locker room? Denise. They really made me feel like they cared. It wasn't just business. She looked at me like I was one of her children. When I left the 49ers, she called me when I was a free agent. She knew I wasn't going to be on the team. She wished me the best. She told me to go win a Super Bowl. "You deserve that," she said.

At the time I didn't like it because I didn't want to go anywhere. I was comfortable. I had 10 years here. I still felt like I was playing well. I just had my eighth 1,000-yard season. The team wasn't doing well, but I still found a way to have success. I didn't want to leave. I was bitter, real bitter. I'm going to be real: I can never look at another franchise like I do the 49ers because that was my first team and I was there 10 years, but I was blessed to go to some good organizations and good people. Despite what team doctors were saying, the 49ers gave me the opportunity from the jump.

I was a 49ers fan when I was younger. They had the stars, especially that '94 team. They had Steve Young, Ricky Watters, Jerry Rice, Deion Sanders. They had everybody. They were winners. I never thought about becoming the 49ers' all-time leading rusher. My main goal was to make sure to let people know they made the right decision drafting me. And I felt like I did. It means everything to be their No. 1 rusher. There's a bunch of great football players in the 49ers' franchise history. When you think about the quarterbacks, Hall of Fame guys. When you think about the receivers, Hall of Fame guys. D-line, we just got one into the Hall of Fame with Bryant Young. Linebackers, we got another one in with Patrick Willis. And hopefully, one day, when people think about the 49ers, they'll think of my name, and hopefully I'll be a Hall of Famer.

There were great guys who paved the way before me with that franchise, and they're all featured in Cam Inman's book. For my name to be with Rice, Steve Young, Ronnie Lott, Bryant Young, Willis...there's so many people. Roger Craig was the first back to have 1,000 rushing and receiving yards in a season. To see my name amongst those guys and my name as the No. 1 guy at the position with the most rushing yards there, it's a blessing.

The year we went to the Super Bowl in 2012 was my signature moment. The reason why is because we went with the same guys who got drafted when we were real young, when we were the laughingstock of the NFL. Just to see us grow every year and get better and have a chance to show what we had in the locker room with the same guys, that was big to me. When you're a young team and you all get drafted at the same time, you look at them as your family. The core guys—like me, Willis, Vernon Davis, Alex Smith, Joe Staley, Dashon Goldson, Ray McDonald, and even Ahmad Brooks coming in—we were young. We were living on our own and all spent that time together like we were in college. We played tough, but we weren't winning. In 2011 we got a chance to go to the playoffs to show what we had. But to get an opportunity to show the world what we were about in 2012, to go to the Super Bowl, that was big. That's one moment and one season I love. If there was one man I know who cared about what I did and if I had a successful year, it was Staley. There was no quit in us.

Jed, Paraag Marathe, Denise, Dr. York, Kyle Shanahan, John Lynch, they're really good people. Now I want to learn how to evaluate talent and understand more than football. As a personnel advisor for the 49ers, I'll sit with Paraag, sit with Lynch. Kyle is a smart guy. From being around him, I know how he really understands and knows players so well. A lot of coaches aren't like that. He really knows football players, bro. He really knows what to look for. I like studying guys. And I like that when the front office challenges me and asks questions about what I think.

Lynch asks me certain questions when we watch film. "What do you think about this? What do you think about that?" But since I haven't been at it long, I want to respect those other guys in the personnel department. Just because I played ball doesn't mean I know everything. I'd rather let them ask me what I feel about something instead of just jumping in. That's their field, man. And now I'm going to try to keep getting better. As I work more and more with the new role, it has me thinking about the 49ers and their great history. And *The Franchise: San Francisco 49ers* captures the best of this historic team.

—Frank Gore

Foreword

I AM HONORED AND PRIVILEGED TO WRITE THIS FOREWORD for Cam Inman as part of his book, *The Franchise: San Francisco 49ers*. It is such a rich and powerful history and one that I am so very proud to be a part of and to have contributed to in my own small way. I'm in my eighth season in the NFL, and all of them have been with the 49ers, and for that all I can say is thank you and that I am grateful.

My time as part of this amazing and wonderful organization and franchise has been nothing short of living in a fairy tale and having (almost) all of my dreams come true. I was part of the teams that helped the 49ers get back into the win column and back into the playoffs. Since our turnaround after 2017–18, we have been a dominant force in the NFL and have continued to make deep playoff runs year after year. Obviously, one goal has still eluded us, and we will continue to fight for that. But being able to do this with other great players, coaches, and ownership who deeply care not only about winning, but also about their staff, players, and fans, has made it even more special. For an NFL player, being a part of the 49ers is about as special as it can get.

I dreamt about being in the NFL since I was a small child playing catch with my dad in the backyard. Throughout grade school, junior high, and high school, that dream never left me. Then in my senior year in high school in 2012—when I got a scholarship offer to attend the University of Iowa (the last one the school offered that year) and the opportunity to play football at a D-I school (where my dad also played)—I felt that this was my path of entry. And indeed it was. Playing at Iowa wasn't easy and it was a grind, but the dream never left me, and after all of that work, when the 2017 draft came around and I got the call from the 49ers, I was thrilled beyond words. I finally had the chance to make my dream into a reality. I had the chance to join this storied franchise and try to add my name to the list of great players who had played there and won championships. And that is when the dream really began.

When I stepped into the 49ers' door as a rookie, it immediately felt like family. The amount of care that everyone had for each other was everywhere. From the head coach and GM to players to equipment managers and the training room, it felt like one big family. That's what I came from and was used to, and it made me fall in love with this team, this franchise, this wonderful place they call the 49ers.

I could see every day how badly everyone in the building wanted to win, to be great. I could feel in everything that we did that we understood this is a franchise with five Super Bowl championships under its belt, and we're trying to add to that legacy. Another cool thing about when I first arrived was they made it a major point to show who the 49ers were, how the previous people sacrificed to bring them there, and how the city and their fans responded to it all. It was bigger and even more amazing than what I had thought, and I was so excited to be with them.

We were reminded very early on that we were all standing on the shoulders of legends—not just on the football field but off it as well. Everything that this organization does emanates winning and trying their best to do that. I've not had an experience other than that since playing with the Niners through my first seven years. Every single day when I walk into the building, that is what everyone is committed to: trying their best to win another Super Bowl. Another reason this has been an awesome experience for me is that they do a great job of letting players be themselves and not trying to fit them into a box of what they think a football player should be. They give you opportunities to express yourself both on the field and off. They let you speak up for whatever you want to talk about. Then they also have your back on the field. It's a fantastic organization that wants to win and approaches it with love and concern.

When I came on my pre-draft visit, it felt almost like everyone was overly friendly, but they were just being who they were, and it was really cool. Over my years here, it's just grown from there, and I know how fortunate I am because I've heard more than a few stories about what it's like elsewhere in the NFL, and it is not even close.

When I showed up for rookie minicamp, I went to my locker and saw that "SF" on the side of the gold helmet. That's a memory I will never forget because I saw that logo and was taken back to how storied of a franchise this is. It made me think of "The Catch," Joe Montana, Jerry Rice, and Ronnie Lott's sacrifice to cut off the tip of a finger to play. I thought of all these amazing plays, these talented and gifted players, the great teams, and the unbelievable coaches who came before me. It made that moment very surreal for me.

I love the game of football. I didn't grow up a 49ers fan by any means. I didn't watch 49ers games all the time. I kind of missed that era when they dominated. But the second I walked into that locker room and saw the logo, it hit me how awesome of an opportunity I had in front of me, and I knew in my heart that I would do anything and everything in my power to add to their story. My goal as a rookie was to make the team, whether that was practice squad or active roster. My teammates and coaches were incredibly helpful in getting me to where I'm at now. My focus each day was: what can I do today and how can I get better?

Every single day of training camp—when I walk from our cafeteria to the locker room—I go by our trophy case in our lobby. I also do this two or three times a week during the season. When I'm in the middle of training camp and about to head out for a 10th padded practice and am beat up, tired, and sore, I walk through there because it's a constant reminder: this is why I'm doing all of the work. This is why I wake up. This is why I do the extra rehab. This is why I go out to practice. This is why I'm dedicated to my craft. This is why my entire life revolves around working out and getting my body ready to play football. It's so that I, George Kittle, can add to this legacy. Seeing those trophies has been an inspiration to me in some of my toughest times. I am grateful to all those who have come before me and have laid the foundation for this franchise. I walk humbly amongst them and am grateful for the history they have handed to me to carry on.

I have a bunch of favorite victories. I had a blast against the New Orleans Saints in 2019. It was just an offensive explosion for both teams when many of our other games were more like street-fight slugfests. The Los Angeles Rams game after that was incredibly important to me because the day before was when C.J. Beathard's brother, Clayton, died. That game carried an emotional toll, and we bumped the Rams from playoff contention. Then came the Seattle Seahawks. To win that and clinch a first-round bye in the playoffs was so amazing. Then beating the Green Bay Packers was so fun as we ran the ball for more than 280 yards!

The 2021 season had some fun ones. Winning on the road against the Cincinnati Bengals was pretty sick, and we did it in overtime. In the playoffs that year, we went into Dallas and beat the Cowboys. Then we went into Green Bay and won against the Packers, even though that wasn't the prettiest first half of football you've ever seen. *Wooo,* I still had a good time, though. That was an old-school fistfight there, and when we finally won, it was an amazing experience. I still remember just looking around that historic field, seeing all of the disappointed fans, and thinking, *This is who we are and what we do.* I was so proud to be a part of that team.

The next year was crazy. We had Trey Lance, who got hurt. Then Jimmy Garoppolo got hurt. Then Brock Purdy got hurt. We won 12 straight that year. I will say that NFC Championship Game in Philadelphia is what made me realize that quarterback might indeed be the most important position in sports! You literally can't play the game without one. But we had some awesome wins like beating the Miami Dolphins with a third-string rookie at quarterback. It was fun in the playoffs beating Dallas again, and I made a catch off my facemask! And it was fun beating Seattle before that. I always love beating Seattle.

In my experiences the best places I've played were at Seattle and New Orleans. In that 2019 game against the Saints, I couldn't hear a single word anybody said the entire game. Yes, the game is about the players and coaches, but it isn't much fun without the awesome fans we play in front of each week. They make it special, and some of the venues we play in and their fans are just flat-out awesome. They bring the juice, and when the teams come together, it is such a blast. I am grateful for all of the fans throughout all of the NFL.

In 2023 we started off 5–0, and the Dallas game was a hoot. It was the night before my birthday, too. So it made it even better, and I had a bunch of friends in town. *Three touchdowns on my 30th birthday?* Hey, that's pretty convenient, isn't it? After that I had a lot of fun in the Jacksonville Jaguars game. I just like that stadium a lot. With the best pregame playlist and the pools up on the deck, it's like a Vegas party. That season's Super Bowl loss was probably a little tougher than the loss in 2019. The more games I play, the more I understand how hard it is to get back—let alone win it. So getting there and not winning is even more difficult. But that is the stuff life (and football) are made of. So all you can do is learn, grow, and keep on going.

I do know the 49ers Faithful are the best fans in sports. Now I don't play soccer in Europe, so I can't attest to that, but from what I've seen and how the Faithful travel with us, cheer for us, mourn for us, have fun with us, they're just fantastic. They're passionate about the team and they love the game. They love sharing those experiences with their kids. The number of complete families I see on the road and at our home stadium is awesome and inspiring. They're introducing the game I love to their families and passing it down through the generations. Every single away stadium we go into, if you give them an inch, they'll take a mile, and they'll buy up all the seats. In 2017 when we were in Houston and Jimmy G was the quarterback, they were like 60 percent of the Texans' stadium. *Holy cow,* I had never seen anything like it. That was just the standard, and it kept going. They're always there, always loud, always proud, and always having a great time. In each road game, I will feel their energy and how much they love the game and us as players.

I do wish I had the opportunity to play in Candlestick Park just to feel that buzz throughout the city. But I do know whenever I pull into a game, there are already a couple of thousand 49ers Faithful there tailgating and waiting for us. And I know it's going to be another great day being a San Francisco 49er. It has been a dream come true, and I am looking for more as I have some dreams left that have not been fulfilled and I am doing everything in my power to make them happen. Just as I enjoy so much being a part of the 49ers history, I am grateful for this rendition and retelling of that history and know you will love reading this book. Bang-Bang, Niner Gang! Let's go get another one!

—George Kittle

PART 1

QUARTERBACKS

1

Joe Cool

Joe Montana's name was kept out of Bill Walsh's mouth as he listed off his three best draft picks of all time. Jerry Rice was a lock as the NFL's most prolific receiver ever. Dwight Clark earned his spot with "The Catch" that launched the San Francisco 49ers' 1980s dynasty. Walsh reserved a nod for Michael Carter, an Olympic shot putter turned All-Pro nose tackle.

Wait, what about Joe? You know, Joe Montana, who merely quarterbacked the 49ers to their first four Super Bowl triumphs? "Joe goes without saying. What the heck! Of course he's in there," Walsh replied in 2004, three years before he passed away at age 75. "Joe's the franchise. There's never a question."

Montana reset the standard for 49ers quarterbacks, for all NFL quarterbacks, for all NFL teams. His ring collection ruled for a generation, eventually surpassed by Tom Brady, a Bay Area native who sat in Candlestick Park's stands as a 49ers-cheering kid during "The Catch." "Joe, of all people in the history of this franchise, is the central figure," Walsh said. "He was just the franchise. Joe made it all work. Hell, he's the greatest player in history."

The 49ers' world revolves around quarterbacks. It did before Montana's 1979 arrival and it hasn't dared stop since his numbing exit in a 1993 trade to the Kansas City Chiefs. And it's all about adding to the Super Bowl legacy he launched. "Every year you come in, if you're not expecting to go to the Super Bowl, something is wrong, especially when you have a team like the 49ers have," Montana said when he returned for an October 2022 game on alumni weekend at Levi's Stadium. "It's an everyday occurrence. It's what we play for every year. People say, 'Well, you've won one, why do you need another one?' I say, 'Ever seen a kid with candy that's never had candy? Give him a piece and what does he want?' All he wants is candy. It's the same as the Super Bowl...Once you win, that's all you want to do. We never lost one. So, to get there and lose, I'm sure it makes you a little more hungry than normal. That's what you play for every year."

Montana worked his magic with late-game comebacks and Super Bowl perfection—four wins in four championship games in which he had 11 touchdown passes and no interceptions. Any recitation of Montana's Pro Football Hall of Fame career will list off the customary accolades: four-time Super Bowl champ, three-time Super Bowl MVP, back-to-back NFL MVP, eight-time Pro Bowler, two-time passer rating leader, five-time completion percentage leader, and, in "Joe Cool" fashion, 31 fourth-quarter comeback wins. "There wasn't any way of predicting how great Joe would be," Walsh said. "We knew he'd be very good, but how can you quantify one of the greatest players of all time? You just don't know that until it happens."

On May 3, 1979, Montana made his entry into the NFL. He did so from The Kettle, a corner restaurant just up from the Manhattan Beach pier in the heart of Southern California paradise. That's where Montana dined and waited until with the last pick of the 1979 NFL Draft's third round, the 49ers selected him No. 82 overall. "They got word to us, and I was excited. I was glad," Montana recalled back in 2004. "It was a great opportunity coming to a great city, and they had a Notre Dame owner."

Eddie DeBartolo Jr. was a Domer, but his 49ers also had a reputation as the worst team in football, to which Montana countered: "That will change. They won't be the worst forever."

Days before the draft, Walsh and then-quarterbacks coach Sam Wyche traveled down the California coast for a follow-up workout with Montana not long after visiting Phil Simms in the Appalachian mountains. "They were putting me through different footwork and watching me throw different passes," Montana said. "You get a reputation you don't have a strong enough arm...I did a lot of things he liked. I didn't throw the ball as hard as I could every play, but I made difficult passes he wanted me to throw."

Walsh saw Joe Namath-like quickness, agility, and fluid movements. After he and fellow 49ers brass surveyed the NFL, they correctly surmised they could wait until the third round to select Montana as Steve DeBerg's eventual successor. "There wasn't any question when Sam and I got on the plane to come back [from Los Angeles] that Joe was in our plans," Walsh said. "Now it was when can we draft him? Our team was in desperate need of virtually every position."

Pick No. 82 originally belonged to the Dallas Cowboys before it was shipped to the Seattle Seahawks, who then swapped it with safety Bob Jury for the 49ers' original third-round pick.

"Joe was there in the third round just as Bill said he would be," Wyche recalled, "another mark of genius."

Brian Billick was a 49ers public relations assistant before becoming a Super Bowl-winning coach with the Baltimore Ravens. "Bill saw more in Joe than a lot of people did," Billick said. "When I went to pick him up [at the airport], I wasn't picking up some slappy, third-round draft choice. There was a quality about Joe, even then. There was a calmness in Joe's eyes you didn't typically see as a rookie."

Walsh never forgot what he saw from Montana in his second season, specifically in a 1980 start at Detroit and on a pass to Charle Young on a slant route. "Joe threw the ball into the stands. I don't mean over Charle's head. That ball went up in the stands," Walsh recalled. "It slipped out of Joe's hands because he was nervous or something. Point being: it was a work in progress with Joe."

A month later Montana delivered the first of 26 fourth-quarter comeback wins in regular-season action—a 38–35 triumph over against the New Orleans Saints at Candlestick Park. His first playoff win was even more dubious: a 28–27 comeback against the Cowboys on January 10, 1982 in the NFC Championship Game. Yes, this was when No. 16 rolled 16 steps to his right, moved away from three onrushing defenders, and then lobbed a six-yard, last-minute touchdown pass to, of course, Clark, who soared to make "The Catch" in the back right corner of Candlestick's north end zone.

That comeback was rivaled only by Montana's game-winning drive to win Super Bowl XXIII, where his last-minute touchdown pass to John Taylor capped a 92-yard, 11-play drive and beat the Cincinnati Bengals 20–16 in Miami.

Rings Nos. 3 and 4 could not quell the quarterback controversy that raged once Steve Young arrived in a 1987 trade from the Tampa Bay Buccaneers. Back and elbow injuries eventually doomed Montana's tenure. Decades later in an ESPN expose, Montana mourned his exit, saying he struggled to understand the whole process and going so far as to say he never should have had to leave town. Montana wanted to keep competing for the throne he made so sacred. The truth is every quarterback to wear the scarlet and gold after him will never challenge his stature, even though the degree of difficulty is much easier with the NFL's increasingly pass-friendly rules.

Although more and more teams deploy three, four, and five receivers, Montana knew how valuable his running backs were in Walsh's West Coast Offense. "A lot of the times in that style of the offense, you use your passing game as part of the running game," Montana said in 2022. "From back when Bill [Walsh] started this phenomenon, so to speak, we had some good running backs, but we didn't have great running backs at the beginning. So you had to catch the ball coming out of the backfield. They were part of the passing game—them and tight ends. Bill would say, 'If you don't like what I'm going to give you down the field, I'm going to give you a couple other guys and you don't need to force it on first down.' If you hand off on first down and gain four yards, [the defense says]: 'You can't give up four yards on a run!' Then you drop back to pass, nobody's open, you drop it underneath, the guy gains four yards. They think they've stopped you. Same four yards, right? Next thing you know you're inside their 20, and they're trying to figure out how you got there. It's an understanding of the offense, how it works, and how to use the guys underneath, as much as trying to force it down the field."

One such next-generation quarterback who's proven that on the way to multiple Super Bowl wins is Patrick Mahomes, who has won two Lombardi Trophies in comebacks against the 49ers in Super Bowl LIV and LVIII. "He's too crazy fun to watch. I mean, the guy does everything you tell every quarterback you can't do or don't do," Montana said. "He does all of it and does it well. 'Don't go off the back foot, don't go this way, don't go sidearm, don't go late down the middle.' He is one of the most talented guys you'll see in that position. He can run the ball, too, but that's not what Patrick is really about. He loves delivering the ball down the field. He has a bunch of weapons to do it with. As they let guys go and guys come in, he makes the transition pretty quickly."

Three decades earlier, Montana's legacy made its own transition from the 49ers to the Chiefs. He's as beloved as ever by the 49ers Faithful when he makes an annual visit to Levi's Stadium. He'll stride in with his wife, Jennifer, wave from the field during pregame warmups, and draw ovations befitting such franchise royalty. "We won four Super Bowls with Joe and we could have very well won a fifth," Walsh said. "We'd have won a Super Bowl along the way without him. I don't know who it would have been or when, but we put together a really good team. It could have been someone else, but never another Joe."

2

Steve Young

THE COOLEST THING STEVE YOUNG DID ON HIS WAY TO becoming the Pro Football Hall of Fame's first left-handed quarterback was...well, there's no shortage of options.

- Like throwing a Super Bowl-record six touchdown passes before hugging the San Francisco 49ers' fifth Lombardi Trophy.
- Like zig-zagging past Minnesota Vikings defenders and staggering across the goal line.
- Like waiting in Joe Montana's shadow after dark days with the Tampa Bay Buccaneers and the United States Football League's Los Angeles Express.
- Like joyously taking a Candlestick Park victory lap after dethroning the two-time reigning champion Dallas Cowboys in the 1994 season's NFC Championship Game.

- Like getting his just due as a league MVP (twice), All-Pro (thrice), Pro Bowler (seven times), and team leader (Len Eshmont Award in 1992 and '94).

The coolest thing about his road to Canton, Ohio, however, was that he first made it there at age 12, when that wishbone quarterback from Greenwich, Connecticut, convinced his parents, LeGrande "Grit" and Sherry, to take a family vacation to football's most cherished museum. "I was for it. The rest of the family voted against it, but we actually went," Grit said. "He wanted to go and he seemed to really like it. Then we went to Hershey's in Pennsylvania to satisfy the other children."

Satisfying the 49ers Faithful would prove a much tougher chore, even though he was enshrined in the Pro Football Hall of Fame in 2005—at age 43—as the NFL's highest-rated passer over his 15-year career. All it took for the 49ers to free him from terrible Tampa Bay in 1987 were second- and fourth-round draft picks plus $1 million from ever-generous Eddie DeBartolo Jr.'s bankroll. "I blame the rest of the NFL for not moving quickly and trading for him. But they had doubts about him actually making it as an NFL quarterback," Bill Walsh said.

Young arrived under the illusion that Montana's back was shot. Instead, Montana produced back-to-back Super Bowl wins (in the 1988 and 1989 seasons), won back-to-back NFL MVP honors, and the NFL's ultimate quarterback controversy raged on year after year. "Watching Joe play and how he prepared," Young said, "it was so beyond anything I've seen before."

It took Young a full year to learn Walsh's offense, but he did so with a familiar tutor in quarterbacks coach Mike Holmgren, who held that same role at BYU as Young rose from No. 8 in the Cougars' depth chart. "Coaching Joe Montana and Steve Young at the same time was one of the great challenges of my coaching career," Holmgren said, "because we would have a meeting, and after everyone left, Joe would come in, 'You know you're spending a little too much time [with Young]. I know he babysat for your kids.' Steve would come in 20 minutes later, 'What happened? You used to coach me. You're not coaching me anymore.' Steve was a perfectionist and very much a runner until he developed the idea of throwing the ball and using the whole offense instead of just getting out of trouble running. Then he became a Hall of Fame player."

But for four years, he toiled in Montana's shadow, aside from the occasional start or relief appearance. "When Joe was hurt, he's sitting on the sideline, and every mistake you make, everyone turns and says, 'Well, Joe wouldn't do that,'" Young said. "It can drive you crazy or it's super important you see the truth: that this is an incredible opportunity so don't get distracted by all the noise, the whispers in the locker room, the issues with the media, the boos you start to hear after a couple of picks."

Exercising discipline over distractions was vital to Young's survival, as it is to any quarterback competition. "Most laymen see the situation and go, 'Oh! Trouble! Trouble! I don't want that guy spying on me, talking behind my back,'" Young said. "Laymen would say it's a disaster. When the truth is if you really step back, it's an incredible opportunity."

Young essentially assumed the starting role in 1991. He annually produced the NFL's best passer rating from 1991 to 1997 (except in 1995 when he still made All-Pro and the Pro Bowl teams). Regular-season stats meant little to a 49ers fan-base, though, that demanded Market Street parades to end seasons.

The Cowboys were Young and the 49ers' postseason kryptonite. They lost to them in the 1992 and 1993 NFC

Championship Games. Then came 1994. None of Young's 87 playoff passes got intercepted, and he pulled off a touchdown run in wins against the Chicago Bears 44–15 and, at long last, the Cowboys 38–28. "We were in a state where the context is hard to imagine, where if you lose the Super Bowl, you need to leave town," Young said. "It was: enough of this. We had a three-peat of championship games. It was elation [to win the 1994 NFC Championship Game]. But it was a relief as well. It had to get done. I'm grateful it worked out. I don't want to think the other way. We screwed up in '92, didn't realize how good [the Cowboys] were going to get. And they were good. Beating the [1994] Cowboys at their peak, that was the best team we beat in the best moment."

Young opened Super Bowl XXIX with a 44-yard touchdown strike to Jerry Rice on their third snap. Once Young finished his six-touchdown masterpiece against the San Diego Chargers, he famously begged teammates to take the proverbial monkey off his back, a move he later regretted for how that sound bite seized the spotlight away from a complete-team win. "My favorite moment still was the five minutes after the Super Bowl when we were alone in the locker room," Young said in his Hall of Fame speech on August 7, 2005. "Just the 50 players and coaches kneeling in the Lord's Prayer, then looking up at each other and realizing that, yes, we were world champions. No media, no one, just us. That feeling when you do something great together is like no other. No MVP or passing title can compare to that feeling."

Young recaptured that feeling in the fall of 2023. For the first time in his life, he found himself coaching his kids and he did so in the sport he forever cherishes: football. Only this version was girls flag football, which enjoyed tremendous popularity and success only months after its approval by the

California Interscholastic Federation. Former 49ers quarterback John Paye asked Young to assist with Menlo School's inaugural team, and that allowed Young the chance to not only share his insights, but also rewarded him with quality time as a girl dad to Summer, a senior who wore her dad's No. 8 as a wide receiver, and Laila, a freshman who was moonlighting as a competitive dancer. "It was so much fun. I didn't expect it. I only went over there to help out. I didn't know what I was going to do," Young said. "There was just something about the girls' earnestness and asking me how to throw a ball and then watching them get better every day."

He admired their inclusion, excitement, and love of learning a totally foreign sport. He estimated that 90 percent of the girls couldn't name a favorite NFL team or player before the season. By the end of it, they'd met NFL commissioner Roger Goodell, attended a 49ers game, and finished their 15–1 season on a 15-game win streak. "Football at its roots, especially offensive football, is choreography. They loved that analogy: 'Oh, it's a dance step,'" Young said. "Everyone, just do your part of the dance, and someone will come open. Once they realized that, they quit roaming around. It was, 'Oh yeah, I get that.'"

One of Young's favorite memories with those Menlo pioneers was a role-reversal scenario from his 49ers infancy under Walsh. One of the Menlo's quarterbacks chucked what Young called a "hairball throw," presumably like a cat gagging, prompting the following dialogue:

Young: "Why did you do that?"

Quarterback: "Well, it was a pass play."

Young: "You know you don't have to pass it on a pass play."

Quarterback: "You don't? Oh, I'm so relieved. It's so hard to think about throwing it every time."

Young went from a mad-scrambling quarterback to one of the NFL's most efficient pocket passers of all time, and that ensured his trek to Canton's hallowed Hall of Fame.

On the eve of his Pro Football Hall of Fame induction in 2005, he acknowledged that Super Bowls—for better or for worst—are "career-makers." He made sure to note, however, that is reliant on a supporting cast. He enjoyed that with the 49ers. And he passed that on decades later as a Menlo assistant coach.

3

John Brodie

As generations pass by, as quarterbacks come and go, John Brodie's spot in San Francisco 49ers lore remains unvanquished. That's not just because he was the National Football League's Most Valuable Player in 1970, the modern era's first season since merging with the American Football League.

Brodie's staying power is unrivaled among the 49ers. He played a franchise-record 17 seasons with them from 1957 to 1973. His presence was cherished anytime he attended 49ers events in the ensuing decades even after a 2000 stroke. Before Joe Montana and Steve Young decorated the 49ers' lobby with the Lombardi Trophy five times over, Brodie delivered their first NFC West title in 1970, then their second in '71, and their third in '72.

No Super Bowls ensued—not after the Dallas Cowboys ended their 1970–72 postseasons—but you know what did come of Brodie's efforts? Repeated attempts by teammates and fans to try getting him elected to the Pro Football Hall of Fame.

In 2006 Brodie gave his blessing for his No. 12 jersey to come out of retirement for Trent Dilfer, a longtime pal, golfing buddy, and friend of Brodie's son-in-law, Chris Chandler. "I really believe John should be in the Hall of Fame, and hopefully this will create some awareness of his career and how spectacular it was," said Dilfer, who spent 2006–07 as Alex Smith's backup on the 49ers.

As a seniors committee candidate in 2015, Brodie reunited with teammates at Kezar Stadium in their push to get him to Canton, Ohio. The San Francisco Chamber of Commerce even bestowed an endorsement letter to a Hall of Fame representative there. Instead, Ken Stabler and Dick Stanfel were the seniors' nominees, and joining them in the Class of 2016 was ex-49ers owner Eddie DeBartolo. Before Brodie's final season in 1973, he not only paid his first visit to the Pro Football Hall of Fame, he also did a television commercial encouraging "every football fan" to visit.

A statue of Brodie, dropping back to pass and gazing upward, resides in a corner of the 49ers' Edward J. DeBartolo Sr. Hall of Fame, located on the north side of Levi's Stadium. He's not the center attraction, but he earned his spot there. He soldiered through four coaches (Frankie Albert, Red Hickey, Jack Christiansen, Dick Nolan) and he endured jeers from home fans whether at Kezar Stadium or Candlestick Park. Amid that stadium switch in 1971, Brodie and the 49ers enjoyed their greatest run, and he pulled it off in the twilight of his career.

Can you imagine in this day and age, a No. 3 overall draft pick (see: Trey Lance) afforded 14 years to deliver his first division title and playoff victory? Brodie did it and he did so with another No. 3 overall draft pick (Steve Spurrier in 1967) waiting in the wings.

Technically, Brodie succeeded a Pro Football Hall of Famer, though Y.A. Tittle didn't rise to prominence until the 49ers unloaded him to the New York Giants in 1961 (for guard Lou Cordileone). Tittle arrived in 1951, waited his 49ers' turn behind Albert, made four Pro Bowls, and then Hickey committed in 1961 to the more athletic and agile Brodie to run his novel "shotgun formation."

Brodie served as a leader through the worst of times and, eventually, in great times. He lost more than he won as a starter (74–76–8), and more passes went for interceptions (224) than touchdowns (214). He also won the NFL's passing title en route to 1970 MVP honors with a NFL-best 2,941 yards and 24 touchdowns. That 1970 regular season ended with Brodie leading the 49ers to a 38–7 win at the Oakland Raiders just down the hill from his childhood home in Montclair and his three-sport days at Oakland Tech High School. "I've had some other years that weren't bad, but I felt I threw as well this year as any," Brodie said of that 1970 season, coinciding with the 25th anniversary of the 49ers' existence.

Then came the NFC playoffs. The 49ers opened with a 17–14 win at top-seeded Minnesota, which he anointed his favorite game. He not only passed well (201 yards, one touchdown, no interceptions), but his fourth-quarter touchdown run provided the eventual winning points against the Vikings. Alas, the 49ers fell 17–10 in the ensuing 1970 NFC Championship Game to the Cowboys, who again finished off the 49ers in the next two postseasons. The 1971 campaign saw Brodie throw three interceptions in a 14–3 loss at Texas Stadium to the eventual Super Bowl VI champs. In 1972 Brodie came off the bench against Minnesota to get the 49ers back into the playoffs, but that run ended with a 30–28 divisional loss to Dallas, as Roger Staubach produced 17 unanswered points in the fourth quarter.

Staubach, by the way, wore No. 12, like Brodie, who had it first and was at the forefront of a procession of elite quarterbacks to don that number. Others in his wake: Joe Namath (New York Jets), Bob Griese (Miami Dolphins), Roger Staubach (Cowboys), Terry Bradshaw (Pittsburgh Steelers), Ken Stabler (Raiders), Jim Kelly (Buffalo Bills), Tom Brady (New England Patriots, Tampa Bay Buccaneers), and Aaron Rodgers (Green Bay Packers).

Brodie's NFL influence carried over to the Bill Walsh era. Brodie was a Stanford star, and the Menlo Park native would pop in on The Farm to talk quarterback shop with Walsh before he took over the 49ers in 1979 and presided over the franchise's Super Bowl-winning dynasty.

4

Jeff Garcia

As the San Francisco 49ers approached 20 years without a Pro Bowl quarterback, Jeff Garcia reflected on what molded him into that role from 2000 to 2002. Actually, he pondered how much greater his tenure could have gone. Pro Bowl honors, after all, are simply part of the job description when you follow the Hall of Fame footsteps of Steve Young and Joe Montana. And Garcia indeed blossomed from Canadian Football League refugee to a three-time Pro Bowler.

"Even though I had a long career and it was successful, I think what could I have done differently, how could I have had a different approach," Garcia said in a spring 2021 interview. "Players today are more knowledgeable about health and taking care of bodies and what they have access...from the standpoint of technology, they're able to watch film from home, things we didn't have access to."

That edge to constantly improve is what propelled Garcia through five seasons wearing the No. 5 jersey on the 49ers. Few, if any, got more out of a chip on their shoulders than this local-boy-makes-good quarterback. Two decades later, it should be no surprise he feels his career could have been so much better if he enjoyed the luxuries afforded to today's quarterbacks in a more offense-friendly NFL.

Garcia, a Gilroy, California, native, took a circuitous route to the 49ers. He morphed from San Jose State redshirt into a three-year star who passed for 6,545 yards, ran for 729 yards, and scored 48 touchdowns. Garcia started his professional career in Canada with the Calgary Stampeders and he led them to the 1998 Grey Cup championship. Then a fellow San Jose State product named Bill Walsh convinced the 49ers they should take a chance on Garcia. "I had to sell Garcia to the coaching staff and I was the general manager," Bill Walsh recalled in a 2004 interview. "The only way was that he'd be an interesting backup. They wouldn't buy the idea he'd be a potential starter, even though I thought he was."

Once Steve Young retired, Garcia became the full-time starter in 2000, but he got benched for Rick Mirer in a Week Two blowout loss to the Carolina Panthers before a clamoring crowd at 3Com Park. "All of a sudden, controversies were sparked up, and I didn't like to have to deal with that sort of situation," Garcia said a month later. "I just wanted to take it upon myself to try to do anything I could to make myself a better player on the field."

Garcia won just two of 13 starts before morphing into a three-time Pro Bowl quarterback in 2000–02. He not only played with a fiery edge, but he also battled through injuries like a 2001 cracked rib that still protrudes from his chest 20 years later. Garcia became the first-ever 49ers quarterback to throw

30 touchdowns in back-to-back seasons, and those three straight Pro Bowls came in his first as a full-time starter.

On January 5, 2003, Garcia engineered what was then the NFL's second greatest comeback in playoff history. The 49ers erased a 24-point deficit in the final 20 minutes as he threw two touchdown passes and ran for a score in that 39–38 triumph against the New York Giants at 3Com Park. "I knew before the snap where I was going with that football," said Garcia, who found Tai Streets for a 13-yard, game-winning touchdown pass with a minute to spare.

"This ranks right up there with our top victories," Walsh said in the 49ers' winning locker room.

It marked the 49ers' first playoff win in four years since Terrell Owens caught a 25-yard touchdown pass from Young with eight seconds left—also in Candlestick Park's south end zone—for a 30–27 home victory against the Green Bay Packers. "When T.O. caught that pass from Steve Young, we weren't down 24. So that makes this more enjoyable and fascinating," 49ers coach Steve Mariucci said after the comeback against the Giants.

A year later Garcia was released—more so because of the 49ers' 2004 salary-cap crunch rather than a highly publicized arrest for drunken driving, to which he pled guilty two weeks after the 49ers cut him. Garcia spent only five seasons with his hometown team, but that was enough to produce the fourth best passing numbers behind Montana, Young, and John Brodie: 16,408 yards, 1,449 completions, 2,360 attempts, 113 touchdowns.

That built up enough respect around the league that Garcia would be a wanted man elsewhere: 2004 Cleveland Browns, 2005 Detroit Lions, 2006 Philadelphia Eagles, 2007–08 Tampa Bay Buccaneers, 2009 Oakland Raiders, 2009 Eagles, 2010

Omaha Nighthawks of the United Football League, and 2011 Houston Texans. The latter club brought him in as an inactive, third-string quarterback for their final four games. The Raiders brought him in to try to push No. 1 draft bust JaMarcus Russell. Garcia was gone before the season began after posting a 67.1 passer rating in the preseason and prompting "concerned season-ticket holders" take out newspaper ads pleading for his release. *Raider Nation hating on an ex-49er? Never!*

After his playing days, Garcia went on to dabble in coaching and broadcasting, making use of all his knowledge from that decade-plus in the NFL—not to mention being the son of former Gavilan College coach Bob Garcia. Taking notes was a staple of his career to help a gritty underdog prove his mettle. "I'd write down everything as a repetitive reminder," Garcia said, "how I handled the ball off, carried out bootlegs, my fake. It was all part of my studying."

Looking back, decades later, Garcia could still recite how Walsh shaped his offensive schemes, saying: "There was a method to the madness of what feet would do according to routes and depth...It's all eyes and feet. Eyes lead feet, and feet lead your arm."

In today's pass-happy NFL, the need to hit receivers in stride is critical. Quarterbacks throw to the open window rather than wait for receivers to break free. "These guys today, the arm strength on some of these guys, it's remarkable," Garcia said. "Everything is based upon timing. When you think of what guys can do playing within the system and a go route, there's a sweet spot. This was emphasized years ago by Walsh."

5

Alex Smith

THE 2005 NFL DRAFT WAS UNDERWAY IN MANHATTAN. ALEX Smith, the No. 1 overall pick, was escorted into a dimly lit corridor beneath the Jacob K. Javits Convention Center crowd. Awaiting him were a few reporters who traveled from the Bay Area for the launch of Smith's uniquely long and twisted San Francisco 49ers career.

Smith was addressed as if he was an innocent victim at a crime scene rather than a Gotham superhero coming to the rescue. He was warned how barren the 49ers' roster was. He had no choice but to accept this impossible mission, the reward for winning coach Mike Nolan's approval over uber-confident Aaron Rodgers as the No. 1 pick. "Obviously, you need people around you," Smith said on Day One as a Niner. "With time and experience, absolutely I can carry more of a load on my shoulders, carry a team, and get a lot done."

Smith, just 20, noted he was "still young," and that "it's not a one-man show." How he lasted eight seasons is a story of turbulence, triumph, and tough breaks. How he spent eight more seasons in the NFL—in Kansas City and Washington—is a testament to his resilience, determination, and professionalism, all of which culminated with him recovering from a life-threatening leg infection to exit the NFL stage as its Comeback Player of the Year in 2020 with the Washington Football Team.

On his first NFL team, Smith played under four 49ers head coaches, including Jim Tomsula's interim stint in the 2010 finale, which could have been Smith's finale if Jim Harbaugh had not convinced him to return in 2011 for a career reboot. The 49ers saw a roulette of seven offensive coordinators in Smith's eight seasons—to say nothing of the supporting cast that was built from the ground up and into a playoff contender—just in time for him to engineer one of the most thrilling playoff victories in franchise history.

That 36–32, divisional-round playoff win had Candlestick Park rocking on January 14, 2012, when the 49ers and the New Orleans Saints traded two touchdowns apiece in the final four minutes, including Smith's 28-yard, bootleg run behind lead blocker Joe Staley with 2:11 remaining and Smith's 14-yard, game-winning touchdown bullet to Vernon Davis with nine seconds to spare. "It might have been 100 miles per hour," Davis said of Smith's velocity. "It was just like practice. He pushed up 12 or 15 yards, I snapped my head around, and the ball was there, just like practice. Great timing on Alex."

"I knew it was going to be a bang-bang play and that you have to get it in there. It wasn't going to be a lob ball," Smith said postgame.

Added Harbaugh: "Might be time to give Alex some credit, huh? Spectacular job."

It made for Smith's sixth fourth-quarter comeback win of the 2011 season. The so-called game manager had managed to escape the dark cloud that hovered above his tenure. Harbaugh called Smith "heroic" in that victory, crediting it to his "great mental toughness." He said: "He has a way to be focused and loose in the most pressure situations. He's got that makeup about him that allows him to play and execute. Experience, demeanor, confidence—all those things give you a chance."

Trent Baalke, then the 49ers' general manager, also praised Smith after that epic playoff performance. "Like I told him after the game, I don't know if I've ever been happier for an individual than I was for Alex to come through in the moments like he did," he said. "And to just see the joy on his face, if anyone deserved it, Alex deserved it."

That playoff win had Smith at his mountaintop for the 49ers. His ensuing 2012 descent did not come at his choosing or doing. Who knew his final full start would see him complete 18-of-19 passes with three touchdowns in a 24–3 win at the Arizona Cardinals on October 29? The following game Smith sustained a concussion against the St. Louis Rams at Candlestick, and Colin Kaepernick entered to seize the quarterback throne on that season's Super Bowl run.

Smith's 49ers rebirth had been sabotaged—just when the going got good. Very good. Not that this was the first tough-luck-kid moment in his tenure. Not that it would turn him into a bad guy, a bad teammate. "He coaches Colin now more than I do, and that speaks high of the kind of person and teammate that Alex Smith is," Harbaugh said in the days before Super Bowl XLVII, which the 49ers would lose 34–31 to the Baltimore Ravens in New Orleans' Superdome.

Three weeks later Smith found a new home. The Kansas City Chiefs agreed to trade two second-round picks for him.

Smith would be following the trail of the other 49ers-turned-Chiefs quarterbacks: Steve DeBerg, Joe Montana, Steve Bono, and Elvis Grbac. And, like in 2005, Smith would be joining a team coming off a 2–14 season and doing so with a new coach (Andy Reid).

Smith's Arrowhead Stadium debut with the Chiefs would come against, of course, the 49ers in an August 16, 2013 pre-season affair. Two days prior Smith sat down for an interview at Missouri Western State University, site of the Chiefs' training camp, and reminisced about his freshly expired 49ers career. Nearby, in a dorm room, his NFC championship ring sat in a box that the 49ers shipped to him, prompting Smith to sincerely ask aloud: "What do you do with them?"

That's not to say he wasn't grateful for contributing to that championship run and having to watch the final half of it on the sideline thanks to a November 11 concussion. "As frustrating as last year was," Smith said, "it's certainly not a memory I'm trying to forget."

Five years before that, Smith battled through the low point of his 49ers tenure, when his 2007 shoulder separation triggered an open feud with Nolan. "The most frustrating thing was, for sure, the first time dealing with my shoulder," Smith said in that August 2013 sit-down at Chiefs camp. "As a youngster I was trying to play through it. I'd do it so differently now if I could go back. It was frustrating at the time how it all got dealt with, how that all played out."

The 2007 season opened with divisional wins against the Cardinals and Rams. Then after a road loss to the Pittsburgh Steelers, the 49ers came home, where Smith promptly had his right shoulder planted into the ground by Rocky Bernard's sack on an opening-drive sack. Smith missed the next two games, then returned to play three in a row. The 49ers lost all three and fell to 2–7. He wouldn't play the rest of the season and he finished with a 48.7 completion percentage, the worst mark of his career. (His all-time mark is 62.6 percent.) "I felt I was getting pushed to come back," Smith recalled. "Then I did, and then it's, 'Well, you're not playing good.' As a young player, that was really hard for me to handle."

Tough times like that hardened Smith up for the road ahead. After that 2011 season's playoff win against New Orleans, the 49ers lost in overtime of the NFC Championship Game to the New York Giants. Then, two months later, the 49ers secretly courted Peyton Manning to replace Smith, who merely called that a "little blurb" in his awkward tenure with the 49ers.

Smith's vast experience on and off the field carried over in a positive way to the Chiefs, as he led them to four playoff berths in five years. Along the way he proved a valuable mentor to Patrick Mahomes, the 10th pick in the 2017 draft (seven spots after the 49ers took defensive tackle Solomon Thomas). Smith was an open book for Mahomes, sharing with him how to game plan, how to recognize coverages, and, foremost, how to be a professional. "He didn't hold anything back from me. He taught me. That's the type of person he was, that he is. I attribute a lot of my success to him," Mahomes said days before winning his first Super Bowl ring to cap the 2019 season against, ironically enough, Smith's original team, the 49ers.

Those 2019 49ers, like Smith's 2012 team, also came away only with NFC championship rings as a consolation prize for their efforts. Think about where that franchise was nearly 15 years before, which put them in the No. 1 draft spot to bring Smith aboard. "I remember doing drills there my first year and looking around and having teammates watching me: 'What's he got?'" Smith recalled in 2013. "The first day of minicamp, there were like 50 photographers out there taking pictures of us stretching. I kind of developed this [mentality of] every single throw I'm going to prove it. I've got to be the No. 1 pick. I've got to be that much better."

He got better. And he got the short straw on occasion. But, looking back, Smith also got the 49ers back into playoff mode over an eight-season tenure.

6

Kap

Colin Kaepernick lined up for a photo with 20 children battling heart disease. The Del Rio Country Club, peacefully isolated in California's Central Valley, was abuzz with excitement. Its hometown star was back—to give back at a fundraiser. "It really is a reality check every time I'm around these kids," Kaepernick said in that 2015 visit to Modesto. "We have kids that go through so many different things, and they have struggles that I have no idea about and have never been through personally. But they walk around with smiles on their faces and they're running around having a good time. It helps me realize how blessed I've been."

Kaepernick, unbeknownst to all, was entering the final stages of his San Francisco 49ers career—and his NFL livelihood. His starfall was almost as sudden as his arrival as a 2011 second-round pick. He was the pretty young thing in a NFL world that craves new stars and by Year Two he was starting in the

Super Bowl and nearly winning it in New Orleans. That comeback fell short. The Niners suffered their first Super Bowl loss. That ignominy was a prelude for his career. He'd yet to become a polarizing force for his quest to make a more equitable society.

Of all the 49ers quarterbacks to seek either a steady job or ambitiously try ending the franchise's decades-long Lombardi Trophy drought, Kaepernick redefined what a powerful platform comes with that job description. A reality check? It came in so many facets in his six NFL seasons and never more so than in his 2016 finale. In 2012 it meant Alex Smith could lose his starting job to injury, when the 49ers delayed clearing him from a concussion to ride Kaepernick's dual-threat talents to a Super Bowl XLVII date with the Baltimore Ravens, who won 34–31. It meant a defense—the Green Bay Packers' in this case—could know what was coming and still have no shot at stopping Kaepernick from rushing for 181 yards (an NFL single-game record by a quarterback) in his victorious playoff debut. He ran for two touchdowns and threw for two, too. His legacy was born. It meant that injuries could swiftly not only derail a career, but also wedge distrust between a player and an organization as happened with Kaepernick's second-opinion shoulder surgery late in the 2015 season. It meant that if you stop and look around at the world, you will not like the evil you see and hear.

How did he react to getting booed every time he took the field in their 2016 exhibition finale at the San Diego Chargers after he and teammate Eric Reid knelt during the national anthem? "It's a misunderstanding. The media painted this as I'm anti-American, anti-men and women of the military, and that's not the case at all," Kaepernick said. "I realize that men and women of the military go out and sacrifice their lives and put themselves in harm's way for my freedom of speech and my freedom in this country and my freedom to take a knee. The message is that we have a lot of issues in this country that we need to deal with. We have a lot of people that are oppressed. We have a lot of people that aren't treated equally. Police brutality is a huge thing that needs to be addressed. There are a lot of issues that need to be talked about, need to be brought to life, and we need to fix those things."

Wide receiver Torrey Smith said of Kaepernick's words in a players-only meeting: "He had an open table to stay exactly why he did it. He stood up for it. He understands the magnitude of it. He's man enough to take that stance and the heat for it. It takes a strong individual to stand up for a belief like that."

Whereas Steve Young had to overcome Joe Montana's shadow, Kaepernick steered his career into a black hole. How it ended up there is in the eyes of the beholder. On the eve of his final season, he opted to kneel during the national anthem prior to that exhibition finale at the Chargers. His goal: to draw attention to social injustice and police misconduct. Controversy and heated conversation would ensue just as he desired—even if it meant receiving death threats that he shrugged off as proof of society's state. The 49ers had his back—to an extent. When he pledged to donate $1 million for community ventures, the franchise vowed to match it.

Once he stood up at a team meeting to explain his motives for kneeling during the national anthem in that 2016 season, teammates (including strident patriots) gained a necessary understanding of his protest. By season's end Kaepernick drew their vote for the Len Eshmont Award, the 49ers' highest honor to reflect courage and inspiration. "This team has given me the opportunity to become the man I am today," Kaepernick said. "And I'm grateful for that. I'm thankful for that, and San Francisco has become my home."

But by March 2017, he was gone. He opted out of the final year of a revised contract before the 49ers could release him, which was the outspoken intention of their new regime under general manager John Lynch and coach Kyle Shanahan.

Kaepernick's final season, while publicly consumed with his social initiatives, saw him throw 16 touchdown passes vs. just four interceptions, while going 1–10 upon reclaiming his starting job from Blaine Gabbert. Statistics can be deceiving. Kaepernick's second-half stats were abominable that final season. Before halftime he completed 72.5 percent of his passes, threw for 11 touchdowns, yielded three interceptions, and posted a 115.5 passer rating. After halftime he had a 48 percent completion rate, five touchdowns, one interception, and a 70.3 rating. Mind you, the 49ers as a whole were horrid under one-and-done coach Chip Kelly, who had other issues to deal with than admonishing Kaepernick for off-field activism. "Colin made it clear that he wasn't trying to discriminate against the military, but I can see where some people take offense to that," then-center Daniel Kilgore said. "Personally, I have family and friends currently serving. When it came out, honestly, I took offense to it. But after Kap stated his case today and seeing where he was coming from, I do stand with Kap when he says enough is enough against crime, violence, discrimination, racism. I do believe that enough is enough."

Was Kaepernick's career long enough? That depends on your view. No player of his generation made a more sweeping impact across the NFL, and, though he initially was known for a dual-threat ability to pass and run, he exited in pursuit of social equality and police reform. "What is this country really standing for?" Kaepernick asked during his final season in the NFL.

7

Jimmy G

Mention Jimmy Garoppolo, and his "Feels Great, Baby!" charisma comes to mind. When Jimmy G stepped out of a black SUV and onto their doorstep on Halloween 2017, his cover-boy smile and winning touch provided the San Francisco 49ers with a desperately needed uplifting vibe. But from a maddening string of injuries to frustrating flirtations in championship games, it didn't always feel great. Even Garoppolo described his 49ers tenure as "a hell of a ride."

Those parting words turned out premature. He said them after his fourth season, figuring he would leave the 49ers. Instead, he underwent shoulder surgery in March 2022, loitered on a side field through training camp, and made an improbable return to flip the 2022 49ers into playoff contenders. Only he wouldn't be around to partake in that postseason. The 49ers were riding a four-game win streak and a 7–4 record before Garoppolo found trouble. Two Miami Dolphins defenders breached the pocket, and as he battled to get back into field-goal range, he sustained a fractured foot on a first-quarter sack, thus opening the door for rookie Brock Purdy's startling emergence.

How to best define Garoppolo's legacy beyond that of a handsome bachelor who endeared his teammates with victories and a one-of-the-guys mentality that traced to his high school linebacker days? "Jimmy was unbelievable here," head coach Kyle Shanahan said in August 2023, when the 49ers held joint practices against Garoppolo's new team, the Las Vegas Raiders. "He was the best quarterback here in about 20 years since Steve Young. He has an unbelievable record, and every time he played and stayed healthy, we were either in the Super Bowl or NFC Championship Game. So, I hope no one insinuates I ever said differently."

Garoppolo indeed had a winning touch with the 49ers, posting a 42–19 record that includes playoff appearances in the 2019 and '21 seasons, where two wins were followed by a come-from-ahead loss in those seasons' Super Bowl and NFC title games, respectively. Some will boil down Jimmy G's shortcomings to one pass: an overthrow of Emmanuel Sanders on a potential touchdown, which could have delivered a Super Bowl LIV triumph in Miami on February 2, 2020. Instead, the 49ers blew a 10-point, fourth-quarter lead and lost 31–20 to the Kansas City Chiefs, and Garoppolo's trophy-less tenure was forever tarnished.

Some will look to Garoppolo's 5–0 debut in December 2017 as a much-needed ray of sunshine under Shanahan, whose tenure began in 0–9 fashion after inheriting a 2–14 franchise.

And some will look at Garoppolo's medical file: ACL tear three games into the 2018 season at Kansas City; high-ankle sprains in 2020; calf, thumb, and shoulder injuries in 2021; and the foot fracture against Miami in December 2022. That final blow did not land him on an injured reserve. The 49ers were hopeful of a playoff or Super Bowl return, and he certainly could have been a godsend after Purdy's elbow injury in the NFC Championship Game loss against the Philadelphia Eagles. "It was wild, man. I was doing my thing, trying to get my foot ready, and it didn't work out the way I wish it would have," Garoppolo recalled in August 2023. "But those guys, going through three quarterbacks and still making it to the NFC Championship Game, I mean, that's damn impressive for a team."

That Garoppolo didn't surface in his final 49ers game was almost fitting. He was the Bay Area's most reclusive sports star ever—not that there is anything wrong with keeping one's private life, well, private. Teammates, especially George Kittle, would publicly tease him about not returning text messages. But as that trend continued over the years, going incommunicado became downright odd. The spotlight did find him and seemingly blind him months after the 49ers signed him to a then-record contract, committing a five-year, $137.5 million package to him in February 2018. That July paparazzi feasted when Garoppolo was spotted on a Beverly Hills dinner date with an adult film star, Kiara Mia. "My life's looked at differently," Garoppolo said upon reporting to training camp a week later. "I'm under a microscope, and like Kyle said, 'It's a good learning experience.'"

He rarely made public appearances afterward and turned down many commercials, endorsements, and reality TV pitches. He did, however, spend a day each spring promoting a tool company's youth scholarships. He made those pitches alongside his father, Tony, a former electrician who worked in the Chicago area and occasionally would bring along his son, Jim, stringing wires to him down in a chilly basement. "That work ethic is not seen every day, and I'm glad I got to witness it firsthand," Garoppolo said of his father. "Anytime you think you're having a rough day, I always think back to that and I'm like, 'Is it as tough as you think it is?'"

Life was indeed tough for the 2017 49ers. But when Garoppolo arrived for a second-round draft pick from the New England Patriots, he liked the young team he joined. "The connection was real, and guys weren't faking it," he said. "That's why I fell in love with this team."

The feeling was mutual. "His competitive edge—every time he stepped out there, you knew he'd give us a chance," linebacker Fred Warner said. "Just seeing his poise out there, he's a leader through and through. I respect him a lot and am grateful for everything he brought to our team."

That's the first impression Christian McCaffrey gathered, though he played only six games with Garoppolo before the December 4, 2022 foot fracture exit. "Jimmy's just one of the guys," McCaffrey said. "He's an interesting guy because he doesn't promote himself ever. But he could. He's won a lot of games. He's a great quarterback who's been successful in the past. He always has a smile on his face."

Garoppolo sure did when he won his first start for the 49ers on December 3, 2017 in Chicago's Soldier Field, some 30 minutes from his hometown of Arlington Heights, Illinois, where Garoppolo got switched from outside linebacker to quarterback after his sophomore season at Rolling Meadows High School. "We've got a quarterback, huh?" left tackle Joe Staley said with glee in the 49ers' victorious locker room after that 15–14 win in Chicago.

The 49ers Faithful fell in love at first sight. "The Joe Montana comparisons, I think it's a little early for those. It's only been one game," Garoppolo said. "We are both Italian. So we have that in common, but it might be a little early."

Indeed. The roller coaster careened toward Earth three games into the 2018 season. Garoppolo scrambled left, cut up the sideline into the red zone, and then his left knee's anterior cruciate ligament blew out on him as a Chiefs defender side-swiped him. Season over.

Garoppolo recovered so well that he started every game for the 2019 49ers, who turned an 8–0 start into an eventual Super Bowl trip. Along the way was a classic shootout pitting Garoppolo against Drew Brees in New Orleans' Superdome, where thousands of 49ers fans rejoiced after a 48–46 triumph against the Saints. Garoppolo passed for 349 yards and four touchdowns, and his most critical pass to Kittle—on fourth and 2—resulted in a 39-yard gain that set up Robbie Gould's walk-off field goal.

Garoppolo threw only five interceptions over his next six games combined. An air attack was unnecessary in the NFC playoffs, which the 49ers qualified for as the No. 1 seed by winning their regular-season finale at the Seattle Seahawks. Garoppolo was 11-of-19 for 131 yards (one touchdown, one interception) in a 27–10 playoff-opening win against the Minnesota Vikings, then he completed 6-of-8 passes for 77 yards in the NFC Championship Game, when Raheem Mostert ran for a franchise-record 220 yards and four touchdowns to key the 37–20 victory at Levi's Stadium.

Garoppolo's passing proficiency, however, had him first in line for Super Bowl MVP honors through three quarters, when he completed 17-of-20 passes for a 20–10 lead. But he was just 3-of-11 for 36 yards in the fateful fourth quarter. His third-down overthrow to Sanders lives in infamy, but Chiefs defensive lineman Chris Jones batted down two earlier passes to throw off the 49ers' rhythm. "The one to 'E,' just missing him, putting a little too much on it," Garoppolo said three days afterward, "but you've got to be a man, you have to own up to those things. Some things I'd rather have back. But this whole year, it's been incredible."

"Obviously people are going to be hard on Jimmy, but Jimmy, to me, is still a baller," Sanders said. "A lot of people want to say this and say that, but this guy took his team to the Super Bowl. He didn't come out victorious, but we had a 10-point lead in the fourth quarter and easily could have come out victorious."

Garoppolo pulled off 11 fourth-quarter comebacks in his No. 10 Niners jersey. The first was that starting debut in Chicago. The second-to-last comeback: a snow-covered playoff win in Lambeau Field, where he passed for just 131 yards, threw no touchdowns, had a pass intercepted in the end zone just before halftime, and in the end delivered completions to Kittle and Deebo Samuel to breach midfield on the winning drive. "F*** the Packers!" Garoppolo, the Chicago-area native, told Gould, the former Bears kicker, amid the postgame frenzy on the snow-covered field.

The legacies of 49ers quarterbacks are ultimately measured on postseason success. That win in Green Bay would be Garoppolo's last postseason triumph. In the ensuing NFC Championship Game, the 49ers took a 17–7 lead into the fourth quarter against the host Los Angeles Rams. Two years after they couldn't hold a 10-point, fourth-quarter cushion in the Super Bowl, it happened again. Jaquiski Tartt would be the scapegoat for dropping a potential interception early in the fourth quarter on the Rams' game-tying drive. Garoppolo didn't help matters, completing 3-of-9 passes for 30 yards and finishing with an interception while being in the grasp of Rams star defender Aaron Donald.

So ended a season in which Garoppolo battled through a midseason calf injury, a torn thumb ligament in a December loss at the Tennessee Titans, and his right shoulder injury in the wild-card win at the Dallas Cowboys. It wasn't the end of his 49ers tenure, but that January 2022 stretch was his last playoff ride. "A lot of people want to talk about what we didn't accomplish with him," general manager John Lynch said as Garoppolo headed for 2023 free agency. "What I know is we won a lot of football games with Jimmy."

It was weird. It was crazy. It was invigorating. It was crushing. It was, indeed, a hell of a ride, as he said during that premature farewell on February 1, 2022. He said something else poignant and true that day: "Since I've gotten here, it's been about me wanting to leave the place better than when I got here." Jimmy G was indeed a driving factor why for many years everyone felt great, baby.

8

Brock Purdy

CHANTS OF "PUR-DY! PUR-DY" RANG OUT FROM THE CROWD. Flat on his back on the green grass in his native Arizona was Brock Purdy. Teammates curiously checked to see what pained him, fearing the worst for the San Francisco 49ers quarterback and the NFL's most unlikely passing leader. Purdy got off the proverbial canvas, walked to the 49ers' sideline with team doctor Tim McAdams, and shook off the stinging sensation of jolted nerves in his left shoulder. Five minutes after getting smashed in the facemask and neck by a 230-pound linebacker, Purdy bounded back into the 49ers' huddle, determined to finish off a drive with a touchdown pass. "Yeah, I didn't want to go in there acting like it was a movie scene," Purdy said after the 45–29, NFC West-clinching victory on December 17, 2023. "It was more about: I'm back in here. Let's actually read out the defense and what are we trying to do. That's what we were trying to do: put up points."

A lot of NFL careers could serve as the basis for a movie script. Purdy's is Oscar worthy. "I mean, if you just look at the whole grand scheme of it, being drafted last and all that, I guess people could start saying stuff about movies," Purdy said. "But for me I'm just taking it one day at a time. I'm playing football, I've dreamed of being able to play in the NFL, and I've got a great team around me. That's just where I'm at, trying to enjoy every day."

The day of April 30, 2022, dragged on as he waited for a phone call and a job offer. Sure, he had a modest frame (6'1", 212 pounds). But Iowa State's captain came packed with experience (school-record 30 wins, 12,170 yards, 81 touchdowns) and intelligence (he aced the S2 Cognition test that reflected his elite processing skills).

As the NFL draft neared its end after Purdy killed time with a nap and a Chick-fil-A run, his phone came alive. He ducked into his parents' bedroom in their 10-year-old, 3,200-square-foot home in Queen Creek, Arizona, a booming suburb 30 miles southeast of Phoenix and 15 miles down the road from Gilbert's Perry High program that he led to the state 6A title game.

He insisted there would be no draft day party. So only his tight-knit family and close friends gathered to learn where he'd launch his NFL career. They weren't privy to the 49ers' call: "This is John Lynch from the 49ers. I'm sorry it took 'til the end. We find you very relevant, but you are going to be 'Mr. Irrelevant.'"

"Yes, sir," Purdy responded. "I appreciate it."

Coach Kyle Shanahan grabbed the draft-room phone and added: "Brock, congrats, dude. Hey, dude, you're coming to an awesome situation for you. We've loved you on tape. You know how to play the position, and it's a hell of a day for you, man."

"I appreciate it," Purdy responded. "Thanks for the opportunity. And, honestly, man, I'm ready to roll for you all. So let's do it."

He wasn't lying. But first, Purdy politely played out his benevolent role as "Mr. Irrelevant." It came with an annual celebration in Newport Beach, California; a June banquet; an inscribed longboard; a key to the city; and a bronze trophy. Irrelevant Week began in 1976 with Paul Salata, who not only played for the 49ers, but also scored their first NFL touchdown in 1950. Two decades after his playing career, he created the inaugural event. Six months after Salata died at age 94, his daughter, Melanie, was at the NFL draft in Las Vegas to announce Purdy's selection with the No. 262 overall pick. "Go Niners!" she said in mic-drop fashion.

When Purdy arrived for minicamp in Santa Clara, he entered the stadium's windowless press room and enlightened reporters with his best assets. "Maybe the craftiness I play with and extending plays," he said. "I have the mentality I always feel I can make something out of nothing in a sense when something breaks down in a play. Other than that, it's being consistent and doing my job."

It would be one thing to beat out Nate Sudfeld in training camp for a backup job to join a most unexpected quarterback room that still included Jimmy Garoppolo and 2021 first-round pick Trey Lance. It would mean more if Purdy could win the trust of his teammates. His first sign of that came before the preseason opener, when he overheard team captains Fred Warner and Trent Williams mention how excited they were to watch him play.

Purdy moved up the depth chart two games into his rookie year when Lance sustained a season-ending ankle injury in the 49ers' home opener. Garoppolo, two years after quarterbacking a Super Bowl-bound team, got his job back, which even seemed remote to him before offseason shoulder injury scuttled any potential offseason trade.

The 49ers fell to 3–3, but then business starting picking up. They traded for running back Christian McCaffrey, who needed a personal tutor for on-field simulations. That would become Purdy's assignment for hours on a side field. On December 4 Purdy rushed to the rescue once Garoppolo suffered a foot fracture. The 49ers' fate was now in the relevant hands of their one-time fourth-string quarterback. He deftly fended off the Miami Dolphins' blitzing defenders, and the 49ers won 33–17 for their fifth straight victory.

Next up, Purdy became the first rookie quarterback (out of seven) to win a starting debut against Tom Brady. Before spoiling Brady's Bay Area farewell, Purdy sustained a broken rib while diving toward a first-down marker in that 35–7 win. Chants of "PUR-DY! PUR-DY!" rang out from the home crowd. FOX's broadcast caught proud father, Shawn Purdy, wiping tears from his eyes. The 49ers had themselves more than a caretaker of Shanahan's offense. They had the first quarterback to produce two touchdown passes, a touchdown run, and a 125-plus passer rating in a starting debut. The 134.0 passer rating actually ranked fourth highest for a first start.

Four days later Purdy's first road start would come in Seattle's deafening amphitheater, and though his rib injury made him a game-time decision, he gutted out a 21–13 win that clinched the NFC West title. The wins kept coming. Down went the Seattle Seahawks 41–23 in the wild-card playoffs, as Purdy produced three touchdown passes, a touchdown run, and the third-most passing yards (332) in 49ers postseason history. Next came a 19–12 dispatching of the 49ers' ultimate playoff rival, the Dallas Cowboys, whose first-half lead didn't intimidate Purdy. A decade earlier he'd rallied Queen Creek's middle-school traveling team from a 20–0 halftime deficit for a 21–20 win at Maricopa en route to a championship.

The 2022 season's NFC Championship Game in Philadelphia would not make for a pleasant memory. It's where a front-side sack by Haason Reddick ruptured Purdy's throwing elbow on the 49ers' first possession and doomed them to a 31–7 defeat. Pain seared through his forearm. Sideline throws convinced him he couldn't pass. Garoppolo remained out with a foot fracture, so the 49ers only had Josh Johnson as their backup. Once Johnson sustained a third-quarter concussion, Purdy returned, somehow managed two completions (for four total yards), and then headed for a most uncertain future.

His ensuing surgery—an internal brace repair of his ulnar collateral ligament on March 10—fast-tracked him back into the lineup for the 2023 season. The 49ers' brass was so confident in his comeback and so assured by backups Sam Darnold and Brandon Allen that Lance got traded to the Cowboys before the preseason finale. "The kid's got poise," Darnold said of Purdy.

When Purdy opened the season with an opening-drive touchdown pass to Brandon Aiyuk, it was the perfectly encouraging start to a 30–7 road rout of the Pittsburgh Steelers. Purdy then took it up a notch with a 19-yard, back-shoulder beauty to a tightly covered Aiyuk, foreshadowing the great accuracy and daring moxie that was to come.

In Week Four, Purdy set a 49ers single-game record by completing 95.2 percent of his passes (20-of-21) in a 35–16 win against the Arizona Cardinals. That preceded a showdown with the Cowboys, and Purdy delivered four touchdown passes with no turnovers in that 42–10 win. He had the NFL's second-best completion percentage (70.4) through 10 career games, and the 49ers were riding high.

Then came the first regular-season loss of his career—a rainy, 19–17 defeat in Cleveland. With McCaffrey and Deebo Samuel sidelined by injuries, Purdy still engineered a late drive to set up a potential winning field goal, but rookie kicker Jake Moody missed wide from 41 yards. Another road loss followed at the Minnesota Vikings that sent Purdy to the NFL's post-concussion protocol. He didn't miss the next game, but he did lose it, producing three turnovers and then apologizing to teammates in a locker room speech after the 31–17 defeat to Cincinnati.

That three-game slide ended with the 49ers' bye week. Purdy used that break to return to Iowa, where he drove a tractor on his fiancee's family farm and drew a hero's welcome at an Iowa State football game. Not only did he give his surgically repaired elbow its first extended rest since he began throwing in May, but he also got mentally recharged. "To step away from the game, take a breather, understand where we're at and what we have to do, it was huge for me," Purdy said, "to clear my mind and come back excited for the second half and this stretch of football, good football, we have to play."

Great football ensued. Purdy threw three touchdown passes in a 34–3 win at the Jacksonville Jaguars, then reached the NFL's highest-attainable passer rating (158.3) in a 27–14 home win against the Tampa Bay Buccaneers (21-of-25, 333 yards, three touchdowns). "The doubters have been silenced," McCaffrey said. "He'll continue to do that. He's one of the best football players in the league, one of the best quarterbacks."

That primed Purdy and the 49ers for the season's ultimate gauntlet, where wins against Seattle would serve as bookends to a 42–19 rout of the NFC-leading Eagles. Chants of "PUR-DY! PUR-DY!" bellowed from the 49ers Faithful as they serenaded Purdy off Lincoln Financial Field. It didn't cancel out the NFC Championship Game trauma from 10 months earlier, but it represented closure of that chapter and the launch point of another playoff push. Darting toward the visitors' tunnel came the 49ers' quarterback. "LET'S GO!" Purdy shouted back.

"I've never had this much confidence in the offense," defensive end Nick Bosa would say after that victory against the Eagles.

More confidence-building wins followed, including Purdy's December 17 homecoming in his first pro appearance in Arizona. After that victory Shanahan praised Purdy's field vision, poise, reactions, and how cool it must have been for him to hear his name chanted by the crowd. "He's had a great command over the offense," Shanhahan said, "but also the amount of plays he's made throughout the two years has been as many plays as any quarterback I have ever been around."

Purdy came up one play short in the Super Bowl. His final, hurried pass overshot an open Jauan Jennings. The 49ers, thus, settled for an overtime field goal, and the Chiefs answered with a championship-defending touchdown drive.

In the ensuing months, Purdy got married in Iowa, honeymooned in Turks and Caicos, and tried mightily to get past his Super Bowl debut. "Obviously, it's still stinging about how we ended the year. We were right there," Purdy recalled in mid-April. "There's going to be a lot of guys that are hungry and have that chip on their shoulder again. For us, we're always going to think we can get it to another level."

Purdy said so while back on the lush grass at Levi's Stadium, where he was the first 49ers quarterback to host a youth football camp there in its decade of existence. "This community, they've gotten behind my back and supported me since I jumped in the role, and it's real love that you can feel," Purdy said while admiring the 650 kids doing drills. "I just want to give back, give them my time, and show them that I'm human, too. I'm not just a guy they see on TV but a guy who is just like them."

9

The Next QB

THE SAN FRANCISCO 49ERS' "FRANCHISE" QUARTERBACKS come and go with a mesmerizing effect, like watching the chilly waters pass under the Golden Gate Bridge before retreating into the Pacific Ocean. A quarter-century's search for "The Next One" has introduced many a quarterback into the most demanding, scrutinized, and unfulfilled job the Bay Area has to offer—with all due respect to Silicon Valley's tech sector or other noble professions. Joe Montana and Steve Young staged this franchise's endless pursuit for passing perfection. They flipped the NFL's standard of quarterback controversy into its most imposing line of throne succession—with all due respect to the 49ers'quarterback pioneers of Frankie Albert, Y.A. Tittle, and John Brodie.

Since Y2K—the turn of the century—the 49ers can't be faulted for casting a wide net to find their next Super Bowl-winning quarterback. They've scoured and scouted. They've overlooked and overpaid. They've imported and exported. They've picked first and picked last.

The 49ers have had a revolving quarterback door since Young took his final snap in 1999. Some took root for years—Jeff Garcia, Alex Smith, Colin Kaepernick, Jimmy Garoppolo, and, at last check, Brock Purdy. But so many others bombed their auditions. Jim Druckenmiller infamously failed his turn. A 1997 first-round pick, he lasted two seasons as Young's understudy, completing 21-of-52 passes with one touchdown and four interceptions before getting traded to Miami in 1999.

Ever since 2000 one man in the 49ers organization caught warm-up passes from any and all quarterbacks. They'd take aim at the bare fingers of "Doc" Dressler, the assistant equipment manager. The hardest throwers: Colin Kaepernick ("By far the hardest thrower," Dressler said. "He'd warm up at 90 [mph].") and Cody Pickett ("Every throw was like a slider," Dressler recalled). The most catchable throws, the ones with appropriate touch, spun off the hands of Smith, Garoppolo, and Purdy.

No matter the throw, no matter the quarterback, the expectations stayed the same: become the next Super Bowl-winning quarterback. These are the ones after Young who came, saw, and did not conquer:

Steve Stenstrom

Five years after setting Stanford's passing records (10,911 yards) and finishing under Bill Walsh, Steve Stenstrom got a chance to reboot his NFL career with the San Francisco 49ers. He inherited a four-game losing streak from Jeff Garcia, then lost all three of his starts in November 1999, yielding an interception in each one without throwing a touchdown pass or for more than 200 yards.

Tim Rattay

The 2000 NFL Draft is infamous for the San Francisco 49ers taking Sacramento native Giovanni Carmazzi in the third round and passing on some San Mateo kid named Tom Brady, who went in the sixth round (No. 199) to the New England Patriots. Well, 13 spots later, the 49ers used a seventh-round pick on Tim Rattay. A record-setter at Louisiana Tech, he drew a vote of confidence early in his career from Hall of Fame-bound Terrell Owens. After going 2–1 as Jeff Garcia's injury replacement in 2003, Rattay went 1–8 the next season on an overhauled roster. Hindered by a cascade of injuries, Rattay would bequeath his job to No. 1 draft pick Alex Smith, and the 49ers traded Rattay to the Tampa Bay Buccaneers in October 2005.

Ken Dorsey

He won North Coast Section championships at Miramonte High School in Orinda in the East Bay. He became the University of Miami's winningest quarterback (38–2) with two national title game appearances and a championship in the Rose Bowl. Then Kenny Dorsey came home to the Bay Area as a mere seventh-round pick in 2003. He went 2–8 as a San Francisco 49ers starter in his two-year tenure. That first win came in 2004 when he had three touchdown passes against the Arizona Cardinals. Said Dorsey: "It means a lot just to be able to go out and perform and play well again. It's kind of a relief." He played two seasons with the Cleveland Browns and became their offensive coordinator in 2024 after previous coaching stints with the Carolina Panthers and Buffalo Bills.

Cody Pickett

"Who's he?" an old-time sportswriter bellowed upon seeing the media encircle the San Francisco 49ers' latest quarterback inside the locker room. Back then, Cody Pickett's rodeo background made for a fun storyline—not to mention his underdog stature as a 2004 seventh-round flyer. Pickett became the quarterback du jour upon relieving an injured Ken Dorsey in a 2005 win against the Tampa Bay Buccaneers. After throwing for 104 yards in his starting debut (a 24–6 home loss to the New York Giants), Pickett's final NFL passes saw him go 1-of-13 for 28 yards in a 17–9 loss to the Bears in gusty Chicago in November 2005.

Trent Dilfer

This Santa Cruz, California, native and Aptos High product wrapped up his 14-year career by joining the San Francisco 49ers for the 2006–07 seasons. These weren't the caliber of teams, mind you, like the dominant 2000 Baltimore Ravens team he rode to a Super Bowl. So, he served as a veteran mentor to Alex Smith, whose shoulder injury in 2007 vaulted Trent Dilfer into the lineup as a 1–5 replacement starter. Nearly a decade later, Dilfer shot down rumors he would leave his role as an ESPN analyst to work in the 49ers' front office with close friend and general manager Trent Baalke. Instead, after broadcasting Dilfer took to coaching both at the high school and collegiate level—with a Super Bowl ring in tow.

Shaun Hill

Who had one of the top winning percentages in San Francisco 49ers quarterback history? This guy. He won 10-of-16 starts between 2007 and 2009 after idling in 2006 on the bench. When then-coach Mike Singletary picked Shaun Hill over Alex Smith as the 2009 Opening Day starter, Hill replied: "I almost made it a whole six seasons without taking a snap in the league. Now here I am with the opportunity to start for one of the most storied franchises in the NFL, a franchise that's had great quarterbacks throughout its history." Hill got off to a 3–1 start that year but got benched for Smith after two straight defeats and then took his remaining NFL snaps with the Detroit Lions, St. Louis Rams, and Minnesota Vikings.

Chris Weinke

As Alex Smith's feud with then-coach Mike Nolan went public over the quarterback's shoulder injury, San Francisco 49ers personnel czar Scot McCloughan called on one of his former baseball teammates in the Toronto Blue Jays' organization, Chris Weinke. "He won't be stealing bases here, I guarantee that," McCloughan said of Weinke, who didn't steal a win either in his only 49ers start—a 20–7 home loss to the Cleveland Browns—with just 104 passing yards in the 2007 finale. The 2000 Heisman Trophy winner, Weinke won his 2001 NFL debut as a Carolina Panthers rookie, then lost his final 14 starts, and finished 2–18 as an NFL starter.

J.T. O'Sullivan

A product of U.C. Davis, J.T. O'Sullivan served as the San Francisco 49ers' grumpy starter the first half of 2008, going 2–6 with eight touchdowns, 11 interceptions, and six lost fumbles. "It's very hard to see the good when the bad outweighs it," Mike Nolan said after a Week Seven loss at the New York Giants, which represented his final game as 49ers coach.

Troy Smith

The 2006 Heisman Trophy winner-turned-Baltimore Ravens castoff replaced Alex Smith as the San Francisco 49ers' starter for a five-game stretch, starting with a 2010 Halloween win in London against the Denver Broncos. Coach Mike Singletary toggled between both Smiths over the final month, and then Singletary (and Troy Smith) would not be welcomed back in 2011.

Blaine Gabbert

A 2011 first-round pick of the Jacksonville Jaguars, Blaine Gabbert got dealt to the San Francisco 49ers in 2014 for a sixth-round pick. "His career was headed out the door," Steve Young said at the time. "He reclaimed an opportunity to play football and this year he might solidify it." By November, Colin Kaepernick got benched, and Gabbert mustered only a 3–5 record in 2015 under coach Jim Tomsula. As Kaepernick recovered from shoulder surgery in the 2016, Gabbert began that ensuing season as new coach Chip Kelly's Week One starter. After a shutout win in the opener against the St. Louis Rams, the 49ers lost their next four, and Gabbert wouldn't play again other than in relief of Kaepernick in a 26–6 loss at the Chicago Bears in December 2016. "You're never going to play your best ball looking over your shoulder," Gabbert said. He, though, can look forward, knowing he earned Super Bowl rings as a backup to Tom Brady and Patrick Mahomes for the Tampa Bay Buccaneers and Kansas City Chiefs, respectively.

Brian Hoyer

Unable to trade for Kirk Cousins from Washington, first-year head coach Kyle Shanahan instead reunited with Brian Hoyer from their days on the 2014 Cleveland Browns, where Shanahan was an offensive coordinator. Hoyer was introduced with the San Francisco 49ers' first wave of 2017 free agents (including fullback Kyle Juszczyk and kicker Robbie Gould). But after a 0–6 start with four touchdowns and four interceptions, Hoyer got benched for rookie C.J. Beathard, and once the 49ers brokered an October 30 trade for Jimmy Garoppolo, Hoyer was released.

C.J. Beathard

Once C.J. Beathard unleashed an 83-yard touchdown pass to Marquise Goodwin, the previously winless San Francisco 49ers sprung to life and bounded toward their first win in 10 games under Shanahan, a 31–21 home win against the New York Giants. Beathard was a 2017 third-round draft pick from Iowa, where the 49ers also uncovered their fifth-round pick, future All-Pro tight end George Kittle. Beathard won only two of 12 starts in his four-year tenure as a bridge between Brian Hoyer and Jimmy Garoppolo in 2017, between Garoppolo and Nick Mullens in 2018, and as the No. 3 option in 2020. Beathard's other victory was intensely emotional. That December 2020 win at the Arizona Cardinals came around the one-year anniversary of the murder of his brother, Clayton, outside a Nashville bar. "It means more than I can put into words," Beathard said. "Everything that I've been through the last year and it being the anniversary of my brother's passing... you can't write a script any different."

Nick Mullens

An 11-year-old fan showed up on the San Francisco 49ers' sideline on November 12, 2018 wearing a gold cape adorned with the phrase: "Mullens Mania." Such was Nick Mullens' star turn following his NFL debut the previous game, when he blistered the Oakland Raiders 34–3 on *Thursday Night Football* by passing for three touchdowns and 262 yards. Those were the third-most passing yards in a 49ers debut, and Mullens posted the second-best passer rating (151.9) in a NFL debut since 1973. Though that only lifted the 49ers to a 2–7 record, the world took notice of this Southern Miss product who went undrafted and spent 2017 on the practice squad. He went 3–5 to close as the 2018 starter, then retreated behind Jimmy Garoppolo in the 2019 Super Bowl season before resurfacing amid the 2020 COVID season and going 2–6. Mullens tore an elbow ligament in his 49ers finale, and though the severity of that injury got overlooked after that December 20, 2020 loss against the Dallas Cowboys, his innovative surgical repair a month later would serve as a blueprint in two years for another future quarterback, Brock Purdy.

Trey Lance

When the San Francisco 49ers dropped three first-round draft picks and a third rounder on the Miami Dolphins on March 26, 2021, it proved the most costly gamble in franchise history. And it backfired. Trey Lance, the No. 3 overall draft pick, appeared in only eight games and posted just a 2–2 starting record during two seasons with the 49ers, who shipped him out August 25, 2023 to, of all teams, the NFC rival Dallas Cowboys for a fourth-round pick.

Lance's downfall was not that he came out of North Dakota State and the Football Championship Subdivision. His lack of game experience carried over from the COVID-aborted season in 2020 in Fargo, North Dakota, to his abbreviated 49ers tenure, starting with finger and knee injuries as a rookie before seizing the starting role for his second season, which ended with a fractured ankle in the Week Two home opener against the Seattle Seahawks on a run up the gut and into the red zone. His departure triggered Jimmy Garoppolo's last stand before rookie Brock Purdy triumphantly entered the picture. Lance spent the 2023 offseason program alternating reps with Sam Darnold for the No. 2 role behind Purdy and, once Darnold won that nod, Lance got scooped up two days later by the Cowboys. The trade went down mere hours before the 49ers' preseason finale against the Los Angeles Chargers. Immediately, the 49ers got panned for trading up in the first place for Lance. Was it the worst trade in NFL history? Heck, it may not have been the worst in 49ers history, considering how poorly trades played out for Jim Plunkett and O.J. Simpson.

PART 2

LEGENDS

10

The Genius

BILL WALSH'S LASTING IMPACT ON THE SAN FRANCISCO 49ERS is at first blush reflected with the Lombardi Trophy collection in the 49ers' lobby of their Santa Clara headquarters. But silver hardware alone does not define Walsh's cherished legacy. "None of us can capture all he's brought to us," Ronnie Lott said after the August 2007 memorial services for Walsh, who died at age 75 after battling leukemia. "We talked about his accomplishments. I relish how he was there for everyone in adverse times. How do you capture that in a quote?"

But perhaps one quote from Walsh does capture part of his essence, and it is painted on a wall above the Levi's Stadium staff room: "Afford each person the same respect, support, and fair treatment you would expect if your roles were reversed. Deal with people individually, not as objects who are part of a herd—that's the critical factor."

While the NFL names its championship trophy after former Green Bay Packers coach Vince Lombardi, the league's persistent push for minority hiring is aptly dubbed: "The Bill Walsh Diversity Coaching Fellowship." Thousands of minority coaches have interned through that program since Walsh launched it in the late 1980s. He did so after approaching Dr. Harry Edwards, America's preeminent sports sociologist who taught at nearby Cal-Berkeley. Walsh was setting up a "Playing To Win!" program, and in his initial 1983 meetings with Edwards, they whittled down a few key topics: "sport and race," "women and sport," and "athlete support programs."

"It was tough to get through to the league owners," Walsh said in 2003 while serving his final year with the 49ers as a consultant. "I wouldn't say that they were racist, but they felt no urgency at all."

So, Walsh challenged the norm.

It's what he did in establishing the West Coast Offense as a short-pass, horizontal-base scheme that thrived—and became trendy throughout the NFL from one generation to the next.

It's what he did in drafting a skinny-legged quarterback out of Notre Dame with the last pick of the 1979's third round, not to mention his discovering of Jerry Rice, Dwight Clark, Michael Carter, and a star-studded 1986 class. It's what he did with a practice structure that became the NFL's model and with the filming of his meetings so others could learn from them in the 49ers' archives.

Walsh set an impossibly high standard for the 49ers' ensuing coaches—with all due respect to George Seifert's two Super Bowl titles in his eight seasons (98–30) after his promotion, as well as other playoff-winning coaches such as Steve Mariucci (1997–2002), Jim Harbaugh (2011–14), and Kyle Shanahan, who, when introduced in 2017, immediately mentioned Walsh's name (after thanking the York family ownership) in establishing the 49ers' aura. Shanahan brought with him a general manager, John Lynch, who played under Walsh at Stanford.

Like those coaches, Walsh knew when to break his serious façade and crack a joke. The most popular anecdote: he dressed up as a hotel bellman and slyly took players' bags as they got off the bus and into town for the 1981 season's Super Bowl in Pontiac, Michigan, which represented the franchise's first appearance in the big game.

Simply put, Walsh's zest for life was matched by his drive to break glass ceilings so others could reap football's great rewards. "What really made Bill special is that he understood the game was bigger than him," said Lott, Walsh's 1981 first-round draft pick. "His genius was not centered around X's and O's. It was centered around his ability to create a platform that made the game inclusive to others."

Hired away from nearby Stanford in 1979 by a desperate-for-success owner in Eddie DeBartolo Jr., Walsh delivered three Super Bowl wins and six division titles as coach from 1979 to 1988. He returned as general manager from 1999 to 2000, then took on consultant duties for three years during the franchise's shaky ownership transition.

Walsh's own staff served as a stepping stone for assistants such as Dennis Green, Ray Rhodes, and Sherm Lewis. Such ties created a Walsh Coaching Tree that is arguably unmatched in NFL history, and that does not even include those who served minority-coaching fellowships.

Edwards noted that Walsh's ambition was such that "we didn't want everyone to apply to the 49ers. We wanted to spread it out and get every team involved."

About 25 years later, the NFL tried to advance that even more with the "Rooney Rule," requiring clubs to diversify their interview pool. Another push came in 2021, as teams began receiving third-round draft picks as compensation for losing a minority coach or executive to another team.

Walsh was way ahead of the curve. "Bill was wise enough to realize that to make the game better, there needed to be inclusion not just on the field of play but with coaches," said Herm Edwards, who parlayed his internship into eventual head coaching roles with the New York Jets and the Kansas City Chiefs. "Bill understood it. He kind of got it early."

Former Cincinnati Bengals coach Marvin Lewis had a summer internship in 1988. "I hadn't thought much of the NFL until that opportunity," he said. "It was different. There was an attraction to that."

When Lewis showed up at the 49ers' headquarters—then up the Bay Area's peninsula in Redwood City—Walsh confidently offered not only a sales pitch, but also an outline of things to come. "You're going to have an opportunity to be part of the best organization in pro sports," Walsh told Lewis. "You know why? Because if I mess it up, I can fix it."

Walsh loved to mentor, to teach, to help others grow. David Shaw is among those forever grateful. Shaw played under Walsh at Stanford from 1992 to 1994, spent 16 years as an assistant at various NFL and college spots, and then ultimately entrenched himself as Stanford's coach from 2011 to 2022. "Bill understood that in order for things to progress, someone like him needs to push it," Shaw said. "It wasn't going to come from the African American coaches to make changes. It was going to come from someone in his position to make change and push change."

What never changed was Walsh's drive for success. He wanted to be the best, to coach the best, to have the best of all worlds. "And for something like race to stand in the middle of it," Shaw said, "it was incomprehensible."

As NFL and pro sports increasingly turn to data analytics, their research and development departments may want to heed Walsh's words on what pointed him to Montana. "It still takes professional judgment. It still takes an intuitive, instinctive feel for athletes and what they can do and how they fit on your squad," Walsh said in 2004. "These are things computer programs don't connect with."

Walsh certainly overcame his own obstacles to become an NFL head coach at the ripe age of 47 and serving in that capacity solely with the 49ers. Twenty years before that gig, he was coaching Washington High School in the Bay Area town of Fremont not long after graduating from San Jose State and serving in the U.S. Army (and boxing for them). He was an assistant at Cal-Berkeley and then rival Stanford before his first pro job came with the Oakland Raiders as their running backs coach in 1966, when Al Davis took majority control of that franchise. So began a bond with Davis that endured for four decades. "We're different, he and I," Davis said. "Bill's more like the opera, the guy leading it with a stick. That's Bill. But if something happens with the musician out of whack, Bill can't stand it."

Davis and John Madden said their goodbyes to Walsh two days before he passed away in his Woodside home July 30, 2007. The following week more than 1,000 VIPs turned out for a private service at Stanford's Memorial Church, and about 8,000 fans came the next day to Candlestick Park to sit on the newly named "Bill Walsh Field" to hear from 49ers legends.

"He made us all," Steve Young said, "feel like champions."

When Walsh passed away, Harbaugh was the 49ers' coach, having followed Walsh's coaching path from Stanford to a first NFL head coaching job with the 49ers. "Like everything else Bill

Walsh did, he had the foresight to see how to get minorities opportunities to have an inside look at how to run a professional program, how to coach a team and a practice," Harbaugh said. "I'm really thankful Bill Walsh had the foresight and emphasis to take a step back and see that something was not right."

11

Dwight Clark

TWO DAYS HAD PASSED SINCE DWIGHT CLARK'S DEATH WHEN John Madden tried to reflect on happier times. Tributes, of course, had poured in from San Francisco 49ers teammates, fans, and family with heartfelt devotion to Clark, author of "The Catch" that triggered the 49ers' 1980s Super Bowl dynasty.

Madden's connection? Upon retiring from his Pro Football Hall of Fame coaching career with the Oakland Raiders, he forged into the broadcasting world. That included interviewing Clark for a syndicated radio show in San Francisco, after which they'd stroll to Enrico's Café in North Beach. "I'd walk the streets with Dwight Clark, and we're talking in 1981 and '82, and he was more popular than any other 49er," Madden recalled in June 2018. "Everyone loved Joe [Montana], and then Jerry Rice came along. But Dwight Clark was like a movie star. I never heard anyone say a bad word about him. He wasn't a big shot, but people treated him as a big shot."

Of all people who fawned over Clark, one in particular sparked a series of fortunate events for the 49ers: Bill Walsh. Entering his first season as coach in 1979, Walsh went to Clemson's campus to scout quarterback Steve Fuller, who, of course, needed to throw to someone. Enter Clark. "Here comes Dwight running out with a bag of footballs in it," John McVay, Walsh's right-hand personnel man, recalled in 2017. "So the quarterback was throwing balls, Dwight was catching them, and Bill kept warming up to him."

Fuller would get drafted in the first round (23rd overall) by the Kansas City Chiefs. Walsh would find his quarterback with the last pick of the third round, a Notre Dame guy named Joe. In the 10th round with the 249th overall pick, Walsh said: "Dwight Clark, let's take him." They did.

"You talk about being lucky in the draft. We were definitely very fortunate to get Dwight," McVay added. "Probably the thing that caused it to happen is Bill personally worked him out on his own campus and seen him. As you know, when you first meet Dwight, you are charmed. He's a charming guy and a hell of a football player."

Clark combined both those attributes to become one of the most beloved athletes in Bay Area history and among the 49ers' initial honorees to their Hall of Fame in 2009. "He was the nicest guy and he never expected to make it, and that's not B.S.," Madden said. "He was surprised to work out with Steve Fuller, surprised to get drafted, surprised to make the team. He was as humble as you could get. His football legacy is The Catch, but he was so much more than that."

Clark delivered 48 regular-season touchdowns and three playoff scores while spending his entire nine NFL seasons with the Niners. You probably can guess what was his only go-ahead, fourth-quarter touchdown catch.

On January 10, 1982, Clark soared into the air toward the back right corner of Candlestick Park's north end zone, where he grabbed Montana's last-minute, six-yard touchdown pass to lift the 49ers to a 28–27 win, thus propelling them to their first Lombardi Trophy and launching the 49ers' Super Bowl dynasty. "When I threw it, I knew it was high. I thought it was above his head," Montana recalled 25 years later. "I always say, 'It's like when you throw paper into the trash can, you kind of have an idea whether you're going to hit it long or short or you're going to make it.' Well, I let it go and got knocked down and I got to the sideline. I still remember [equipment manager] Chico Norton coming to me and saying, 'Your buddy saved your ass that time. He jumped out of the stadium.' I said, 'Get out of here. He can't jump that high.' I thought Chico was just playing around, so I was playing around with him. It wasn't until I went back and saw the replay...I didn't realize the ball was that high. Thank God he could get off of his feet."

Vin Scully's call on CBS' telecast poetically captured The Catch: "Clark caught it! Dwight Clark! It's a madhouse at Candlestick with 51 seconds left. Dwight Clark is 6'4". He stands about 10 feet tall in this crowd's estimation."

Cornerback Eric Wright's game-saving tackle of Drew Pearson on the Dallas Cowboys' ensuing possession locked in Clark's place in NFL lore.

Clark and Montana were brought back 25 years later to recreate that play at a November 5, 2006 game, in which the host 49ers beat the Minnesota Vikings 9–3 in a game with no sign of a touchdown other than the Montana-Clark redux. In the days leading up that return, Clark had his daughter, Casey, find the 49ers' game-winning drive on YouTube so he could appreciate it all over again. "Some of the throws and the play calling, the blocks, it's all an amazing drive," Clark said in 2006.

"And to do that against America's Team was just too sweet... It just seemed like it was destiny. No matter what happened, we were going to find a way to win that game."

Clark and the 49ers kept winning and he kept making catches—506 in all. He produced an NFL-best 60 receptions in 1982 to earn his second straight Pro Bowl berth. "With Dwight you always saw the talent, the soft hands, and he'd run routes based on the way the defender was trying to work him, so he had the latitude to either run inside or out," safety Carlton Williamson said. "He ran routes in smart ways, and that's why he really had a lot of catches. With his soft hands, he had a lot of great catches for us."

Clark reached 250 receptions quicker than any previous 49ers receiver, doing so in 59 games. That's the same amount it took Deebo Samuel from 2019 to 2023 in a much more passing-friendly league; Jerry Rice and Michael Crabtree reached the 250-catch mark in 57 games. Of Clark's 48 regular-season touchdowns, 41 came on throws from Montana, and that was just a tiny reflection of their connection that began in 1979. "I remember when we were having our training camp at Sierra College, and Dwight and Joe Montana bonded," McVay said. "They were together all the time. They were, as you can recall, young and full of vigor. They enjoyed playing tricks on some of the coaches. One time they went a step almost too far, where they took Bill Walsh's bicycle and put it on the roof of a building."

Clark, though, also had misplaced a treasured item of his own. For years Clark thought he safely stashed The Catch football inside the closet of his North Carolina home. But in 2005 a fan, William F. McDonagh Jr., claimed to have purchased the true football for $50,000 a few years earlier from Jack McGuire, a ballboy in the 1982 NFC title game who told *Sports Illustrated* he gave Clark a different ball. Front and center in the 49ers' museum at Levi's Stadium is a glass case displaying the original football, and it's duly noted that it is on loan by McDonagh.

As fans enter the stadium's northwest A gate, they see two statues of the most iconic moment in 49ers history: Clark in midair making The Catch, and Montana in the distance with arms raised in celebration. "At the time I felt very fortunate to be a part of the team and be on the team with guys like Joe Montana, Ronnie Lott, Bill Walsh, and Eddie DeBartolo, our owner, and all the great players from that team," Clark said in 2006. "It was like a dream."

After his playing days, he moved into the 49ers' front office and eventually the Cleveland Browns' before returning to the 49ers as an ambassador and a television analyst. His life took a tragic turn in 2015, when he learned he had ALS, also known as Lou Gehrig's Disease. Clark went public with his diagnosis in March 2017 and he received an outpouring of support, especially from DeBartolo; Lott; Clark's wife, Kelly; and his brother, Jeff.

Former 49ers coach Steve Mariucci was among the parade of former teammates and friends who'd travel from all over the country to see Clark and have emotion-packed lunches at a Capitola café just south of Santa Cruz. "For a couple hours, we'd tell stories and laugh and cry and reminisce," Mariucci said. "Each time you saw him, you knew it was getting closer."

Mariucci and his wife, Gayle, followed by Lott and his wife, Karen, paid their final respects to Clark just before he passed away in Whitefish, Montana, on June 4, 2018. Clark bid farewell to "my 49ers Faithful" eight months earlier, when he addressed the Levi's Stadium crowd at halftime of an October 2017 game against, fittingly, the Cowboys. More than 50 teammates gathered on the field for a halftime ceremony, and Montana grabbed the mic. "We started in '79, rookies and roommates," Montana told the crowd. "He never unpacked his bag. He always thought he was going to get cut. Here he is standing the test of time. We thank you for the joy you brought to our life and we all love you."

With that Montana passed the mic, so to speak, to Clark, who gave his address from a suite behind the south end zone. "I want to thank you for all the support as a player," Clark began. "You all know I'm going through a little thing right now, and I need your prayers and thoughts and I appreciate those you've given me."

12
Ronnie Lott

Any time a four-time Super Bowl champion starts building a mansion atop a hill in your neighborhood, it's kind of a big deal. It certainly was back in about 1990. Ronnie Lott's 6,000-square-foot abode overlooked Silicon Valley, an area renowned for computer startups and also home to an NFL franchise whose stock soared thanks in large part to Lott.

Imagine being a teenager who lived down the hill from a sports hero and occasionally driving by or riding bikes to perhaps catch a glimpse of one of the NFL's ultimate gladiators.

Bill Walsh considered him the greatest defensive back ever. Teammates cherished Lott's leadership and humanitarianism. Fans knew the sacrifice Lott was willing to make for his team and his sport. "Sacrifice" is such an overblown word in sports. When it comes to Lott, however, it's a deeply earned title.

Flash back to November 5, 2003. Lott descended from his Cupertino hilltop to the San Francisco 49ers' Santa Clara headquarters. In the team's meeting room, Lott sat before reporters with two of his red, No. 42 jerseys hanging in the backdrop. This was a press conference about his jersey retirement more than 20 years since he burst on the scene as a playmaking cornerback, an eventual hard-hitting safety, and arguably the greatest locker room leader ever. The ceremonial retirement of a jersey number, an automatic nod for such prestigious players, actually seemed trivial for what Lott meant to the franchise and his sport. And what it meant to him.

Lott wiped away tears, paused for 15 seconds, then explained "The Pinkie." Actually, he described how he'd tell his children why the tip of his left hand's pinkie finger was missing. It had been caught in a Dallas Cowboys player's facemask. He tried playing with a cast covering it and weeks later had it amputated. "You try to explain there are sacrifices that you make," Lott said. "Sometimes those sacrifices you make, people don't understand it. But at some point, they'll get it. That's what I'm hoping they'll get. At some point in their life, they'll be able to make sacrifices for their teammates, they'll make sacrifices for their friends. But it's kind of hard to get people to understand why would you do that. So my kids right now probably think it looks like E.T.'s head. But at some point, they'll realize that's an important aspect of the Lott family—making sacrifices for others."

Jersey retirements typically are a festive occasion filled with blubbery and embellished stories. Not Lott. This appropriately was a hard-hitting affair that symbolized his commitment, pride, and leadership. "For all the guys that play the game and see they can't wear 42, hopefully they'll know it's because of a certain honor of how I honored the game, and that it wasn't given to me," Lott said. "I earned it and played the game for the right reasons."

His career resonates for a multitude of reasons beyond grainy highlights of crushing hits or acrobatic interception returns for touchdowns (he had five, including three as a rookie). Quarterback Steve Young pinpoints Lott's impact for the inspiration he provided during the peak of the 49ers' quarterback controversy between Young and Joe Montana. "One of my darkest moments came in '90 or '91," Young said, "Ronnie could see it. So he grabs my shoulder, looks me in the eye, and screams at me, 'I got your back! You don't need to worry!...It meant the world to me he did that."

Young relays that story to modern-day 49ers to demonstrate that such brotherhood will pay off and that insecurity has no place in pro football.

Lott, Montana, Keena Turner, Eric Wright, and Mike Wilson played on the franchise's first four Super Bowl-winning teams from 1981 to 1989. It was a dynasty, and that meant a lot to Lott, who grew up admiring the Boston Celtics' run that produced 11 championships from 1957 to 1969. Basketball is forever embedded in Lott's soul. He said with sincerity that making a basket for USC's basketball team was "bigger than playing in the Rose Bowl."

Lott has long had courtside seats for the Golden State Warriors, and in 2022, as they closed in on their fourth NBA championship in eight years, they had Lott's backing. "I'm rooting for them," Lott said, "just for the greatness of winning."

13
Jerry Rice

Jerry Rice obliged San Francisco 49ers fans with selfie photos, then stepped over a three-foot tall partition and onto Levi's Stadium's field, where he naturally headed for the end zone. Nearly 20 years after his retirement, he went there again. This was before the 2023 home-opening win against the New York Giants, when Rice resumed his pregame ritual of greeting and hyping up the 49ers' modern-day wide receivers. Eventually, Rice retreated to his front-row seat in a red, leather recliner situated behind the end zone—an area that no one in NFL history knew better than he.

It was the perfect time and place to ask him this question: which of his NFL-record 208 touchdowns is his fondest? Rice considered his spectrum of scores and concluded: No. 127. "I had the opportunity to break Jim Brown's record on *Monday Night Football* against the Raiders," Rice responded. "The greatest football player ever, Jim Brown. So I broke his record. I had to get three touchdowns. The last one was No. 127, and I'll never forget it. And I got a chance to celebrate it with my teammates and my family."

Rice's record-breaking moment came in the September 5, 1994 season opener at Candlestick Park. He started in motion to the left, turned up field, and jumped at the 2-yard line to beat out cornerback Albert Lewis for Steve Young's 38-yard touchdown pass. It came with five minutes, 29 seconds left in a 44–14 rout of the then-Los Angeles Raiders. Candlestick's crowd rose in unison and chanted "Jer-ry! Jer-ry!" Teammates soaked in the moment, and Young afterward correctly predicted that Rice's touchdown totals had "a lot more to go."

Rice's 49ers tenure spanned from 1985 to 2000, so he was entering Year 10 when it came time to surpass Brown, who piled up his points in just nine seasons with the Cleveland Browns (1957–65). Rice had no touchdowns in his three previous games against the Raiders. Then he caught up with three in that 1994 opener. He started with a 69-yard touchdown catch in the first quarter to tie Walter Payton for No. 2 on the all-time list. Rice's second score was a 23-yard run (his seventh of 10 career rushing touchdowns). Since Rice eclipsed Brown's bar, nine other players followed suit to reflect the NFL's high-scoring popularity: Emmitt Smith (175), LaDanian Tomlinson (162), Randy Moss (157), Terrell Owens (156), Marcus Allen (145), Marshall Faulk (136), Cris Carter (131), Marvin Harrison (128), and Adrian Peterson (126).

Touchdowns don't define Rice's career. Heck, he left the NFL also owning all the significant receiving records (1,549 receptions and 22,895 yards). His scores, however, encapsulate his greatness to deliver points for a perennial contender that had won two Super Bowl titles in the four years before he arrived and then hoisted the Lombardi Trophy three more times with him.

The 208 regular-season touchdowns are an indelible standard. Playoffs are where legacies are truly defined or emboldened, and Rice excelled on that stage, too. He produced a record 22 touchdowns in the playoffs. Eight came in his four Super Bowl appearances, and the last came with him in a Raiders uniform during their 2002 team's title-game drubbing by the Tampa Bay Bucs. "They all were different," Rice said of his Super Bowl scores. "All of those Super Bowls meant something different to me. I couldn't say one was better than the other one. The most important thing for me, it was not losing. We had to win for the fans, and that was it."

Sure enough, a 14-yard touchdown catch pulled the 49ers into a 13–13 tie in their 1988 team's Super Bowl XXIII win, which is known more for John Taylor's last-minute touchdown to topple the Cincinnati Bengals 20–16. But Rice won Super Bowl MVP honors with 215 yards on 11 catches. The next year's Super Bowl, Rice had three touchdowns. His 20-yard touchdown catch provided a 7–0 lead, a 38-yarder pushed it to 27–3, and a 28-yarder extended the margin to 34–3 in the 55–10 blowout of the Denver Broncos in New Orleans' Superdome.

Once the 49ers returned to the Super Bowl with their star-studded 1994 team, Rice again produced three touchdowns, starting with a 44-yard scoring strike from Young on the game's third snap to set the tone in their 49–26 rout of the San Diego Chargers in Miami. Maybe that touchdown sticks with the younger generation of 49ers Faithful. Or maybe they've uncovered YouTube videos of his regular-season masterpieces like a last-second touchdown for a 1987 win at the Bengals or a last-minute, 78-yard Hail Mary catch to beat the New York Giants the following September. "Oh, the Hail Mary, where

Eddie DeBartolo had gone into the locker room, ready to curse everybody out," Rice recalled, "then we went in, said we had won, and he was so excited."

There was the 1988 game against the Minnesota Vikings when Rice threw a block to help clear Young's zigzagged path on a legendary, 49-yard touchdown run. There was a 1995 game in Atlanta where Rice scored first on a fumble recovery against the Falcons then later threw his only career touchdown pass—to J.J. Stokes.

A decade earlier in October of 1984, Bill Walsh was in his Houston hotel room, sipping his drink of the night (a margarita) and watching local college highlights the night before the 49ers faced the Houston Oilers. Sprinting across his television screen was a Mississippi Valley State wide receiver. Rice had 17 catches for 199 yards in a 55–42 win against Texas Southern. The 49ers traded up to draft him 16th overall in 1985.

The records piled up before his surreal yet anticipated June 2001 release. "Jerry is my favorite player, favorite person. It's been a great run," Walsh said in the run-up to Rice's final home game in 2000. "Who is to have ever considered the possibility that we had the greatest player of all time here?"

News broke just as Rice was about to tee off at his annual charity golf tournament at Los Altos Golf and Country Club in 2001. Speculation was that he'd stay in the Bay Area, and though he wouldn't confirm it, Walsh essentially did. "The closure of this is great, and I'm glad it's the Raiders," Walsh said in the golf course's parking lot. "I'm glad he's right here close to home and that [his release] was not difficult, that he doesn't feel he was sent to Devil's Island or somewhere out in the Midwest."

49ers Faithful may have seen the Raiders as a devilish defection, but Rice added to his legacy with three-plus seasons there, then made his swan song in 11 games with the 2004 Seattle

Seahawks. In 2010 the Pro Football Hall of Fame welcomed him in as a first-ballot lock, and a month later, the 49ers retired No. 80, making him the 16th player in team history to receive such an honor.

He didn't go quietly into retirement. His crave of the spotlight carried over to *Dancing with the Stars*, golf tournaments, commercials, and speaking engagements. He never looks more at home than when he unabashedly graces—and sometimes runs 100-yard sprints or plays catch—pregame warmups on the 49ers' home field, 37 miles south of Candlestick at Levi's Stadium in Santa Clara. Even at age 60, he looked capable of another go route despite being adorned in white, Dolce & Gabbana sneakers with red jeans while wearing a necklace of a bejeweled, fist-size 49ers helmet.

No need, though. His touchdown record looks safely out of reach. Or is it? "Well, in today's football, the ball is in the air a majority of time," Rice said before adding this caveat: "I don't know if anyone is willing to sacrifice and commit to it."

14

Roger Craig

Just up the road from the San Francisco 49ers' old training facility and just 23 miles south of Candlestick Park, The Hill awaits its challengers. Find a parking spot on Edgewood Road, stretch the legs, then start the ascent, initially veering left up a narrow trail. Switchbacks await, as does the climb in elevation, until the summit appears at the 20-minute (or understandably longer) mark. The payoff is not merely a scenic view to the east of the Bay Area waters or a glance to the west of more hills obstructing Half Moon Bay. This hill run became a famous training method for Roger Craig, as he became an NFL pioneer and the 49ers' multi-dimensional running back in the 1980s.

Others followed Craig's trailblazing training method, including a teammate who also adopted The Hill as his own secret weapon. "I remember when he went up the first time, he stopped two or three times, and we didn't see Jerry Rice again for about three weeks," Craig recalled. "I said, 'You've got to finish that hill.'"

Bay Area outdoorsmen can relate. When it comes to the football field, however, Craig's pioneering spirit carved a path that few dared to follow. Craig's 1985 season, his third with the 49ers, was the NFL's first in which a player produced 1,000 yards rushing (1,050) and receiving (1,016 on an NFL best 92 catches). Marshall Faulk became the next 1K/1K player for the 1999 Super Bowl-champion St. Louis Rams. When Christian McCaffrey joined that fraternity in 2019—also his third season—Craig celebrated. "He sent me a really nice message. I was very appreciative," McCaffrey recalled in 2022 when he joined the 49ers. "He didn't have to do that, but that was definitely good company to be a part of...He's the man. He's special."

Paying homage to Craig is a rite of passage for any 49ers star running back and vice versa because Craig's class and character were exemplary. When Frank Gore's 2010 season was cut short because of a hip fracture, Craig was among those championing his ensuing comeback, even though Gore was poised to pass Craig for the No. 2 spot on the 49ers' all-time rushing list. "He's happy for me," Gore said upon surpassing Craig in 2011 (and eventually overtaking Joe "The Jet" Perry for the franchise's all-time record). "Roger and I became really close these last two years. When I got injured, he called me a lot this offseason, telling me what I had to do and I'd be fine, that this year I'd come back and prove a lot of people wrong who thought I couldn't be the guy I've always been."

Entering the 1983 draft, Bill Walsh thought Craig could be the perfect guy for his state-of-the-art West Coast Offense. "He loved Roger. He loved his versatility," then-owner Eddie DeBartolo recalled. "He knew what he could do when he came to the pros. Roger gave us a different dimension."

Craig ran for 7,064 yards and 50 touchdowns from 1983 to 1990 and he produced 4,442 more yards on 508 receptions, 16 of which went for touchdowns. He set franchise records with nine rushing touchdowns in 1985 and then again in '88, marks that would be surpassed by Ricky Watters, Derek Loville, Gore, and ultimately McCaffrey. Craig scored the most touchdowns in a season by a 49ers running back with 12 in 1983, then he raised that bar to 15 in 1985, and it stood until 2023 when a record-breaking, 21-touchdown effort came from McCaffrey.

Craig's production and presence were instrumental as he won three Super Bowl rings, starting with a three-touchdown showing in the 1984 team's 38–16 win against the Miami Dolphins. With 84,059 fans crammed into Stanford Stadium—a 10-mile trek from The Hill—Craig scored the go-ahead touchdown on an eight-yard pass from Joe Montana, then came a two-yard touchdown run for a 28–10 halftime lead, and, for the hat trick, Craig and his high-knee style ran 16 yards into the end zone for a third-quarter score to cap the barrage.

Craig proved just as successful in the next two Super Bowl wins. He opened their 1988 team's playoff run by rushing for 135 yards and two touchdowns in a 34–9 win against the Minnesota Vikings, he followed that with 101 total yards in the NFC Championship Game win against the Chicago Bears, and in a 20–16 Super Bowl win against the Cincinnati Bengals Craig rang up 101 receiving yards with 71 rushing yards.

The 49ers opened their title defense the following postseason with another win against Minnesota, and Craig rushed for 125 yards and a touchdown. He'd deliver a touchdown run in all three of their playoff triumphs, and it was his one-yard run that capped the scoring barrage in a 55–10 thrashing of the Denver Broncos in Super Bowl XXIV in New Orleans.

Craig appeared in 16 playoff games for the 49ers, but the 16th had an infamous ending in the 1990 season's NFC Championship Game. Craig collided with linemen on a run up the middle and fumbled at the New York Giants' 43-yard line with two-and-a-half minutes remaining. The Giants converted that turnover—arguably the most notorious fumble in 49ers history—into Matt Bahr's 42-yard field goal as time expired on the 49ers' three-peat bid. "Joe [Montana] got hurt [on a sack with 10 minutes remaining], and that set us back, and then other unfortunate things happened in the game with me fumbling," Craig recalled in 2005. "Then our defense couldn't stop the Giants from driving down field."

Some two months later, Craig left the 49ers in free agency and followed Ronnie Lott's path to the Los Angeles Raiders. By the way, when the 49ers retired Lott's No. 42 jersey in 2003, Lott lobbied for them to do the same in honor of Craig's No. 33, to no avail. Craig finished his career with two seasons on the Vikings, then returned to the Bay Area, where he'd work 25 years for TIBCO Software.

Craig also took up marathon running, a reminder of his conditioning days in the 49ers' offseasons and those grueling climbs up The Hill. "Your offseason will make or break you as a running back," Craig said in 2004. "You have nagging injuries during a season. What helps you get through is what you have in the tank, and that comes from what you did in the offseason."

Craig got that advice from Walter Payton at the 1986 Pro Bowl. Sure, the 49ers and the Bears were NFC rivals at the time, but Payton's mentorship reflected his pure heart. "He told me to help the next young guy to come up. I thought about Jerry Rice," said Craig, who approached Rice after his 1985 rookie season and introduced him to something special: The Hill.

Tom Rathman ran it just once with them. “When you run it with Jerry and Roger, they were flying,” Rathman said. “And you’re terrified you’re going to get lost.”

Rathman and Craig formed a cohesive backfield for five seasons with the 49ers and they were able to switch positions between fullback and running back when Craig needed a breather as the lead rusher. Their backfield bond traced back to college. “Some of my best memories were at Nebraska when I was a freshman, and he was an upperclassman who took me under his wing,” Rathman recalled. “We had the same view of the game and how to be successful.”

15

Edd-ie! Edd-ie!

SUCCEEDING EDDIE DEBARTOLO AS THE SAN FRANCISCO 49ers' primary owner was an unenviable task. He is a beloved icon after all as the most popular owner in the history of Bay Area pro sports and he rightfully has a bust in the Pro Football Hall of Fame. So, the 49ers were in Y2K chaos as ownership officially transferred to his sister, Denise DeBartolo York, and her husband, Dr. John York, with their oldest son, Jed, eventually shifting from CEO to principal owner.

Every failed run at a Super Bowl, every coaching change, every management blunder, every quarterback switch, and every budget cut invited the 49ers Faithful's fury. "I had it rougher than Jed," DeBartolo recalled of his infancy as an owner in the late 1970s during a 2016 interview. "When I came to Candlestick Park a couple of times, I mean I had people throw things at me. I got hit with a full beer can once.

I had people spit at me. That's how much they cared and felt about their team."

All in all, DeBartolo's passion matched and likely surpassed even the most fervent fan during his ownership reign, which delivered the Lombardi Trophy five times along with an all-time great coach in Bill Walsh, two Hall of Fame quarterbacks in Joe Montana and Steve Young, and a stream of football legends such as Jerry Rice and Ronnie Lott.

How adored did DeBartolo become? Imagine going to someone else's memorial service and having thousands chant your name. That is what happened at Candlestick Park in August 2007, when 8,000 fans graciously serenaded "Edd-ie! Edd-ie!" at Walsh's public memorial.

DeBartolo drew that adoration not simply as a visible owner from the franchise's Camelot heyday, but also, as he acknowledged, "a lot of it has to do with the success we had."

It wasn't just DeBartolo's financial generosity that fueled the 49ers' dynasty. He desperately needed help to turn around a moribund franchise bought in 1977 by his father, Edward J. DeBartolo Sr. The turning point came after a 1978 season that produced two wins, 14 losses, a nine-game losing streak, two coaches, and the rueful arrival of a past-his-prime O.J. Simpson. Come 1979, Walsh was hired as coach, Montana was drafted at the end of the third round, and away they went. "Mr. DeBartolo came in with the idea he could make a turnaround. When he found Bill," Montana said, "it was a match made in heaven."

After that rough start, they made it to pro football's winner circle five times under DeBartolo in the 1981, '84, '88, '89, and '94 seasons. "I just said to myself, *I have to do something about this because this can't go on,*" DeBartolo recalled. "Bill came in;

we had a tough year. He didn't turn things around right away. Then we had our drafts and brought good people in. Besides players, we brought good management people in, turned things around, and there we are."

It took until 2016 for the Pro Football Hall of Fame to enshrine him. Those two decades in between were—in a word—awkward for DeBartolo's legacy. He essentially got run out of the NFL because of a scandal, in which he pled guilty for failing to report a felony after paying $400,000 to former Louisiana governor Edwin Edwards in pursuit of a gambling license. DeBartolo got pardoned in 2020 by then-president Donald Trump, and among those attending a White House ceremony for it were Rice, Lott, and Charles Haley.

Such loyal support was nothing new. Flash back to 2008 when DeBartolo was entering the Bay Area Sports Hall of Fame much to the chagrin of bittersweet ex-players who campaigned for his inclusion into Canton's hallowed Hall. "This is great, but we want to get him the real deal," Rice said at a gathering of 49ers greats on DeBartolo's behalf at a Union Square hotel in downtown San Francisco. "What he did for the NFL, having a dynasty, and having a team that represented the NFL the right way with a lot of character, I think it's time."

Montana, who greeted DeBartolo with a kiss on his cheek at that event, said: "It went way beyond the football field. Guys noticed that when they had issues, like with their families, he was the first person there to help. He had genuine love for players, and you could feel that in the locker room."

"Playing for Eddie was a pleasure. We bet the farm," Steve Young said at his Pro Football Hall of Fame induction. "How could you not love playing for Eddie? The rumors were true. He was the best."

The 49ers Faithful returns that sentiment any time DeBartolo surfaces at Levi's Stadium. He's typically lured from his Tampa-area home to celebrate 49ers alumni in halftime ceremonies. And chants of "Edd-ie! Edd-ie!" still follow.

16
Bryant Young

BRYANT YOUNG WORE HIS RED, NO. 97 JERSEY AND A SAN Francisco 49ers ballcap turned backward. Off he rode on teammates' shoulders in his Candlestick Park finale on December 23, 2007. Hoisting up Young was both symbolic and ironic on so many levels. He left as the 49ers' all-time leader with 89 ½ sacks over his 14-year career and he headed for Canton, Ohio, making it there as part of their Pro Football Hall of Fame's 2022 class. When he arrived in San Francisco in 1994 as a first-round draft pick out of Notre Dame, Young would prove tough to move—much less lift—whether it be on the field or off it.

Rookies back then were responsible for bringing breakfast sandwiches to work, and when Young forgot to do so once, that didn't go down so well with hungry, veteran linemen such as Dana Stubblefield, Richard Dent, Rickey Jackson, Tim Harris, Charles Mann, and Dennis Brown. "They said, 'Hey, rook, next time you don't bring sandwiches, we're going to throw your ass in the pool,'" Young recalled in 2022. "So, next time I got up, I was a little late. I said, 'If I go get breakfast sandwiches, I'll be late for this meeting. I'm not getting fined.' So I go to the facility without breakfast."

He faced the consequences. Nine defensive linemen tried to get Young out of the defensive line room and into the team facility's indoor pool. "I scratched, I clawed, I was pulling ankles. People were falling to the ground. I was fighting nine or 10 dudes," Young said. "Finally, we got to the door about 10 yards from the pool, and I just put my hands on the door and they couldn't budge me. I was picking angles, and finally they gave up."

Such an immovable object helped the 49ers' defense win a Super Bowl his rookie year. He became so admired by teammates that he received the Len Eshmont Award, their highest honor in reflecting inspirational and courageous play, eight times. No other Niners figure had won it more than twice—not Joe Montana (two), Steve Young (two), Jerry Rice (two), or Roger Craig (two).

Bryant Young's 1994–2007 teure overlapped with that of another Hall of Fame-bound 49er: Terrell Owens, who attended the Dwight Clark Legacy Series in 2022 to pay homage to Young while sharing a stage with Steve Young and Charles Haley in Walnut Creek, California. "I wouldn't be here or even considering going to the Hall of Fame if it wasn't for B.Y.," Owens said. "As far as my relationship with the Hall of Fame, I don't have one. But when it comes to being there for your brothers and a teammate like B.Y., the way he showed up every day and his professionalism, he's a gentle giant. He's quiet, but when the beast needed to come out, you saw it on the field...I'd walk in the locker room every day, marvel at his work, his professionalism, and the way he played."

Young started every game that Super Bowl-winning season as a rookie and all 208 regular-season games he would play in his career. Two years later, he had two safeties and his first double-digit sack season (11 ½). Two seasons later, he had nine-and-a-half sacks and two forced fumbles a dozen games into the 1998 season. Then his right leg's fibula and tibula were snapped in a nasty collision with teammate Ken Norton Jr.

Young returned to win the 1999 season's NFL Comeback Player of the Year award, notching 11 sacks and earning his second Pro Bowl berth but only after overcoming post-surgical complications and playing with an 18-inch stabilizing rod. "It was about really earning the respect of those guys," Young said. "How can I do that best? I'm not going to go out there and talk. Those guys can talk and do the rant and raving. Let me go show you and earn the respect of my teammates."

He didn't speak up often, but when he did, teammates were wise enough to listen. The 49ers were down 14–0 at Atlanta in 2001, and with defensive players slumped on the bench, Young stood up before them to give an impassioned speech. "We weren't playing up to our standard. That's what I was emphasizing," Young said after the 37–31 overtime win against the Falcons. "Regardless of the situation during the game, we have to play up to our standard."

Young's soft-spoken nature was instilled in him by his father, Tommy, who was a big proponent that talk is cheap, and actions speak louder than words. "You were a baller, man. When I came back my last year [in 1999], I saw a lion, and you roared. I'm proud to have played with you," Haley told Young on that 2022 Walnut Creek stage. "You taught me a lot. I'd never been around a guy that could be humble and smile and still play with such tenacity. I just wanted you to know you did help me."

Haley said those touching words a couple of months before Young's Pro Football Hall of Fame induction. Young, a father of six with his wife, Kristin, reflected on life's lessons as he headed to Canton 15 years after teammates carried him off the Candlestick Park field. "We go through hard things in life, and the hard things are meant for good as difficult as that may sound," Young said. "Think about the hard things in life that made you better. We experienced things in life that challenge us to our core whether it's injury or losing a child or losing a loved one."

His son Colby was only 15 when he passed away from brain cancer in 2016. Pressing on, Young and his family drew compassion from all corners, and he continues to reciprocate with both actions and words. "It's great to get good things sometimes," Young said, "and be excited to celebrate life."

Such was the case when Haley, dressed in his gold jacket as a Hall of Famer, knocked on the Youngs' front door in Charlotte, North Carolina. Haley came to deliver long-awaited news before the public unveiling of the Pro Football Hall of Fame's Class of 2022. "It was one of the best moments in my life," Haley said, "just to be able to go a teammate and a friend, knock on the door, give him a hug, and say, 'Hey man, welcome to the Hall of Fame.'"

Young, surrounded by his family, was overwhelmed with emotion and he noted that being in the Class of '22 was extra special considering the No. 22 was his late son's favorite. An NFL Films crew was in tow with Haley for the special door knock, and as quite a fitting celebration: Haley pushed Young into the backyard pool. "One guy did what nine people couldn't," Haley proudly said in reference to the attempted 1994 rookie breakfast punishment.

17

T.O.

Terrell Owens got emotional in a heart-wrenching way, as he sat on the lacquered bench inside the San Francisco 49ers locker room. Looming on the 2021 schedule was an October 14 visit to Atlanta, only two-and-a-half hours from his hometown of Alexander City, Alabama, loomed. Owens was entering the prime of his Pro Football Hall of Fame career. Reflecting on his childhood challenges offered a cathartic explanation to how his self-preserving, self-promoting T.O. persona came to be.

At age 10 Owens won a Michael Jackson look-alike contest. He got more than a $25 first-place prize and his picture in *The Alexander City Outlook.* As he danced his way home, he attracted neighbors' attention. "Everybody was looking at him, and he said, 'Mama, I like to be looked at,'" Owens' mother, Marilyn Heard, recalled in 2001. "He wore some black loafers, I put some glitter on his socks, he had a white glove, a hat, and he did a little moonwalk at the end. It was fun. I knew he always had a lot of talent. He had the moves and everything."

At age 11 Owens became smitten with a girl across the street from his little red house at 106 Emerson Street. Then he discovered from her dad that she was Owens' half-sister, and he, L.C. Russell, had fathered Owens, too. "We're fine. I've grown to really understand stuff," Owens said of his relationship with his father. "I just take things for what they're worth. Why be upset about something that happened so long ago?"

The same can be said about the ending of his 49ers career, which to the very end was complicated. A three-team trade sent him to the Philadelphia Eagles after his agent was late to fax in the paperwork that would have made him a free agent. Fifteen years later Owens was inducted to the 49ers' Hall of Fame. That came a year after the Pro Football Hall of Fame enshrined him three years into his eligibility, which angered him so much that he bypassed the ceremony in Canton, Ohio. His acceptance speech instead came at his alma mater, the University of Tennessee-Chattanooga. Owens, though, didn't miss his 49ers' enshrinement. "That's where I started my career," Owens said in 2019. "So this is only right or fitting because I did great things in the Bay Area."

In fact, Owens returned to the 49ers' home of Levi's Stadium in April 2024 to watch his son, Terique, compete in a tryout for local prospects, which was enough to convince the 49ers to sign the younger Owens after he went undrafted.

For someone constantly seeking adoration and validation, Terrell Owens didn't take an easy path to becoming one of the best football players ever. His truly was a rags-to-riches story. In Alexander City's Tallapoosa County, the hometown hero wasn't Owens as much as Russell Athletic, a clothing apparel giant that ran its headquarters there for years and where his mother worked a double shift. Football—and the weight room—became Owens' passion after his junior year at Benjamin Russell High, where he also excelled in basketball and track.

Drafted in the third round, Owens came to the 1996 49ers with Southern manners and unlisted expectations. "I was raw, I was green, and I had no idea what I was going to do and what I was going to become," Owens said in 2019.

He would learn, practice, and compete alongside Jerry Rice, the NFL's best-ever receiver, scorer, and practice field example. What a passing of the torch it was in the 49ers' 2000 home finale when Owens set an NFL record with 20 receptions (for 283 yards) to overshadow Rice's farewell game. As Rice cleaned out his locker months later, Owens helped take boxes to Rice's car, and Rice gave him the ceremonial gameball from that game against the Chicago Bears, as witnessed by the Associated Press' Dennis Georgatos.

Owens crested 1,000 yards in five of his final six seasons with the 49ers. "I wanted to bring another championship to the Bay Area, and unfortunately that didn't happen," Owens said in 2019. "But it wasn't because I didn't put my heart and soul into that uniform."

No one ever questioned Owens' passion for excellence. That heart and soul was on full display when he cried on coach Steve Mariucci's shoulder after making The Catch II—a 25-yard, game-winning touchdown grab against the Green Bay Packers with eight seconds left for a 30–27 wild-card playoff win on January 3, 1999 at 3Com Park.

Owens' relationship with Mariucci took a nasty turn 21 months later. Owens scored two touchdowns to spark a September 2000 win at the Dallas Cowboys and twice he celebrated by racing to the Cowboys' midfield logo. Mariucci suspended him a week and fined him $24,294, though Owens did recoup $8,000 in a settlement with the team. Banished from the 49ers' facility, Owens fled home—not to his 4,000-square-foot mansion in Fremont, California, but rather back to Alexander City.

Two decades later, Owens still held a grudge against his former coach, claiming Mariucci fueled his reputation as a selfish player who was a headache in the locker room. Owens said Mariucci "never took the time to really get to know who I was. That's what's really, really sad...I didn't really play the politics game. That's what he was about—more of the politics than being more as a coach and getting to know me as a person. He had his favorites. It was a double standard, and I didn't care too much about that."

It wasn't that simple, however. Politics aside, Owens was a handful. He'd certainly play hard for the 49ers, but along the way, he could alienate teammates, even getting into a training camp brawl with one of his few allies, offensive lineman Derrick Deese. Wide receiver coaches Larry Kirksey and George Stewart proved instrumental in Owens' maturation. "He is a complex human being with a lot of emotion and a lot of fire," 49ers coowner Dr. John York said in 2003. "I don't think either one of us knew each other in Dallas. We've come a long way since then. He's just truly a great player who's unique both in football and outside of football. Nobody's going to ever change that."

Owens radiated drama—whether through on-field actions that were good and bad—or postgame words that could be daggers at a quarterback, such as Jeff Garcia, who fed Owens the football in his prime years.

Owens made All-Pro and Pro Bowl teams from 2000 to 2002 while annually totaling more than 1,300 receiving yards. He led the NFL in touchdown receptions in 2001 with 16 and in 2002 with 13. He made a fourth Pro Bowl in 2003 before his NFL journey took him to the Philadelphia Eagles (2004–05), Dallas Cowboys (2006–08), Buffalo Bills (2009), and the Cincinnati Bengals (2010). He entered the Pro Football Hall of Fame ranking third all time with 15,934 receiving yards and 153 touchdowns. While wearing jersey No. 81 with the 49ers, he totaled 81 regular-season touchdowns, which ranked second only to Rice's 176. Owens also trailed only Rice in the 49ers' record book with 592 receptions, 8,572 receiving yards, 25 100-yard games, and five 1,000-yard seasons. "From the outside looking in, you'd think I've got a glamorous life," Owens said in 2001. "It's sad sometimes. It's hard, man. It's frustrating."

Not long after saying so, Owens took center stage in Atlanta and scored three touchdowns in a 37–31 overtime win against the Falcons, including a 17-yard scoring grab with 17 seconds left in regulation and then the game-winner on a 52-yard bomb from Garcia to end it.

It was his only three-touchdown game as a 49ers player, though he went on to have two with the Eagles and two with the Cowboys, one of which saw him produce a career-high four touchdowns on just eight catches in a 2007 win against Washington.

Owens appeared in one Super Bowl, making nine catches for 122 yards on a recently fractured fibula and sprained ankle, but that wasn't enough to prevent the Eagles' 24–21 loss to the New England Patriots in Super Bowl XXXIX on February 6, 2005 in Jacksonville, Florida.

There would be no pulling a Sharpie out of his sock to autograph a touchdown ball like he did in Seattle. There would be no grabbing a cheerleader's pompoms or a fan's popcorn to celebrate. There would be no dunking over the goalposts like he did to rock the Georgia Dome after that overtime winner in 2001. "I'm satisfied as long as we win," Owens said of that hometown win in Atlanta. "It was tough in the first half...I wasn't going to let that shake me."

Such is life for one of the most flamboyant, fantastic, and perplexing players in 49ers' history.

18
Frank Gore

Frank Gore was standing on the finely manicured grass at Levi's Stadium under the California sunshine. He was watching running backs, of course. Not even a year into retirement, Gore couldn't pull himself away from the game—and franchise—he loves. On this sunny spring day in April 2022, NFL draft prospects were auditioning as long shots in the San Francisco 49ers' annual tryout for local players. None went on to get drafted, but it made for a nice community outreach event at the very least. So why was Gore there? An aspiring scout? Indeed and he was officially hired in 2023 as a personnel advisor who'd travel to college games and eye talent.

Truth be told, he was a longshot himself back in the 2005 draft. The 49ers, at the urging of Scot McCloughan, saw something in the University of Miami running back who came with a surgically repaired anterior cruciate ligament in each knee. But Gore's passion for football burned like an eternal flame inside his 5'9" cauldron. The 49ers saw that spark, and it only cost them a 2005 third-round draft pick (No. 65 overall).

Fast forward 17 years later, Gore played the most games in the history of NFL running backs and ran for the third most yards, an even 16,000. "Frank Gore was their bell cow, kind of like a queen bee," John Madden, the Pro Football Hall of Fame coach, said of Gore in 2015.

Gore won the 49ers' most prestigious honor, the Len Eshmont Award given by teammates to their most courageous and inspiring leader, on his way out the 2014 door. He took away something else to show for his 10 seasons: the title of 49ers' all-time leading rusher. When Gore passed Joe "The Jet" Perry for that crown in 2011, then-coach Jim Harbaugh marveled at Gore's "superhuman powers" and suggested the soon-to-be-built Levi's Stadium come with a statue of Gore "about six inches off the ground, one leg going one way, the other going the other, twisting and turning."

Gore put up 1,000-yard seasons almost annually after unseating Kevan Barlow as the starter in 2006. The lone exception came in 2010 because of a hip fracture. Gore made second-team All-Pro in that 2006 season with a franchise-record 1,695 yards and the first of five Pro Bowl invitations. Gore used his combination of football smarts, great feet, and truly remarkable vision to find running room. "When you see certain movements in the defensive line," he said, "you know where you can punch the ball through."

Gore's lone Super Bowl season came in 2012, and on the way to that not-so-grand finale, he memorably delivered a season-high 131-yard effort in an October win against the rival Seattle Seahawks. Only four days earlier, Gore and the 49ers were battered by the reigning Super Bowl champion New York Giants. "He didn't get enough credit," Madden said of the

Seattle win. "The way he runs, it's like being in a car wreck. [Against the Giants] he was in a car wreck, then went to the hospital, came back, and got in another car wreck."

That 2012 season was in jeopardy of crashing and burning in Atlanta with a Super Bowl berth on the line. Gore came to the rescue against the Falcons. His second-half touchdown runs (five yards in the third quarter, nine yards with 8:23 remaining in the fourth) catapulted the 49ers to a 28–24 win against the top-seeded Falcons in the NFC Championship Game. Gore played 42 of 53 snaps that game, and while he carried the ball half those snaps (90 yards), his pass-protection prowess was vital.

That reliability in protecting the quarterback was almost unmatched in the NFL. At one point late in his 49ers career, Gore earned a 100 percent score on picking up over 30 blocking assignments, to which he quipped: "Damn, I may as well be a fullback."

"He wishes," quipped Tom Rathman, Gore's position coach and a franchise icon who played fullback in his 49ers days. Rathman adored Gore and indeed considered him one of his best blocking backs, along with Garrison Hearst and Charlie Garner.

Ultimately, Gore's 16,000 career rushing yards speak volumes about his remarkable longevity despite surgically repaired knees, shoulders, and much more. In 2013 Gore defiantly would say he was "not ready to pass the baton yet," and teammates fully understood. "That's what makes him great," offensive tackle Anthony Davis said. "If you look at him on the field, he looks like a rookie. Coaches have to pull him out of drills. He's trying to impress himself."

Establishing a legacy was important to him, something he was able to do despite being on some awful teams as the franchise rebooted itself into a playoff contender before he left. He never got the Super Bowl ring. He sure came close, though. How close? Seven yards. The 49ers' incredulous comeback attempt in Super Bowl XLVII saw Gore take Colin Kaepernick's handoff out of the pistol formation and burst loose 33 yards toward paydirt before getting knocked out of bounds at the Ravens' 7-yard line with 2:39 remaining.

Gore never touched the ball again, as the 49ers' hopes instead were dashed as three consecutive fade passes by Kaepernick failed to connect with Michael Crabtree. Limited to just 29 yards at halftime, Gore finished with 110 yards in his lone Super Bowl, and 67 of those came on a quartet of fourth-quarter carries. Gore came away distraught. "He's the type of guy where losing destroys him," said Pete Bommarito, who trained Gore and many other NFL stars.

Two years later, Gore was gone, cast loose into free agency by then-general manager Trent Baalke. Gore stayed productive (2,953 yards with the 2015–17 Indianapolis Colts followed by one-year stints through the AFC East with his hometown Miami Dolphins, the Buffalo Bills, and the New York Jets). The 49ers had no 1,000-yard rushers in eight seasons after his exit. He went into their Edward J. DeBartolo Sr. 49ers Hall of Fame in 2022 and, when he finally returned to Levi's Stadium for a December 4 cameo as the 49ers beat the Dolphins, he said: "I love this place."

Six months later he quietly signed a ceremonial contract to retire as a 49er. He did so without a press conference or really much fanfare at all. He simply issued a statement that encapsulated his 49ers tenure. "One of the very first things I told the 49ers organization when they drafted me in 2005 was that they got the right guy," Gore said. "I knew early on that I wouldn't let my college career define me in regards to injuries and that I would have to outwork a lot of people to get to where I wanted to be. After 10 years in San Francisco and 16 years in the NFL, I can confidently say that I put all I had into the game of football. Football was and is everything to me. From meetings and film study to practice and just being in the locker room, all of it meant the world to me. I am happy to officially close this chapter of my life and proud of what I was able to accomplish and the legacy I leave behind...I will talk about San Francisco as 'we' and 'us' for the rest of my life and will support the 49ers and The Faithful in every way possible."

19

Patrick Willis

Patrick Willis' retirement from the San Francisco 49ers came like one of his signature tackles: a sudden, hard-hitting, ground-shaking impact. "Speed kills, and to have running back speed at 238 pounds is remarkable," former 49ers linebacker Gary Plummer said upon Willis' March 2015 retirement. "He was so aggressive. What you want as a linebacker is no wasted steps."

Willis' feet cruelly ran out of steps before he could finish his eighth season as one of the NFL's best-ever linebackers. Even after his toe surgery in November 2014, Willis hoped to prolong his days in a No. 52 jersey. He relayed to his fans via Instagram that he was determined to get back on the field, to be better than ever, and that "the road back starts now."

Alas, that was the end of the road in a career that began with him winning NFL Rookie of the Year honors in 2007 with a league-leading 174 tackles for a 5–11 team. Seven straight

Pro Bowl nods came his way as did six All-Pro selections up until that final 2014 season, which was limited to six games. At age 30, however, he was done. "I always heard [NFL] football was for Not For Long," Willis said in May 2023. "Whether it ended tomorrow or four years from now, I wanted to be able to evaluate and stop and say, 'Look at this time. I was giving it everything I had.' That's what I was graded on—not what could have been, what I should have done. Take what you see and do what you will with it."

Various Hall of Fames beckoned. The year he retired from the NFL, his alma mater welcomed him into the Ole Miss Sports Hall of Fame. Four years later the College Football Hall of Fame did so, too. In 2021 the 49ers ushered him into their Edward J. DeBartolo Sr. 49ers Hall of Fame complete with a statue of him celebrating a tackle. In 2023 Willis entered the Bay Area Sports Hall of Fame (BASHOF) alongside San Francisco Giants baseball star Buster Posey, who took the Bay Area by storm alongside Steph Curry in their prime. The Pro Football Hall of Fame passed in his first four years of eligibility, but he earned induction in 2024. "He was a throwback player that could have played in our era, could have played with Ronnie Lott, could have played with Dick Butkus," said Plummer, a 49ers linebacker from 1994 to 1997 who served as their radio color analyst as Willis helped build a playoff contender. "He wasn't a showboat. He went out and was a beast on the field."

Mike Singletary, who had a hand in Willis' development—begrudgingly at first—agreed. While presenting Willis at the 2023 BASHOF ceremony, Singletary recalled scouting Willis in college, how he saw an "okay" linebacker who often played hurt with bandages on his hand and knee and foot. "Then someone told me before his last year he had a devastating situation where his brother drowned," Singletary recalled. "Patrick played that year lights out. I didn't really need to see any film on him after that. I said, 'Man we have to get this guy.'"

Singletary, a Hall of Fame linebacker with the Chicago Bears in the 1980s, joined the 49ers in 2005 as linebackers coach, eventually replacing Mike Nolan during the 2008 season. Coaching Willis wasn't a pet project. It was a passion. Willis was drafted No. 11 overall, 17 spots before the 49ers found their franchise left tackle in Joe Staley. Willis would have to abandon his childhood ties rooting for the rival Dallas Cowboys. Two other things crossed his mind when he heard Singletary on a congratulatory call: bag drills in practice and California's taxes.

It was time to leave Tennessee, where his challenging childhood in Bruceton included an abusive, alcoholic father. Willis and his siblings would move in under the guardianship of his high school basketball coach, Chris Finley, and his wife, Julie. "I grew up watching *Baywatch* and *Crocodile Dundee* and being a kid from the South. It's hot summers with some ponds, but you didn't see the ocean," Willis recalled. "I remember as a kid saying, 'One day I want to live somewhere like that and drive a nice car on a nice open highway.' Then I got drafted by the 49ers, and it wasn't long before I had this moment. I walked out on my balcony, the sun was shining and hitting me just right. I said, 'I'm having a real-time moment. I'm exactly where I'm supposed to be.'"

He made an instant impact all right. After Willis' first practice, Singletary told Nolan:

"This guy is going to be All-Pro this year."

"Come on now, don't overdo it, Mike," Nolan responded.

"I'm telling you, man. I just came from Baltimore, coaching Ray Lewis, and I'm telling you: this guy has the ability to be the best ever."

They'd already coached Willis in the Senior Bowl. So his potential wasn't hidden, and even Nolan suggested on draft day how great it would be if Willis drew comparisons to Lewis "in three or four years."

Well, four years later Lewis, the Baltimore Ravens great, told ESPN that Willis "emulates me a lot. I just love the way he plays the game. He plays the game with a fire. He reminds me of myself—a lot, a lot, a lot."

Willis thrived in a starring role on the 49ers' defense, eventually forming an All-Pro tandem with NaVorro Bowman as the 49ers reached three consecutive NFC Championship Games in the 2011–13 seasons. Willis became only the third defensive player in NFL history to earn Pro Bowl berths in each of his first seven seasons. The others were Pro Football Hall of Famers Lawrence Taylor and Derrick Thomas. Ronnie Lott was the only other 49ers player to make the Pro Bowl in his first four seasons. "When you buckle the chin strap, there are no friends," Willis said in 2023. "It's straight business. It's game time. I'd have to tell Marshawn [Lynch] that because he'd try to talk between the lines and I'd say, 'Man, stop talking to me. We'll talk when the game's over.' It's just about knowing what needs to get done and getting it done."

Willis' chatter was limited to pregame huddles. That's where he would look at his teammates, give them a fierce look, and shout: "THIS! IS! THE! DAY!" He'd pause, shoot that look again, and continue: "The day that we put an end to all the critics!"

The best days, or at least the most meaningful and triumphant ones, came as Willis unknowingly entered the twilight of his career. He'd paid his dues before his first winning season came in 2011 with coach Jim Harbaugh and defensive coordinator Vic Fangio pulling the strings instead of Nolan and Singletary.

The 49ers were 9–1 when they marched into Baltimore on Thanksgiving Night that 2011 season. They lost 16–6 to a Ravens team that didn't suit up Lewis because—of all things—a toe injury. The following season Willis and the 49ers lost in the Super Bowl to the Ravens in Lewis' final game as a first-ballot Hall of Famer.

Willis' finale unsuspectingly came October 13, 2014, in St. Louis, where his toe got caught in the Edward Jones Dome's artificial turf amid a 31–17 victory against the Rams. The left toe, he revealed two days later, had bothered him for years, comparing it to the tread wearing thin on a car's tires and preventing him from going full speed in case of a tire blowout. When it did blow out and he had to retire, former NFL quarterback Matt Leinart posted on Twitter. "Still have a chipped tooth from [Willis] knocking me out," he wrote "Congrats on a GREAT career man! Not a nicer guy out there!"

Willis indeed got up and on with his life after his career's abrupt ending. Ole Miss brought him back as a commencement speaker, prompting these inspiring words: "Purpose, vision, and passion when aligned creates a force, a will that is hard to stop. So, for the Class of 2020, as you go forward, do it with purpose, do it with vision, and do it with passion."

As Bay Area native Tom Brady headed for his sixth Super Bowl win with the New England Patriots, a retired Willis couldn't fathom what Brady was doing at age 41—or envision him winning a seventh ring two years later with the Tampa Bay Buccaneers. "That's crazy," Willis said in a January 2019 interview. "Mentally, when I finished, I felt so old and tired. How can guys play forever like that all those years?"

In the end it wasn't about how long he played but rather how he played. With Willis' blazing speed, brick-wall force, and resilience in triumphing over life's obstacles, his legacy is stamped forever in 49ers lore. "I saw this young man overcome one thing after another," Singletary said. "Every time he got punched, every time he got knocked down, he just kept getting back up. I love a man that gets up every time."

PART 3

COACHES

20

George Seifert

When fans rank the San Francisco 49ers' best coaches, No. 1 is Bill Walsh, and No. 2 is whoever just presided over their most recent win. George Seifert should be considered No. 1A, however. Heck, he's won more games than any of the other 19 coaches in 49ers history. Then again, he's also lost more playoff games (five) than any other 49ers coach. Seifert's legacy lurks in the shadows of the franchise's trophy case, which includes championships from his 1989 and 1994 teams.

November 24, 2014 served as a sweet reminder about Seifert's contributions beyond his eight seasons as Walsh's successor as head coach. On that day at the 49ers' new home of Levi's Stadium, Seifert was introduced as a "five-time Super Bowl champion" during a halftime ceremony, honoring his induction into the Edward J. DeBartolo Sr. 49ers Hall of Fame. That's right: Seifert played critical roles for the 49ers' defense on their first three Super Bowl-winning teams, arriving in 1980 as their defensive backs coach, then getting promoted in 1983 to defensive coordinator. Notably, Seifert presided over a 1984 defense that is arguably the 49ers' greatest of all time, a unit that stymied Dan Marino and the high-flying Miami Dolphins in Super Bowl XIX.

But if not for the events of January 10, 1982, who knows where Seifert's 49ers tenure was headed. That landmark date, of course, is when Dwight Clark made "The Catch" for the winning touchdown against the Dallas Cowboys in the NFC Championship Game. What happened next is not underappreciated by Seifert. "The Catch was great," Seifert recalled. "The tackle was great. Eric Wright's tackle of Drew Pearson to save the win, to save my rear end, was special."

Indeed, Wright, a rookie, made an open-field, horse-collar tackle of Pearson to prevent a 75-yard touchdown. That kept the 49ers on track to launch their dynasty.

But Seifert's connection to the franchise goes way beyond his 17 years with the team. "I grew up as a young man in San Francisco and played high school football [for Polytechnic High] at Kezar Stadium and I became a fan of so many great players—Y.A. Tittle, R.C. Owens, Gordy Soltau, and so many others," Seifert said while re-introducing himself to 49ers fans during that 2014 halftime ceremony also attended by Ronnie Lott, Steve Young, Clark, and Jimmy Johnson. "My foundation was Kezar, and then my professional foundation was at Candlestick Park with so many outstanding players, some of which I'm proud to have on the stage here. Now to be honored and enter the Hall of Fame here in the new Levi's Stadium, I've gone full circle. I'm just lucky, lucky, lucky."

For decades others valiantly stated his case to enter the Pro Football Hall of Fame in Canton, Ohio. Two Super Bowl championships got arguably less accomplished coaches there before him. Seifert's contributions to the 49ers and the NFL go beyond those two wins. One perceived knock on him could be viewed as a strength. Yes, he inherited a talent-rich team from Walsh and defended their Super Bowl crown in 1989. Filling legendary shoes is a task others tried and failed to do. "George stepped into an extremely difficult situation and handled it very well," John McVay, then the 49ers' vice president, said after Super Bowl XXIV. "He did a great job. We're happy to have him."

Three decades have passed since a Super Bowl was won by a coach who got elevated as an in-house hire. Those thwarted at such a Walsh-to-Seifert transition on the NFL's biggest stage: Jeff Fisher (1999 Tennessee Titans), Mike Martz (2001 St. Louis Rams), Bill Callahan (2002 Oakland Raiders), and Jim Caldwell (2009 Indianapolis Colts). Martz and Caldwell followed Hall of Fame-bound coaches in Dick Vermeil and Tony Dungy, respectively. Fisher actually served as the 49ers' defensive backs coach in 1992–93 before becoming the then-Houston Oilers defensive coordinator and he was promoted later in that 1994 season to replace Jack Pardee as head coach.

Only four Super Bowl-winning coaches won the game after an internal promotion. Don McCafferty followed Don Shula on the 1970 Baltimore Colts and won in Year One, John Madden followed John Rauch on the 1969 Raiders and won in Year Eight, Tom Flores followed Madden on the 1979 Raiders and won in Years Two and Five, and Bill Parcells followed Ray Perkins on the 1983 New York Giants and won in Years Four and Eight.

The 49ers' promotions that did not pan out after Seifert include Mike Singletary (2008–10, 18–22 record) and Jim Tomsula (2010, 2015, 6–11 record) after they tasted interim roles.

Seifert's coaching path to the 49ers included two stints as Stanford's defensive backs coach (1972–74, 1977-79), and those were wrapped around two years as Cornell's head coach in the Ivy League. Walsh overlapped as Stanford's coach during those 1977–78 seasons. So a year later, it shouldn't have been surprising that Seifert reunited with him on the 49ers.

It shouldn't have been startling that Seifert replaced Walsh as 49ers coach four days after their 1988 team's 20–16 win against the Cincinnati Bengals in Super Bowl XXIII. Seifert was flying to Cleveland as the Browns courted him before the 49ers lured him home. "Probably the most enjoyable period of my coaching career was working with Bill as an assistant," Seifert said. "When I became the head coach, I was familiar with the development of how we operated so it was a natural flow."

Stoic on the sideline, Seifert captained the ship into playoff waters in seven of his eight seasons at the helm. The exception came in 1991, and the 49ers still went 10–6 despite season-ending injuries to Joe Montana and Steve Young. Seifert's job came with some of the franchise's biggest personnel moves of all time: the transition from Montana to Young and the trade of Charles Haley to the Cowboys. But with double-digit win totals each season, it's no wonder Seifert racked up more wins than Walsh, who took over a moribund franchise. In regular-season action, Seifert went 98–30, and Walsh went 92–59–1. In the playoffs Seifert was 10–5, and Walsh was 10–4.

Seifert's tenure ended after his franchise-high fifth playoff loss—35–14 in the 1996 season's divisional round on the road to the eventual Super Bowl champion Green Bay Packers. Their coach? Mike Holmgren, a fellow San Francisco native and the 49ers' offensive coordinator from 1989–91 under Seifert. Seifert's exodus from his 49ers post was foreshadowed a month earlier, when a 30–24 loss to the Carolina Panthers spoiled alumni weekend honoring the franchise's 50th anniversary.

Nearly 20 years later, he returned with 49ers alumni to become the 20th enshrine of the franchise's Hall of Fame.

What had he missed most from his 49ers coaching days? "The interaction with all the people and the players and coaches, even the tension of it all sometimes," Seifert said. "At the same time, I have to say I thoroughly enjoyed it and I realized there's no way I can do it again. I learned that the hard way."

Two years after leaving the 49ers and after bombing as a CBS analyst, Seifert restarted his coaching career with the Panthers. They went 8–8 in 1999, 7–9 in 2000, and won their 2001 opener but lost the remaining 15. Still, Seifert had more to accomplish in life: "I enjoy having a martini with my wife, walking my dog, and watching my grandchildren play sports and being involved in 4-H, and going on trips with my buddies, and going hunting and fishing."

21

Mooch

Joyful bedlam broke out inside 3Com Park's home locker room. Unbeknownst to him at the time, it would be Steve Mariucci's final appearance inside those walls as the San Francisco 49ers' coach. His team had just pulled off the second greatest comeback in NFL playoff history, erasing a 24-point deficit in the second half for a 39–38, down-to-the-wire win against the New York Giants in a wild-card thriller. "It was the loudest, wildest, craziest game I've ever been a part of and it was my last game there because I got whacked the next week in Tampa," Mariucci said in a December 2023 interview. "There were people in the locker room—women, kids. It was the biggest celebration. I've got photos of my father-in-law in there and of John York hugging my wife, Gayle. It was crazy. It was just a party. Then that was it, never went back in that locker room again."

A week later, a 31–6 loss at the Tampa Bay Buccaneers in the divisional playoffs would serve as the official 49ers finale for "Mooch," even though 49ers coowner Dr. John York said afterward: "To sit there and throw rocks at the coach when you won the western division and a playoff game, that's foolish."

Mariucci two nights later was watching the reality-television show *Joe Millionaire* when an upset York phoned him. A meeting was scheduled for the next day. Mariucci had refused to fire a few loyal assistants, and once he entered York's office, the door closed, and his firing instantly was on ESPN's crawl, stunning his staff, family, and friends. Mariucci and his wife would try slipping out of the facility hours later in the back of a janitor's van.

It was a poorly handled dismissal, which York acknowledged as the next season (2003) got underway with Mariucci coaching the Detroit Lions. "I still regret sort of how that it came down. It came down a little messy," York said. "So I've tried to make my apologies to Steve and through Steve to Gayle because that should not have happened as it did."

A cordial relationship ensued between Mariucci and York, benefitting both as they've crossed paths at NFL functions (both are on the player-safety committee) and, sadly, at memorial services, such as John Madden's in February 2022.

Mariucci's six seasons from 1997–2002 coincided with the franchise's biggest transition period in 20 years—a two-decade span upon which the 49ers' five-championship foundation was built. In the dour backdrop, ownership control was transferred from Eddie DeBartolo to his sister, Denise DeBartolo York, and her husband, Dr. York. That convoluted process wasn't completed until 2000. "Having been invited in by Eddie and Carmen [Policy] and then transitioning to new ownership, then new front office, new players, and new everything over the years, it was interesting," Mariucci recalled. "There was never a dull moment. Bill [Walsh] coming and going, Terry [Donahue] coming and staying. It was interesting times, wasn't it?"

Mariucci's 57 regular-season wins were third most in franchise history until Kyle Shanahan passed him during his seventh season in 2023. Mariucci dutifully won playoff games, albeit only the openers in three of four postseason trips. His 49ers offenses kept churning out points and Pro Bowlers even after Steve Young's Pro Football Hall of Fame career jarringly stopped three games into the 1999 season and even after Jerry Rice's record-setting tenure stopped after the 2000 season.

Mariucci joined the 49ers after one season as a first-time head coach at Cal, but his previous role with the Green Bay Packers as Brett Favre's quarterbacks coach made Mariucci a hot NFL prospect. At Cal he won his first five games before losing six of seven and exiting via the Aloha Bowl. Setting his 49ers tenure in motion was a January 1997 clandestine meeting with Policy, then the 49ers' president, at the Hotel Mac in the bayfront region of Richmond. The pitch: become the 49ers' offensive coordinator and eventual successor to two-time Super Bowl-winning coach George Seifert. A few days later, on January 14, 1997, Seifert resigned, and Mariucci became the 13th coach of "the most successful franchise in pro football over the last 15 years," as he described it at the time.

Tampa Bay is where he'd make his coaching debut and oddly enough it's where he'd oversee his final game six years later. Neither game went great. Or good. But the first one was a harbinger of tough times ahead: the 49ers lost 13–6, Young sustained a concussion, and Rice blew out his knee. The first-year coach with charming blue eyes and an affable personality was headed for way more highs, lows, and good deeds that endeared him to Bay Area communities perhaps more so than any other 49ers coach.

His second season produced arguably the hallmark moment of his 49ers sideline days: Mariucci embraced Terrell Owens and his tears of joy after Owens' game-winning touchdown—The Catch II—with eight seconds remaining in a 30–27 wild-card win against the Green Bay Packers. "The T.O. Catch game was huge," Mariucci recalled. "We'd gotten beaten by the Packers in the championship game the year before. That was kind of a payback to get them in the playoffs."

Tears of pain came with the next playoff game when the 49ers promptly lost Garrison Hearst to a lower-leg fracture on Atlanta's unforgiving artificial turf, dooming the 49ers to defeat against the Falcons and sending Hearst into a two-year hiatus with multiple surgeries. Hearst had opened that season with a 96-yard touchdown run for an overtime win against the New York Jets, and that launched him toward the 49ers' single-season rushing record (1,570 yards).

The cloud darkened over the 49ers franchise when three games into the next season, Young sustained his final concussion on his final play. That robbed Mariucci's offense of a Hall of Fame quarterback, and the ensuing 2000 season would be earmarked as Rice's final one, too.

Passing the torch from Rice to Owens was one thing. What Mariucci had to oversee was the dramatic emergence of Owens' "T.O." persona. The scene: Texas Stadium in Irving, Texas, Week Four of the 2000 season. Owens, or T.O., made two touchdown catches in a bittersweet victory marred by his controversial celebrations at midfield, where he raced to Dallas' Star logo, spread his arms wide, and struck a pose while staring through the halo of the stadium's roof. A suspension and fine followed, as did a grudge that Owens held against Mariucci for decades to come. After Owens' Texas Two-Step, the 49ers lost in overtime, and he blamed Mariucci for taking it easy on Chicago Bears counterpart Dick Jauron, citing a "buddy system with all the coaches." Mariucci fired back, calling it: "Maybe the most utterly ridiculous statement I've ever read and completely void of any deep thought."

Confrontation and adversarial tactics are not Mariucci's vibe, though he'll fiercely defend his honor and that of the sport he's made his life's work. He is a people person, one who loves to share stories and explain football principles, where he'll unabashedly interrupt himself to mix in a funny anecdote to keep things loose and enjoyable. Truth be told, it's not uncommon for people to assume he won a Super Bowl or two, seeing how he coached Young and Rice albeit as dust collected on the 49ers' lobby's trophy case.

Twenty years after his tenure, he still owned a unique place in the franchise's pantheon of coaches, most of whom come and go. None have remained as much a fixture in the Bay Area sports scene. That's in part because of his philanthropic efforts in the community, and it's also because the pride of Iron Mountain, Michigan, put down roots in the foothills of the Santa Cruz Mountains and maintains his primary residence near the town of Los Gatos. "Even when I got let go by the Niners and then went to Detroit, I kept that house. I figured someday we would be back," Mariucci said. "I mean, I moved my wife 18 times in my coaching career. You have to think where you might want have a home base. Was it going to be in Green Bay, Wisconsin, or Louisville, Kentucky, or Orlando or Los Angeles or Berkeley? I coached all over the place. There were a lot of stops. We just felt Los Gatos would be a good place to have our home base when that time came. So we moved back into it. We have a lot of friends in the Bay and the bocce tournament, our Camp for the Stars. There are so many things. To go somewhere else and start over would be silly."

Football Camp for the Stars is an annual event for dozens of athletes and cheerleaders with Down syndrome. They show up at Valley Christian High School in San Jose, where Mariucci and others, including active 49ers, help coach, and everyone involved draws inspiration. When Mariucci hosted his 25th annual charity bocce tournament in June 2023, he was in his natural element: rolling bocce balls, rubbing elbows with Silicon Valley VIPs, hugging 49ers legends like Ronnie Lott, and downing Italian cuisine at Los Gatos' Campo di Bocce. That is where his bocce tournament started. Then it migrated to the East Bay suburb of Livermore when Madden joined as cohost up until his December 28, 2021 passing. The goal is to benefit children's charities, and while more than $8 million has been raised, the spring event annually attracted representatives from Bay Area sports teams and big-time businesses. "Here is the guy who started it all, a very special guy who puts a lot into this, and this tournament has really evolved," Madden said in introducing Mariucci at the 2011 edition of their Battle of the Bay bocce tournament.

Mariucci's friendship with Madden was always a treat to watch. After starting their annual tournament with a "grudge match," they razzed each other. Mariucci said: "Grudge match means nothing."

Madden: "Grudge match means you got your butt kicked."

Mariucci: "Grudge match is like kissing your sister. It doesn't count."

Madden: "Grudge match is the most important match."

Mariucci: "Grudge match is like a fourth exhibition game, where you don't play your best guys."

Like Madden, Mariucci took his passion for football to broadcasting after his coaching days, which ended with the Lions 11 games into the 2005 season. The NFL Network provided the perfect platform for Mooch's enthusiasm, knowledge, and helpful coach-speak. Honestly, the same could be said of his years with the 49ers, which made for the perfect learning ground for young reporters, who could enjoy full access to practices and interviews with his assistants before the advent of social media and NFL teams' paranoia for privacy.

That didn't mean he required a lot of words to capture the moment or explain situations. Think back to that Candlestick Park finale. Before the locker room revelry, their January 5, 2003 win ended with controversy. The Giants botched a field-goal attempt on a bad snap, then attempted a desperation throw down the field. Mike Pereira, the NFL's supervisor of officials, later said a pass-interference penalty should have been called on the 49ers' Chike Okeafor. But the end result stood. Mariucci's epic, sarcastic response to the Giants' day-after plight: "Bummer." Oh, Mooch, gotta love him, and the Bay Area still does.

22

Dennis Erickson

DENNIS ERICKSON BOARDED HIS EVENING FLIGHT FROM Portland, Oregon, to San Jose, California, on the way to his introductory press conference as San Francisco 49ers coach, when into first class walked Terrell Owens. Call it karma. The 49ers had sought a coach to spruce up their air attack, and here he was in the friendly skies with the NFL's leader in touchdown catches the previous two seasons.

Owens, who'd spent his day at Nike's nearby headquarters, met his new coach, and they briefly talked ball, as in getting it to him more at the height of his Pro Football Hall of Fame career. "Everybody wants the ball, and we'd be pretty stupid if we didn't get it to him," Erickson said at his February 12, 2003, press conference at San Francisco's posh Four Seasons Hotel.

Less than two years later, Owens was gone—part of a roster teardown that doomed not only the 2004 49ers, but also Erickson's NFL career. "The big thing for us was the purge in the second year," Erickson said January 19, 2005, upon returning to the 49ers to turn in his keys two weeks after he got fired along with general manager Terry Donahue.

How did it all unravel so fast? Erickson inherited a playoff roster from Steve Mariucci but would never even string together back-to-back wins. The 49ers fell out of contention with a 7–9 record in 2003. Then in a surprise to Erickson, Donahue blew up the roster as his cure for their "salary cap hell." While Owens left in a convoluted trade to the Philadelphia Eagles, the 49ers also excommunicated quarterback Jeff Garcia, running back Garrison Hearst, and offensive linemen Derrick Deese and Ron Stone.

Erickson had scraps to work with in 2004, leading to a 2–14 death march that spelled the end of his second and final NFL coaching job. It was the 49ers' worst record in 25 years and it gifted the 2005 NFL Draft's No. 1 overall pick to Erickson's successor, Mike Nolan, and personnel czar Scot McCloughan. Erickson's advice to the new brass: "They've all got to be on the same page. That's basically it. The personnel director gets the players, the coach coaches them, and go from there. The coach has got to tell him what players he wants, and you've got to go get 'em."

Donahue had covertly hired Erickson, a former peer from the collegiate coaching ranks, rather than one of three NFL coordinators announced as finalists. Jim Mora adamantly wanted an in-house promotion from defensive coordinator. The other two finalists also were defensive coordinators: Ted Cottrell of the New York Jets and Greg Blache of the Chicago Bears, and both were bidding to become the 49ers' first-ever Black coach. All took a turn getting interviewed by media in the 49ers' lobby, which made for a strange dog-and-pony show in a coaching search that began with Donahue interviewing candidates at his Newport Beach-area home.

Erickson was almost 56 when he swooped in for that 49ers' job after flourishing from 1999 to 2002 at Oregon State, where the 2000 Beavers finished 11–1 and beat Notre Dame in the Fiesta Bowl. Such college success wasn't surprising. He'd won two national championships at the University of Miami and went 63–9 there from 1989 to 1994. Erickson's first NFL gig, however, produced annual mediocrity with the Seattle Seahawks—8–8 in 1995, 7–9 in 1996, 8–8 in 1997, and 8–8 in 1998. But those Seahawks offered an air show with quarterback Warren Moon, who said of Erickson: "He's always looking to throw the ball down field, looking for the big plays first. Everything else is secondary."

Erickson's experience was seen as an asset by the 49ers. The last time they had hired a head coach with previous experience in that role: Norman "Red" Strader in 1955 who succeeded their first-ever coach in Lawrence "Buck" Shaw. Bill Walsh, acting as a consultant after bequeathing general manager duties to Donahue in 2001, gave Erickson's hiring his public blessing: "I'm excited about what he does. He brings a new dimension to our offensive team. We've been concerned about getting the football down the field all last season."

The 49ers, mind you, had Garcia and Owens coming off their third straight season as a Pro Bowl combination. So the offense was not inept—except for in a 31–6 divisional playoff loss at the eventual Super Bowl champion Tampa Bay Buccaneers, a defeat that ended Steve Mariucci's tenure. Then again, Garcia's 2002 average of 10.2 yards per completion set the lowest mark by a 49ers full-time starter. Garcia himself questioned the 49ers' aggressiveness. Upon Erickson's hiring, he said: "If Dennis can bring that to this team, a finishing attitude in terms of philosophy and mentality, then that is a great thing for this organization."

The four-week span between Mariucci's firing and Erickson's hiring worked against fortifying a coaching staff. Erickson thus retained Mora as defensive coordinator and Greg Knapp as offensive coordinator, at least until Mora became the Atlanta Falcons coach in 2004 and took Knapp with him.

Mora and Owens presented Erickson the game ball after he won his 49ers debut in 49–7 fashion against the Bears. Never again did the 49ers have above a .500 winning percentage under Erickson. Their only wins in 2004 were overtime victories against the Arizona Cardinals. Tim Rattay quarterbacked one win, and rookie Ken Dorsey quarterbacked the other.

Before that 2–14 season, Erickson hosted a golf tournament between his 49ers coaching staff and the media in an attempt to bridge relationships and forge others. Those were the final days before social media engulfed our world and radicalized so much, including the coverage of pro sports. Erickson was right at home, hosting everyone at his Silver Creek Valley Country Club, throwing down a few "BLs" (Bud Lights), and golfing without fear of something going viral on a blog, Twitter, or YouTube. When a 16-handicap reporter nearly holed a shot from about 170 yards, Erickson raced his golf cart up to him and playfully sneered, "You sandbaggin' motherfucker."

Looking back on his two-year tenure, it was the 49ers' front office that sandbagged Erickson, promising a championship-contending roster that would instead be razed amid salary cap woes to torpedo Erickson's NFL coaching career. As he left the 49ers' upstairs corner office to Mike Nolan, Erickson said: "I've met him before, but I don't really know him. I'm sure he'll do a good job. He's got a good reputation."

23
Mike Nolan

STROLL THROUGH THE SAN FRANCISCO 49ERS' MUSEUM AT Levi's Stadium and you'll find a headless mannequin dressed in a black suit, white-collared shirt, and a black tie with red-and-gold stripes. It makes visitors pause before their eyes shift to the neighboring displays of Patrick Willis' No. 52 jersey and Joe Nedney's ceremonial game ball. This is Mike Nolan's legacy? The sideline suit?

Nolan's suit, to be fair, recognizes at least one battle he won in his three-and-a-half-season tenure. He petitioned the NFL to wear it as a tribute to his father, Dick, who coached the 49ers in a suit from 1968 to 1975 from their Kezar Stadium days to their Candlestick Park infancy. The NFL acquiesced for two suit games in 2006 before NFL sponsor Reebok hired Joseph Abboud to customize Nolan's attire for 2007. "I never dreamed he would be the head football coach of a team I coached," Dick Nolan said through a team spokesman upon his son's hiring. "I never thought it would be that way. It is great to see that happen."

The 49ers' ownership led by the York family thought so, too, in hiring Mike Nolan after interviewing other NFL coordinators, including Mike Heimerdinger (Tennessee Titans), Tim Lewis (New York Giants), Jim Schwartz (Titans), and Romeo Crennel (New England Patriots).

In the years that followed, the Nolan-coached 49ers went through too much quarterback drama, too many offensive coordinators, and too little talent on a roster. And they didn't win enough: 4–12 in 2005, 7–9 in 2006, 5–11 in 2007, and 2–5 before Nolan got fired. Of those 37 defeats, 25 were by double digits.

Nolan, after 11 years as an NFL defensive coordinator, had come aboard with personnel control despite being a first-time head coach. Three years later after losing two-thirds of his games, Nolan passed that ballyhooed trigger of roster power to Scot McCloughan, who'd been promoted to general manager after Nolan hired him in 2005 as a personnel guru. No personnel move loomed larger for them than the 2005 draft's No. 1 overall pick. Would it be Alex or Aaron? Aaron or Alex? One day Nolan and McCloughan would attend Utah star Alex Smith's workout, and the next day they'd be in Berkeley watching Aaron Rodgers' flawless showcase. One day Smith would visit the 49ers' facility (and be put in front of the trophy case to speak to reporters), and the next day would be Rodgers' turn. Smith was steady and heady. Rodgers showed a strong-willed, chip-on-the-shoulder demeanor. Those character differences tilted the scales. Nolan even said so a decade later on the NFL Network how Smith was the "safe choice, always trying to please" and Rodgers was "very cocky, very confident, arrogant."

By Year Three, Smith and Nolan were publicly feuding over the quarterback's ability (or inability) to play with a shoulder that had been separated and would require surgery. Truth be told, neither Smith nor Nolan stood much of a chance to resurrect the 49ers' Super Bowl ways, much less "Win The West," as a 2005 banner demanded outside the 49ers' locker room. That at least was a sentimental rallying cry in that Dick Nolan's 49ers won the West from 1970 to 1972.

When the 2012 team did clinch a Super Bowl berth—with Smith relegated to backup duties and with Nolan in attendance for that NFC Championship Game win in Atlanta—49ers CEO Jed York did give Nolan some credit. In a postgame Twitter post, York apologized for not seeing Nolan there but heard he had congratulated players and added: "#ClassAct. He set the foundation."

York never held it against Nolan for bypassing Rodgers, working under the assumption that the 49ers were too much of a mess to add such a combustible quarterback. Nolan proved adept at handling a disgruntled running back. When Kevan Barlow got traded before the 2006 season, he lashed out to the media, calling Nolan a "dictator" who had players "walking on eggshells" and never should have been given personnel control as a first-time coach. Nolan's response was not to attack Barlow's character but rather defend his coaching style: "I try to run a tight ship. I want people to do their job and not look over their shoulders."

One of Nolan's first challenges, outside of the quarterback call, was the unimaginable horror that happened in the 49ers' locker room on their first road trip. After an exhibition loss at the Denver Broncos, rookie lineman Thomas Herrion collapsed and would die from a heart condition. Some two years later, on November 11, 2007, Dick Nolan died at 75 in Grapevine,

Texas, after battling Alzheimer's disease and prostate cancer. The next year, after the 49ers fell to 2–5 and lost their fourth straight game to the host Giants, Nolan got fired in his corner office by York.

Fast forward 15 years. Nolan was again a head coach just not in the NFL, where his post-49ers tenure led to defensive coordinator roles for seven seasons with four teams. It was June 18, 2023, and Nolan's Michigan Panthers had just posted a second-half shutout to clinch a United States Football League playoff berth. "I've been saying it all my career: it's all about players," Nolan said on FOX Sports' broadcast. "We had some good players on defense, and they played their hearts out."

The 64-year-old grandfather beamed with pride for those players and for the fans who showed up to Detroit's Ford Field. He was a long way from his last head coaching gig back in the Bay Area, where he'd attended high school and where he'd roam the same Candlestick Park sideline as his father—in a suit, to boot.

24

Mike Singletary

MIKE SINGLETARY WANTED MORE THAN JUST WINNERS. HE wanted his San Francisco 49ers coaching tenure to serve as a stepping stone to the top of his profession. Getting fired after the 2010 season did not crush Singletary's coaching vision. "I've learned a lot in the past year and a half, and a lot goes into the progress and process of becoming the best coach ever," Singletary said in August 2012 ahead of his Candlestick Park return as a Minnesota Vikings assistant.

Singletary should not be scorned for seeking greatness. His wide-eyed determination combined with physical and mental aptitude made him a first-ballot entrant to the Pro Football Hall of Fame in 1998 as a Chicago Bears linebacker. And when Singletary replaced Mike Nolan as the 49ers' coach, fans embraced his passionate yet unconventional approach until the losses started piling up and he got dismissed with an 18–22 record.

Singletary was the first Black head coach in the 49ers' 63-year history. "No. 1, I'll always be indebted to the 49ers," Singletary said before that 2012 exhibition opener return with Minnesota. "They gave me an opportunity when they could have chosen many others in their organization. I'm grateful to have had the opportunity to get a firsthand look at an organization that really wants to win."

The 49ers certainly won in his wake as Jim Harbaugh promptly delivered them to three straight NFC Championship Games and a Super Bowl. Whether Singletary gets or deserves credit for laying that foundation is up to interpretation. Singletary knew plenty about the squad he bequeathed to Harbaugh: "I'm very proud of the team and of some of the guys that stepped up. I'm happy for them."

Once upon a time, Singletary wasn't so happy with Vernon Davis, a star tight end who Singletary vehemently dispatched to the locker room after a personal-foul penalty in the third quarter of an October 26, 2008 loss to the Seattle Seahawks. That was Singletary's first game as the interim successor to Mike Nolan, and it proved as much a doozy in public if not more so behind the scenes. Singletary also swapped out quarterbacks (J.T. O'Sullivan for Shaun Hill), dropped his pants during a halftime locker room speech, failed to stop a fifth straight loss, and then delivered his legendary "I Want Winners" address to the media: "I would rather play with 10 people...than play with 11 when I know that person is not sold out to be part of this team. Cannot play with them. Cannot win with them. Cannot coach with them. Can't do it. I want winners. I want people that want to win. Go ahead. What's up next?"

What came next was a full-time appointment to that job as announced in Candlestick Park's catacombs immediately after a season-ending, walk-off win against Washington. What a day that was, and it began with the owners' son, Jed York, being named team president, a key step toward his long-term oversight as CEO and then principal owner.

To understand how wildly popular Singletary had become in winning four of eight games to that point, consider this pregame scene: a swarm of 40 fans encircled Singletary as he walked off the Candlestick Park's field after warmups, and rather than rush into the locker room, he stopped under the south end zone's goal posts to sign autographs and take pictures with the Faithful. When 49ers security director Fred Formosa told Singletary "Let's go, let's go," Singletary responded simply, "No, it's okay." He was being worshiped like a rock star off-stage and in a mosh pit. "It's fun to watch him," Formosa said in admiring the view. "He's so loved. He gets everybody working."

Davis worked his way into becoming a 49ers playoff hero—albeit under Harbaugh—by making a game-winning touchdown catch against the New Orleans Saints for the franchise's first postseason win in nine years. Reflecting on that catch a few months afterward, Singletary noted how "it was big" and showed Davis' growth, adding: "He and Pat [Willis] still haven't scratched their potential yet, and it's scary."

Singletary wasn't initially sold on Willis in the 2007 NFL Draft. General manager Scot McCloughan told him to look closer at the middle linebacker. At the Senior Bowl for college football All-Stars, the 49ers coached the South squad, allowing Singletary to shadow Willis, and vice versa. Willis would be the 49ers' pick at No. 11 overall and he'd be mentored by Singletary, a 10-time Pro Bowler, eight-time All-Pro, and two-time NFL Defensive Player of the Year, including on the 1985 Bears' championship squad.

After winning NFL Defensive Rookie of the Year honors in 2007 on a 5–11 team, Willis blossomed into a perennial Pro

Bowler until toe injuries cut short his career in 2014. One game in particular stands out in Singletary's mind. It was a 24–21 loss at the Houston Texans during Singletary's first season as head coach on October 25, 2009. From the sideline Singletary said to Willis: "Pat! Let's go! Get them going!"

Later, when the 49ers were flying home after the defeat, Singletary got up on the plane and walked back to talk more calmly to Willis, to ask how he was doing. Willis replied, "I'm good, Coach." Singletary saw he wasn't and asked again. Willis' response: "Coach, you yelled at me today. I was like the only one you were yelling at."

Singletary took a seat next to him and said: "Pat, you're the only one I could yell at. You know why? Because I know you can take it, because I know you will get up and fight. I know you will lead. I know you will work through it. You're like my son."

And just like that, Willis replied: "Coach, you can yell at me any time."

Singletary recounted that story while presenting Willis for induction into the Bay Area Sports Hall of Fame in May 2023 at a downtown San Francisco hotel. Providing motivational speeches proved the best coaching trait of Singletary, whose strong faith was reflected beyond words and with a cross necklace he'd wear on the sideline. One motivational technique included a 2008 halftime act for the boxers-wearing 49ers coach who dropped drawers. "I used my pants to illustrate that we were getting our tails whipped on Sunday and how humiliating that should feel for all of us," Singletary said. "I needed to do something to dramatize my point."

He'd "have to look at the film," was a familiar refrain as the 49ers stacked losses. "Don't tell me. Show me," was a Singletary mantra. No one would confuse him with an X's and O's genius, and his 49ers offenses struggled with a carousel of coordinators

(Mike Martz, Jimmy Raye, Mike Johnson) and quarterbacks (O'Sullivan, Hill, Alex Smith, Troy Smith). Singletary, upon replacing Nolan, posted a five-step plan for the "49ers Formula For Success": One, total ball security; two, execute; three, dominate the trenches; four, create great field position; five, finish.

Missing from that list: quarterback excellence or—at minimum—efficiency. One of Singletary's downfalls was ignoring the importance of a quarterback. That went beyond berating Alex Smith on the sideline of a 2010 loss to the Philadelphia Eagles. The 49ers, with Hill at quarterback, beat each of their division foes in a 3–1 start to the 2009 season. A four-game skid followed en route to an 8–8 record that extended the 49ers' playoff drought to seven seasons.

With the 2010 season came chaos, including McCloughan's ouster in March as general manager amid personal issues, the Smith/Smith juggling act at quarterback, and bell-cow running back Frank Gore's season-ending hip fracture in Week 11. Singletary's final season had opened in 0–5 fashion, making for an inevitable firing, which came almost two years to the day he traded his interim label for a four-year contract. After losing that season's penultimate game in St. Louis, York emphatically told reporters in the locker room that the 49ers' objective is to be an annual contender for the Super Bowl. "We're going to make sure we get this right," he said after the loss to the Rams.

Singletary got fired that night from a job that his predecessor and friend, Nolan, needed to convince him to accept on the day of his own firing. Singletary exited with the playoff drought reaching eight seasons, and Jim Tomsula was elevated to interim coach for the 2010 finale. Singletary's next coaching stops came as an NFL assistant with the Vikings (2011–13) and Los Angeles Rams (2016) before taking on head coaching duties in Addison, Texas (Trinity Christian Academy went 1–21 in his two seasons) and in the since-defunct Alliance of American Football (Memphis Express went 2–6 before the league went bankrupt). All of which is to show how determined Singletary was in his continued pursuit for coaching excellence no matter the level.

25
Jim Harbaugh

JIM HARBAUGH'S CORNER OFFICE UPSTAIRS AT THE SAN Francisco 49ers facility looked as you'd expect four years into his coaching term. His desk had piles of folders, his kids' artwork made for homey décor, and lurking near the door was a supersized white board scrawled with messages, words, numbers, and mottos. Only a month remained before moving boxes would be needed after what the 49ers called a "mutual parting" as he left to coach his alma mater, the University of Michigan.

For this rare office visit and one-on-one interview, neither Michigan nor the 49ers were the topic as the 2014 season and his tenure neared an end. Rather, Harbaugh was excited to discuss his NFL entry with the Raiders ahead of the 49ers' ensuing game December 7 in Oakland. Harbaugh glowed about his "tremendous insight and opportunity to learn" from Al Davis, saying he'd often retreat to his humble office and write down notes. Those could end up in his own book someday, though he said at the time: "I never thought about that. I think books are about people that are retired or at the end of their careers. I still think I'm in the moment."

Quintessential Harbaugh: maximizing the moment at hand, living with enthusiasm unknown to mankind, challenging any perceived obstacle in his or his team's path to success.

Harbaugh's four seasons with the 49ers spanned from exhilarating to exhausting. His eccentricities and intensity made for a daily eye-opener. For a reporter it was tremendous in that lazy questions yielded to more challenging inquires that Harbaugh could launch into oratory excellence.

His reign can't be summed up by three consecutive NFC Championship Game appearances his first three years plus a down-to-the-wire Super Bowl loss to his older brother, John, and the Baltimore Ravens. To truly capture the spirit of Harbaugh, here are the highs, lows, and good deeds from that 2012 Super Bowl season:

* * *

August 8, training camp

Kyle Williams was banished from the field by Jim Harbaugh after Williams headbutted cornerback Deante' Purvis. Two drops earlier in practice ignited Williams' frustration, which eventually faded in time for a calm, post-practice chat with Harbaugh. The next day Harbaugh announced that Williams would reprise his role as a punt returner despite two fumbled returns that triggered last season's NFC Championship Game loss to the New York Giants. "He's a 49er. He's one of us," Harbaugh said in solidarity.

August 10, preseason opener

In a harbinger of Harbaugh's quarterback change, Alex Smith engineered a 12-play touchdown drive in his only series in their 17–6 win against the Minnesota Vikings. Then Colin Kaepernick took over—and took off down the right sideline for a 78-yard touchdown run on an option-read fake to LaMichael James.

August 12, Fan Fest, Candlestick Park

A shaggy-haired fan wearing only shorts and shoes darted from the sun-splashed crowd of 32,000 and onto the field to approach Harbaugh. "They locked eyes," Joe Staley said, "and Harbaugh made him withdraw with his Chuck Norris eyes." The fan scurried away to awaiting police officers on the sideline. Harbaugh said: "I'm glad he was clothed, glad he wasn't naked."

August 16, final practice of camp

Alex Smith commanded the offense with such noticeable conviction that Harbaugh said: "It takes about two years in the system to be a real expert at it from the quarterback position, but he's cut that in half." Smith confirmed he knew this offense better than others in his first six seasons but disputed being an expert: "No, no, no, not at all, a lot to learn."

August 18, 20–9 preseason loss to the Houston Texans

Harbaugh "per instruction" declined to rip the replacement officials at least until he said: "Some crazy, wild calls. Were they accurate? Weren't they? We'll see. I have a headache, though. I've got a darn headache. A lot of them didn't seem like they were in the ballpark."

September 1

Those who made the roster's final cut were awarded blue, mechanic shirts with personalized patches at the team meeting as was the case the previous season in a tradition Harbaugh brought from Stanford. Also, Justin Smith and Alex Smith were selected captains to join incumbents Frank Gore and Patrick Wills because Harbaugh said captainships carry two-year terms.

September 4

Harbaugh circled the locker room, bid farewell to players, then rushed to attend the birth of his son, Jack, who wasn't due for another 10 days. "The good ones like to come in early and also I think it bodes well for the 49ers," he said. "It's a sign of good luck to come perhaps: Jack Jr. being born on the fourth day of the ninth month of this year."

September 9, Game One

Harbaugh called the season-opening 30–22 win against the Green Bay Packers in Lambeau Field "a great victory." Added NaVorro Bowman: "Knowing [Green Bay] is the hotshot team or the best team in the last couple years, it just makes a huge statement all across the league."

September 16, Game Two

Harbaugh and Detroit Lions coach Jim Schwartz exchanged friendly handshakes before and after the San Francisco 49ers' 27–19 win, a far cry from last season's postgame confrontation in Detroit. That 2011 scrum started once Harbaugh slapped Schwartz's back after a 49ers victory at Ford Field, prompting Schwartz to chase down Harbaugh exiting the field, only to have

49ers public relations chief Bob Lange step between them and holler: "Whoa! Whoa! Whoa!"

September 24

Harbaugh talked about football's evolution with Hall of Famer Jim Brown over lunch at the Holiday Inn in Boardman, Ohio, where the 49ers were embedded for a second straight year between back-to-back road games. Harbaugh called it enlightening to meet "Mr. Brown." As for losing a day earlier in Minnesota, he said: "It's not our mindset, but I sense this from people who live in a mythical, magical fantasy world of just expecting that game would be a win."

September 30, Game Four

The 49ers ran for 247 yards, and their defense posted a shutout in a 34–0 win at the New York Jets. Harbaugh deployed Kaepernick in the "WildKap" offense, and it led to a seven-yard touchdown.

October 3

Say Hey, baseball icon Willie Mays granted Harbaugh's wish and attended practice, signed autographs, and posed for pictures, including one with Harbaugh, who immediately e-mailed it to his father, Jack. "Who would have ever thought a Harbaugh would be sitting next to Willie Mays with a smile on his face," Harbaugh said. "We're feeling pretty good about ourselves. We got to meet Willie Mays. It doesn't get much better than that."

October 7, Game Five

The 49ers became the first NFL team to tally more than 300 yards both rushing and passing in a 45–3 home rout of the

Buffalo Bills, to which Alex Smith said: "When you think of the 49ers, you think of great offenses, so this is quite an honor."

October 9

After practice Jim Harbaugh took his dad, Jack, to Mays' house for an epic visit that Jack called "one of the great thrills I've had."

October 24

Nearly a week after the 49ers went to 5–2 with a 13–6 win against Seattle, Seahawks cornerback Richard Sherman responded to Harbaugh's comments about Seattle's physical coverage tactics, stating: "Sometimes, man, when the bully gets bullied, that's how that happens." Sherman played under Harbaugh at Stanford.

October 29

After a 24–3 win at the Arizona Cardinals on *Monday Night Football,* Harbaugh presented the ceremonial game ball to two-day-old Jaxon York, the son of CEO Jed York and his wife, Danielle. Alex Smith completed 18-of-19 passes that game, earning him his first NFC Player of the Week award.

November 11

Harbaugh and several players struggled to grasp the relevance of the 49ers' first tie since 1986, a 24–24 draw with the St. Louis Rams. Nor was it obvious that Alex Smith's second-quarter concussion would effectively end his 49ers active service and usher in the Kaepernick era.

November 19

After Kaepernick won his starting debut on Monday night against the Chicago Bears—a 32–7 triumph in which Aldon Smith costarred with five-and-a-half sacks—a quarterback controversy was afoot. "Usually, I tend to go with the guy with the hot hand," a non-committal Harbaugh said. "And we've got two quarterbacks with hot hands."

November 21

Before news broke that Kaepernick would remain the starter over Smith, Harbaugh tried to quell any drama: "It's the opposite of a controversy. A controversy is an argument from opposing points of view. This is coming at it from a team aspect."

November 24

At a team meeting on the eve of their road game against the New Orleans Saints, Harbaugh announced Kaepernick would start over Smith, who was medically cleared earlier in the day from his concussion.

November 28

Kaepernick remained the starter for their next game at the Rams, to which Harbaugh said: "Both have earned it. Both deserve it—Alex over a long period of time, Colin by virtue of the last three games. It tips the scales. Colin, we believe, has the hot hand. We'll go with Colin. And we'll go with Alex. They're both our guys."

December 2, Game 12

The worst play call of the Harbaugh era—at least until the Super Bowl—was Kaepernick's failed execution of an option pitch that resulted in a game-tying touchdown for the Rams, who won 16–13 in overtime.

December 3

Harbaugh stuck with Kaepernick but said Smith was "not out of this" and should continue to prepare as if he might regain the starting job.

December 15, Game 14

The 49ers blew a 31–3 lead, but a playoff berth was ultimately clinched with a 41–34, wild win at New England, the Patriots' first December loss at home since 2002. Harbaugh said: "[I] loved the way our team sucked it up so many times. We didn't make all the plays...But we made more than them."

December 17

Harbaugh offered an optimistic outlook on Justin Smith's elbow injury: "'The Cowboy' should be ropin' and riding" at practice. Smith went on a two-game hiatus and returned for the playoffs but recorded no quarterback sacks or hits in those three games.

December 19

Asked to describe the "hallmark" of Pete Carroll-coached teams, Harbaugh said, "I don't remember getting any cards from him at the holidays." The joke bombed until Carroll caught wind of it and said later on a media conference call: "I heard he didn't get [a card] from us yet. I'll go back and check my list to see how that happened."

January 7

A week after attending practice, baseball manager Tony La Russa said of Harbaugh before the playoff opener: "He's a players' coach but only for the players that do it right. He'll set someone straight if need be. I really admire him."

January 12

Kaepernick ran for 181 yards and two touchdowns in a 45–31, playoff-opening win against the Packers, who opened the game with a 52-yard pick-six on Kaepernick's second career playoff pass. Harbaugh tried to spread the offensive credit afterward: "Everybody was in on it."

January 14

Parents Jack and Jackie Harbaugh held a media conference call and delivered tales about their sons, playoff-coaching counterparts Jim and John. The latter called in as "John from Baltimore" and asked his parents if it's true they like Jim best, resulting in a pregnant pause before unanimous laughter.

January 15

Sports Illustrated's cover featured Kaepernick running with the headline "HOLY…" next to a mugshot of Harbaugh's shouting face.

January 18

The 49ers arrived safely in Atlanta, having made Harbaugh "really happy" after an outstanding week of practice. But on the team's flight, news broke that Michael Crabtree was the subject of a sexual assault investigation. Crabtree was allowed to play through the playoffs and would not get charged in the San Francisco case.

January 19

Rain fell on Saturday's practice for the NFC Championship Game, which delighted Harbaugh. He said: "I noticed when I was standing on my balcony today at about 6:20, 6:30. [I] looked out and saw a very red sky. That means that, 'Red sky at night, sailor's delight. Red sky in morning, sailor take warning.' So, I anticipate that we'll have some precipitation today, some weather, and that will be a great thing for us. Admiral Bull Halsey once said, 'If you're going to fight in the North Atlantic, then you got to prepare in the North Atlantic.'"

January 20, NFC Championship Game

A sixth Super Bowl berth finally came to fruition for the 49ers, and Harbaugh gave Kaepernick a hug as they swapped spots at the postgame media podium following the 28–24 comeback win in Atlanta. Frank Gore's second rushing touchdown had given their first and final lead, and the 49ers defense got Ahmad Brooks and NaVorro Bowman to break up passes and halt the Falcons' last-ditch drive. "You love to have Coach on your side. He puts his guys first," York said after the win. "He might not put the media first, might not put the rest of the league first. I understand that, and he is who he is and he's comfortable with it, and I respect him. I respect the job he's done. I give him a ton of credit for getting this team ready for a big game like this and for getting us back to the Super Bowl."

January 21

Calling it a "blessing and a curse" to oppose his brother in the upcoming Super Bowl, Jim downplayed the "Har-Bowl" hype because, "every moment you're talking about myself or John, that's less time that the players are going to be talked about."

January 25

Jim Harbaugh called into John Madden's daily radio segment on KCBS 740-AM and asked for advice from the Oakland Raiders' first Super Bowl-winning coach, to which Madden replied: "You're a heck of a lot better coach than I ever was."

Harbaugh responded: "Bullcrap. Bullcrap."

Madden countered: "No bullcrap. The job you've done there—and I say this when you're not on here—is one of the all-time great coaching jobs."

January 29

Asked if he's worried his brother can read his mind, Jim Harbaugh answered: "No, worried about a lot of things, but I have not noticed that he has any clairvoyant powers."

February 1

As the Harbaugh brothers shared a stage for a joint press conference, Jim was asked about their commonalities and differences in terms of coaching philosophies: "Philosophical commonalities? I would be hard-pressed to spell philosophical right now," Jim said. Then older brother John chimed in: "I know he can't spell commonalities."

Their parents, Jack and Jackie, were in the audience, to which Jim noted: "There's nobody in the family that has more competitive fire than my mother...She believed in me."

February 3, Super Bowl XLVII

The 49ers' comeback bid fell apart with three consecutive incompletions on Kaepernick throws to Crabtree, and in response to that fourth-down failure, Harbaugh stripped off his black cap and pleaded in vain with officials for not calling defensive penalties. After the 34–31 defeat, Harbaugh said in a quick media scrum: "I really want to handle this with class and grace. Our guys battled back and competed to win. No question in my mind there was a pass interference and a hold on Crabtree on the last one."

February 10, AT&T Pebble Beach National Pro-Am

A week after coming up five yards shy of a winning score, Harbaugh finished five strokes out of the Pro-Am title with partner Jason Day at Pebble Beach. Harbaugh said: "Just the support out here from 49er fans probably first and foremost was the best part of the experience. It was a real treat to play Pebble Beach, and to be in this tournament is a great honor. Everything is just A-plus-plus."

26

Jim Tomsula

CARMINE'S BARBER SHOP IS ANCHORED EIGHT MILES EAST of downtown Pittsburgh and across the Monongahela River. It's on Main Street in humble Munhall, Pennsylvania, and it's where barbers Carmine Caveek and Rich Cavicchia have the inside scoop on town business. "You're going to be hard-pressed to find anybody who says anything bad about Jimmy," Caveek said. "He's a stand-up guy."

Jimmy Tomsula was a feisty lineman a mile up the street at Steel Valley Senior High School. He went to Carmine's Barber Shop. So did his father and grandfather. Family loyalty and town pride aside, it's indeed a tough task to say anything bad about Tomsula. As a humanitarian he'd consistently ask: "Hey, how you doin'? How's your family?" As a defensive line coach, he'd passionately scream at his players: "Bludgeon!"

As head coach of the San Francisco 49ers, however, even he'd say that gig just was not for him. His turn at the helm in

2015 proved that fact beyond just a 5–11, last-place record that was the 49ers' worst since 2007. Press conferences were unbearably awkward, starting with his introductory one. Tomsula's time at the lectern didn't get smoother. He'd be unsure what to divulge, especially in terms of injury information that might reveal strategy or draw the ire of general manager Trent Baalke.

Tomsula's uncomfortable tenure lasted 354 days after his promotion from defensive line coach. He had replaced his boss, Jim Harbaugh, in what some viewed as a palace coup or so it even appeared on the practice field, where the final days saw Tomsula seemingly alienated from Harbaugh and defensive coordinator Vic Fangio.

In eight previous seasons as the 49ers' defensive line coach, Tomsula packed so much gusto. He was genuine. He oozed personality and passion. He wanted the best out of those around him, which during the 49ers' 2011–13 playoff runs included defensive linemen Justin Smith, Aldon Smith, and Ahmad Brooks.

A wave of retirements preceded Tomsula's promotion, including those of Justin Smith, linebacker Patrick Willis, right tackle Anthony Davis, and linebacker Chris Borland, Willis' would-be replacement. Frank Gore, the 49ers' all-time leading rusher and their offensive heartbeat, got cast aside in free agency as did wide receiver Michael Crabtree. Then, a month before the season opener, Aldon Smith got released after his third arrest for suspicion of drunken driving. And yet in the opening *Monday Night Football* game of the 2015 season, Tomsula's team triumphed 20–3 against the Minnesota Vikings at one-year-old Levi's Stadium.

That season would take a wicked U-turn, however. A four-game losing streak followed the opening win. Distractions surfaced, such as Australian rugby-league star Jarryd Hayne's failed experiment as an NFL punt returner, and then the big whammy: Colin Kaepernick discovering he required season-ending shoulder surgery after going 2–6 and getting benched for Blaine Gabbert.

Long gone were the feel-good vibes from that opening win against the Vikings. That 2015 debut played out late at night on a television inside the Thomas Jefferson High School football office back in Pennsylvania. Coach Bill Cherpak was Tomsula's childhood pal who used to cruise with him in an orange Chevelle through the boroughs of Homestead, West Homestead, and Munhall. "We didn't hang out with a lot of people," Cherpak recalled. "They didn't like us or didn't know us. Or we didn't care."

Growing up in Steel Valley, Tomsula made all-conference as a 5'10", 240-pound nose tackle and guard. Could winning a WPIAL AAA championship in 1982 be a stepping stone to becoming a Super Bowl-winning coach? "When I was coming through there, the Pittsburgh Steelers were winning Super Bowls and in their heyday with the Steel Curtain," Tomsula said in 2015. "Those things were happening at the same time the mills were closing, and the economy was dropping."

Tomusla also went through personal adversity on his circuitous route to the 49ers. His playing career bounced from Middle Tennessee State to Catawba College before a knee injury sidetracked him. He would sell medical equipment and food services before coaching became his calling. Eventually, NFL Europe offered fertile ground for him to teach football and to grow as a coach. He circled back there in 2022 and, in a wonderful renaissance, he led the undefeated Rhein Fire to a European League championship and earned Coach of the Year honors.

That is the fairy-tale ending the 49ers dreamed of when they elevated him—only to fire him a year later. A day after that termination, Jed York closed his 30-minute press conference with this mission statement: "We're in need of somebody that can win Super Bowls. We haven't won a Super Bowl since 1994."

Tomsula's one-and-done fate was sealed ahead of his closing act, and despite the franchise's freefall, fans did not hold it against him. Chants of "Jim-my! Jim-my!" rang out as he autographed hats and flags dropped to him from the stands as he stood with a smile in the Levi's Stadium locker room tunnel. What followed was a 19–16 win against the Rams—their final game representing St. Louis and Tomsula's final game with the 49ers. "I've been with Jimmy my whole career. I love Jimmy," linebacker NaVorro Bowman said afterward. "It's always been a good time with him. Today we won a game and let's give some praise for that."

27

Chip Kelly

Coaches typically don't phone up reporters the day after they get fired—much less to thank them for providing fair and responsible coverage of a historically horrid season. So Chip Kelly's call came as a surprise. A casual, amicable chat ensued. Before he hung up and exited the NFL realm, he made sure to note that he got along just fine with outgoing general manager Trent Baalke, which went contrary to a late-emerging narrative.

A day earlier, both Kelly and Baalke got fired—to no one's surprise—after a 2–14 season. Jed York, the San Francisco 49ers CEO, took the stage for a third straight January to explain why he was searching for another coach. "Baalke was defensive-minded, Kelly was an offensive mind," York said. "The marriage didn't work, and I probably should have seen it."

That pairing, honestly, is not what the 2016 season will be remembered for in 49ers lore. Baalke's talent-lacking roster obviously fed the freefall, but even a franchise-record, 13-game losing streak is an afterthought considering what Kelly presided over during his one-and-done tenure. Specifically, Kelly found himself in the middle of an international incident once quarterback Colin Kaepernick used the national anthem to protest social inequality and police misconduct.

All coaches face distractions and personnel juggling. Not many have to navigate as polarizing a situation as Kaepernick created—without tearing apart a locker room awash in on-field defeats. The 49ers' ownership supported Kaepernick's quest from the outset, and Kelly went along with that stance, too, though he essentially let players decide for themselves whether Kaepernick's intentions were for society's greater good.

Kaepernick had not tipped off teammates of his plans and he inconspicuously sat during the anthem their first three preseason games. A picture taken from the press box by reporter Jennifer Lee Chan showed Kaepernick sitting on a cooler before an August 26, Friday night exhibition against the Green Bay Packers. It caught the media's attention. Kaepernick explained his protest afterward to the NFL Network's Steve Wyche, and two days later, teammates listened to Kaepernick in a team meeting discuss why he sought justice for those oppressed in society.

Swarms of news crews invaded the 49ers' locker room in the ensuing weeks to interview a backup quarterback who was still recovering from offseason shoulder surgery. Actually, to interview a social-justice crusader. "We recognize and respect Kap's decision and his constitutional rights to do what he's doing, and it sounds like it's been a positive change," Kelly said. "There's been a lot of positive things that have come out of it."

Kaepernick's protest wasn't a sideshow. It was the main attraction all while Blaine Gabbert had remained in the starting role bequeathed to him during the 2015 season because of Kaepernick's ineffectiveness and injured shoulder. In fact, Kaepernick missed the first two preseason games of Kelly's tenure because of a sore arm, then played just 12 snaps in that exhibition against the Packers. Once the protest drew a firestorm of attention, there was still an exhibition finale to play in military-centric San Diego, where he'd take a knee with teammate Eric Reid at the suggestion of U.S. Army green beret Nate Boyer.

No longer was the scrutiny on Kelly's offensive innovations, sideline signals, scientific strategies, nutritional orders, or his reputation for being so impersonal at his last stop with the Philadelphia Eagles. When Kelly made his official debut as the 49ers' coach, they pinned a 28–0 shutout on the Los Angeles Rams, who saw star Aaron Donald get ejected as the Levi's Stadium crowd erupted in "Beat LA!" chants. The biggest drama happened before kickoff when Kaepernick and Reid knelt during the anthem, while other players on both sidelines raised their fists as part of the call for racial equality. "We recognize his right to [protest], but it doesn't affect what we do when we get here at 8:00 in the morning through 8:00 at night," Kelly said. "When he's here, he's all about ball and he's been great with that."

After four straight losses, Kelly summoned Kaepernick from the bullpen to start in the hostile territory of Buffalo, where chants of "U-S-A! U-S-A!" rang out as Kaepernick and Reid took a knee during the anthem on October 16. The Bills beat the 49ers 45–16. Kaepernick completed just 5-of-18 passes for 52 yards after halftime and he ran for 66 yards overall in the game, all while the Bills rushed for 312 yards, the second-most ever by a 49ers opponent. "He did an okay job," Kelly said. "We have to be better on offense, not just the quarterback."

Things didn't get better. Their defense had lost linebacker NaVorro Bowman to an Achilles tear in Week Four, and as the on-field losses piled up, Kelly was having to defend Baalke's weekend recruiting trips away from the team. "If people want to push blame, find it, look right here," Baalke said just before their eighth straight loss in mid-November. "Because I've been given everything I need to be successful. If we don't get it done here, it's not because of ownership. They've been giving us every resource possible."

Former 49ers owner Eddie DeBartolo gave Kelly an endorsement when in town to receive his Pro Football Hall of Fame ring during a halftime ceremony amid a rainy, half-filled Levi's Stadium. DeBartolo referred to Kelly as "a good coach. This man really wants to win. He certainly has a great football mind."

New England Patriots coach Bill Belichick chimed in as well, doing so before handing the 49ers their ninth straight loss. Kelly was an Oregon assistant when he would drift over from his New Hampshire offseason home and visit the Patriots facility to talk shop. "Chip's got a lot of great ideas: his overall organization, whether it's an offensive system, practice schedule, training," Belichick said. "He had some great ideas that we've incorporated into things we're doing on a number of different levels. Some are X's and O's, but I'd say less that and more other things involved with the program."

As Thanksgiving approached, John Madden summed up Kelly's plight by saying: "He's a good coach in a bad situation." Madden described Kelly having a "unique" approach to coaching, and the 49ers' mistakes traced to: "First of all, they made a mistake in getting rid of Jim Harbaugh. Secondly, they don't have many good players."

The 49ers also picked an odd spot for an East Coast layover between their November 27 loss at Miami—when Kaepernick was stopped two yards short of a game-tying touchdown as time expired—and a December 4 road defeat to the Chicago Bears. In between, they bunkered in Orlando and practiced at the University of Central Florida, whose coach, Scott Frost, was tight with Kelly. At the same time, Kelly was fending off rumors he'd return to Oregon, where from 2009 to 2012 he'd won three straight Pac-10 titles and taken his 2010 team to the national championship game.

Practicing in Florida amid scorching heat and humidity wasn't the 49ers' shrewdest move before descending into a snowy Soldier Field for a 26–6 loss. Two days before that loss, Kelly detoured home to New Hampshire as his father, Paul, passed away at age 87. Kelly returned to Chicago as the 49ers lost their 11th straight and in the process benched Kaepernick after the quarterback completed just 1-of-5 passes for four yards through three quarters. He was the first quarterback in NFL history who had fewer than five passing yards and got sacked five times.

Kelly left Soldier Field via private car and returned to New Hampshire to be with his mother, Jean. Two days later, Paul Kelly, showing loyalty to his son's career, was buried wearing 49ers gear. "He did not want to wear a suit in his coffin," Chip said. "He wore a suit his entire career as a trial lawyer. He wanted to wear a 49ers sweatsuit and he did that when he passed away."

The 49ers' 12th straight loss followed. It was an overtime doozy after blowing an 11-point fourth-quarter lead, and Kaepernick passed for just four yards in the second half. Loss No. 13 came in Atlanta against a Falcons team whose offensive coordinator would be Kelly's successor, Kyle Shanahan. "Kyle's great. Eventually, when he gets an opportunity, he'll do a great job as a head coach," Falcons quarterback Matt Ryan said before their 41–13 win.

Kelly's second and final win as 49ers coach came on Christmas Eve at the Los Angeles Memorial Coliseum, when Kaepernick led two touchdown drives and ran in the go-ahead, two-point conversion for a 22–21 comeback win. So much for competing with the Cleveland Browns for the No. 1 overall draft pick and the right to draft Myles Garrett.

Two hours after a 25–23 home loss to the Seattle Seahawks, Kelly and Baalke were formally dismissed by York. Kaepernick's parting message: "I appreciate Chip and what he's done as far as coming to work every day and making sure this team stays focused and being resilient under not very good circumstances in terms of how our team was playing win/loss record wise."

York vowed to find a coach and general manager who could work with a shared vision. That pairing indeed was found almost accidentally when Kelly's successor, Shanahan, took up John Lynch's offer to leave the FOX broadcast booth and become a first-time general manager.

The Shanahan-Lynch regime opened with nine straight defeats, making that 23 losses in 25 games dating back to the roster Kelly inherited. That 2016 team not only set a franchise mark with 13 consecutive defeats, points allowed (480), touchdowns allowed (55), overall yards allowed (6,502), and rushing yards (2,654), but they also had 20 players go on injured reserve during the year.

Off Kelly went with three years and $15 million left on his contract. It was too late for him to find another major college gig, so he took to the ESPN studio until UCLA summoned him in November 2017. He wasn't in L.A. long before TMZ cameras caught up to him outside a trendy restaurant, and, sure enough, familiar questions came at him from his 49ers days. Should Kaepernick be in the NFL? "Yes," he said. Who would be a good fit? "Anybody that wants a good quarterback," responded Kelly, whose loyalty didn't wane during a 13-game losing streak nor years later out of the NFL.

28

Kyle Shanahan

Some lead by example. Coach Kyle Shanahan leads by explanation. That struck San Francisco 49ers players from the instant he arrived in 2017, and it held true as they marched into the 2023 season's playoffs. Film sessions are where the 49ers obtain their degrees from the School of Shanahan. As details of plays are surgically dissected, players learn not only about their respective jobs, but also those of all 22 players on the field. They also learn about their coach's passion and humility.

Shanahan certainly didn't lack great plays to review after the 49ers' December 3, 2023 rout of the defending NFC champion Philadelphia Eagles. They scored touchdowns on six consecutive drives, won 42–19 in the NFL's most hostile of road environments, and moved into the driver's seat for the NFC playoffs. A few days later in a team meeting, what players saw and heard surprised them. Of course, it wasn't a perfect victory even if it seemingly closed a chapter on their traumatic defeat there in the previous season's NFC Championship Game. Shanahan didn't take a victory lap in film review. "He showed us two drives where he felt like he almost screwed us by chasing a play call. He shows that humility," fullback Kyle Juszczyk said. "A lot of coaches, it's never their fault, they never made the wrong call. 'You just need to execute it better.' That's not how he sees it all the time. It's a cool, unique thing that he does."

Fresh off losing the Super Bowl as the Atlanta Falcons' offensive coordinator, Shanahan was hired in February 2017. He lugged with him a reputation as a young, arrogant know-it-all. Yes, he was young (age: 37) and, for as much as he knew, he shared that knowledge to immediately defuse any alleged arrogance toward players or reporters in a surprisingly transparent fashion. "He's brutally honest. That's the best thing about him," said tight end George Kittle, the fifth-round star of Shanahan's initial 2017 draft class. "He does a good job being very clear with the team with his message. If you were having an issue with something and you wanted to talk to him, he's going to tell you exactly what his thoughts are. That's incredibly healthy for the football ecosystem because if you have a coach telling one guy something and another guy another thing, that's conflicted. And if that gets out, you lose trust. Whether it's one on one, a team meeting, offensive install, he's incredibly honest with everything he coaches and what he says."

That doesn't just go for the offensive side of the ball. Tapping into Shanahan's mind also pays off for the 49ers defense such as when they encountered elite quarterbacks Jalen Hurts of the Eagles and Lamar Jackson of the Baltimore Ravens in 2023. Nick Bosa credited Shanahan for insight that led pass rushers to practice patience and fluster Hurts in that decisive win in Philadelphia. "I definitely pay attention when he's talking because you get all the perspectives from the defensive-side people, but hearing what they might be planning against you is good," Bosa said. "He's the head coach. So if he sees something in the defensive gameplan in the beginning of the week that he doesn't like, he's changing it, and it goes down the line from there."

John Lynch, Shanahan's hand-picked general manager and a Pro Football Hall of Fame safety, marveled at his initial team meetings. "I knew the offensive mind that I thought was really special and ahead of the curve," Lynch said at the 49ers' State of the Franchise event in 2017. "But what I've been so impressed with is watching him in front of the team, the way guys respond to him, the way he stimulates them by teaching them, by educating them, and by having fun."

Teaching players the intricacies of football beyond his scheme showed a willingness to relate to them. Of course, from his fashionable sneakers (Yeezys) and snapback cap ("The Shanahat") to his devotion to rapper Lil Wayne, his personality also meshed with the modern-day athlete. Wide receiver Emmanuel Sanders, upon being traded to the 49ers in October 2019, captured that with his first impression of Shanahan: "In the team meeting, I was like, 'I can't wait to get home and tell my wife that the head coach is wearing Yeezys.' That's cool. This is one cool coach...But we have concentration and are focused on the task at hand. His team is a reflection of him, and it's cool to see."

Juszczyk was part of the 49ers' initial free agency crop under Shanahan. Juszczyk, a Harvard graduate, was enamored with how Shanahan spoke to the team. "He has a unique way of speaking to you as a coach but also speaking to you as an equal, as a friend," Juszczyk said. "You feel he understands what you're going through. It's just a unique thing that I hadn't experienced before, and he does a good job of motivating in that way."

Shanahan wishes he were an equal in terms of fulfilling his childhood dream of becoming an NFL wide receiver. While his father, Mike, served a three-year tenure as the 49ers' offensive coordinator from 1992 to 1994, Kyle would spend his summers in Rocklin, California, at training camp. Beyond just sleeping on a rollout bed in his dad's room, he absorbed the NFL life. He competed in late-night Ping-Pong games with Super Bowl XXIII hero John Taylor and he learned football under offensive line coach Bobb McKittrick. "What a great guy and teacher [McKittrick] was," Mike Shanahan said. "You take three years right there, then go to high school, and have the Denver situation all the way through that and college. He's been around."

Once that 1994 49ers team won the Super Bowl, the Shanahans were on the move to Denver. As his dad began a 14-year tenure that included back-to-back Super Bowl titles, Kyle Shanahan took notes in becoming a master tactician and strategist, though he also was a Cherry Creek High School wide receiver with grand ambitions. "He was an athlete. So that has a lot to do with how well he relates to people, especially when you're talking his language, which is football," said left tackle Trent Williams, who played under the Shanahans in Washington before reuniting with Kyle on the 49ers in 2020.

Kyle Shanahan took his playing career to Duke before transferring to Texas as a walk-on and earning a scholarship. After exhausting his dreams of playing in the NFL, Shanahan insisted on paying his dues anywhere but at his father's shop. So that led him first to UCLA as a 2003 graduate assistant. Then came a monumental coaching spark. He joined the Tampa Bay Buccaneers in an entry-level role. There, he followed his dad's advice to study defense before mastering offense. "When you start out coaching offense, you have to learn from the best on defense," Mike Shanahan said. "Because as you're attacking a defense on a day-to-day basis, you have to know how it's taught."

Jon Gruden's defensive staff on the Tampa Bay Buccaneers offered ideal mentors—Monte Kiffin, Rod Marinelli, Mike Tomlin, Raheem Morris, Joe Barry, and Joe Woods—in those 2004–05 seasons. Shanahan took notes and he took them along on his future coaching stops all the way to a filing cabinet in his 49ers office. "It was learning the defense that allowed me to know why I liked plays, what plays I didn't like, and how to put stuff together," Kyle said, "if I ever got my own offense."

At age 28 he began calling plays with the 2008 Houston Texans. Two years later he went to work for his father in Washington. Four years there included working for one of the NFL's most despised owners, Daniel Snyder, but that didn't shield them from criticism, quarterback controversies, and so much more. When it came time for Kyle Shanahan to become a head coach—after offensive coordinator stints with the 2014 Cleveland Browns and the 2015–16 Atlanta Falcons—his father would serve as a valued voice and behind-the-scenes consultant.

But this was Kyle's show, his chance to establish himself not only as the rare NFL coach who could juggle play-calling duties, but also as his own man. "I'm very close with my dad," Kyle said as he headed into his rookie season as 49ers coach. "But after Washington I got a little insecure about perception. I just hated an S being added to my last name. I felt I worked real hard. I felt I was good and I just got sick of the perception."

Fast forward to 2019: the 49ers claimed a 9–0 win in rain-soaked Washington, defenders celebrated by doing belly slides on FedEx Field, and in the victorious locker room, Kyle Shanahan bestowed a ceremonial game ball to his father. And then at the end of the NFC playoffs, Mike Shanahan presented his son with the George Halas Trophy on Levi's Stadium's field after the 49ers beat the Green Bay Packers en route to the Super Bowl.

That 2019 season Super Bowl ended in heartbreaking fashion, however. The 49ers blew a 10-point, fourth-quarter lead. Four days later, with coffee cup in hand, Shanahan still looked gutted at his end-of-season press conference. Comparisons, naturally and cruelly, went to the 2016 season's Super Bowl, when Shanahan and the Falcons blew a 28–3 lead en route to an overtime loss to Tom Brady and the New England Patriots. "I've lost the Super Bowl before, I've been a part of a bigger lead that was lost, so I'm very well aware of what goes with that," Shanahan said in that February 2020 post-mortem. "I also am not a good liar. How you guys hear me talk is exactly how I feel. I'm really upset about the loss because it's hard to get there. I personally thought we had the best team in the NFL this year. We weren't. We've got to deal with that."

Shanahan's truth-telling is especially appreciated by players even if it's in the form of criticism. Speaking bluntly and truthfully has kept Shanahan in players' good graces in a sport where mixed messages in public can rot away at trust. "Obviously with experience on the job over the years, he's gotten a lot more detailed, and I think that's why his explanations go over so well," Williams said. "He can basically walk somebody without any football knowledge through a gameplan. You'll feel so enlightened by the end of the conversation."

Although several coaches were born out of Mike Shanahan's Washington's staff—his son, Kyle; Matt LaFleur (Green Bay Packers); Sean McVay (Los Angeles Rams)—another wave of hires came from the younger Shanahan's 49ers coaching tree: Robert Saleh (New York Jets), Mike McDaniel (Miami Dolphins), and DeMeco Ryans (Houston Texans). At the 2020

Super Bowl, McDaniel described Shanahan as "a weird mix of dad, brother, and boss. It's a very cool dynamic because when you have a collection of likeminded individuals who are just trying to be the best coaches they can be."

Shanahan's collaborative efforts roll through gameplan strategy sessions on Tuesday night to in-game adjustments Sunday. As impressive as he's been as a playcaller, Shanahan downplays any creativity, often saying it's not as if he sits around inventing plays for his motion-based offense. But cornerback Richard Sherman recalled playing for the Seattle Seahawks when Shanahan's Atlanta offense bewildered them in 2016. "He had drawn up some concepts that we had never seen," Sherman said. "He had broken a few of our rules. He fundamentally broke our defense, or we fundamentally changed it after that game because the rules he broke were rules that nobody had ever broken before."

Once Shanahan orchestrated a 45–29 win at Arizona to clinch the 49ers' second straight NFC West crown—in Week 15 of the 2023 season—Cardinals cornerback Antonio Hamilton Sr. had a simple explanation for the 49ers' diverse dominance. "Kyle Shanahan, he has it. He is an offensive mad scientist," Hamilton said. "He knows how to get those run schemes set up. He's been around the game for a long time and he understands how to rush the ball, how to screen the ball, how to get these short passes out to get those guys into a rhythm. He does a great job with those guys. Hats off to them."

Actually, the 49ers proudly put on their free hats and T-shirts to pose for locker-room pictures in honor of their division championship. It was their third NFC West crown in seven seasons under Shanahan and it was running back Christian McCaffrey's second in as many seasons since arriving in an October 2022 trade from the Carolina Panthers. McCaffrey was more than the perfect, multi-talented offensive catalyst who could rack up yards and touchdowns for the 49ers' system. The Stanford product had the intellectual capacity to soak up Shanahan's teachings.

Like Shanahan, McCaffrey also had 49ers roots. Christian's father, Ed McCaffrey, was a wide receiver on that 1994 championship team before going on to win two more rings under the senior Shanahan in Denver. Getting traded to the 49ers "meant the world" to Christian McCaffrey. "I've had a lot of different coaches over my career and I've learned a lot. Then in getting here, seeing why and how they do things is so cool," he said. "Every day I feel like a kid in a candy store, just learning all the different ways to run the ball, the purpose behind a lot of the routes in the pass scheme, and just continuing to grow and learn as a fan of this game and as a player on this team."

Shanahan smirked upon hearing those October 2023 words. "It makes me feel like a kid in a candy store because sometimes people get bored with it," he said. "It's how much [McCaffrey] loves football not just with his heart but also his mind. It's all he thinks about is what it seems like."

Takes one to know one. Shanahan put his whole fingerprint on the 49ers' franchise, having been given the power and financial backing from the York-led ownership. "The faith they have, the control he has, the freedom he has to be able to build his team as he sees it, the way him and John work together, it's kind of hand in hand," Williams said. "They feed off each other and facilitate each other's needs. That's why he's been so successful because he could put his whole fingerprint on this team from top to bottom. He puts a lot into it. He's a workaholic, and it shows."

PART 4

SUPER BOWLS

29

Super Bowl XVI: Smoke and Mirrors

An Amazon warehouse spans 823,000 square feet on a sacred patch of land 30 miles north of downtown Detroit. Books, electronics, beauty products, and toys get boxed and sent on their way. In July 2023, workers picketed outside, demanding better wages ($16 an hour to start) and safer working conditions. America, at its core. Forty years before this fulfillment center opened, the San Francisco 49ers did some heavy lifting of their own on that land's previous tenement, the Pontiac Silverdome. There, they packed up the franchise's first Lombardi Trophy and eventually delivered it amid a Market Street parade. "All of a sudden, you win the Super Bowl, and people want to buy you drinks, dinner, shoes, clothes," linebacker Dan Bunz said. "It was like going from the outhouse to the penthouse."

The 49ers were not exactly primed for sudden success. They had not reached the playoffs in eight straight seasons. Their coach, Bill Walsh, produced 2–14 and 6–10 records his first two years. Their quarterback, Joe Montana, was a third-year, third-round pick from Notre Dame. "The first Super Bowl, my God, it was mirrors," Walsh recalled some 20 years later about that 1981 season. "And Joe was a big part of that."

The franchise's great rebuild culminated in a 26–21 victory against the Cincinnati Bengals in Super Bowl XVI, where 81,270 sheltered inside the Silverdome after enduring freezing conditions and traffic gridlock. That fairy-tale ending was unimaginable to some when the 49ers opened the season losing two of three. "I was up for a new contract in '81, and after we started out bad—to show how good I was at judging talent—I told my agent to get me the hell out of there. I was frustrated," recalled Keith Fahnhorst, a 49ers offensive tackle from 1974 to 1987. Once they won the Super Bowl, 49ers personnel czar John McVay sauntered up to Fahnhorst with a quick question: "Aren't you glad I didn't listen to you?"

Bunz could relate after all the sorrow and criticism he endured in his earlier three seasons. The 49ers won 10 games combined from 1978 to 1980. Then they started the '81 season by losing two of their first three games before going 12–1 the rest of the way. "It was miserable," said Bunz, whose post-NFL career saw him teach for 22 years at Sutter Junior High School in Sacramento, California. "You're supposed to be proud to be in the NFL. But when I'd go out to eat and people would say, 'What do you do?' I would say I drove a truck. Demolition guy was a good one, too. I'd say my wrecking ball could knock down a six-story building in three swings. It was kind of a nightmare. I kept getting chewed out and I hated to lose. I was calling the [defensive] signals and I felt responsible. I almost became an alcoholic."

Instead, he became a Super Bowl champion at the end of the 1981 season. The turnaround coincided with the addition of veterans Jack "Hacksaw" Reynolds and Fred Dean, as well as the arrival of rookie defensive backs Ronnie Lott, Eric Wright, and Carlton Williamson.

"You could see we had good players, but the thing was they got older guys that helped the younger ones," Dwaine Board said. "That's what this [current] team needs to win. The one thing that's obvious when you're playing the game is you have to find somebody to look up to."

Added Walsh: "It just takes time to develop it. You win with [great] players on defense. You can coach offense. Dwight Clark [for example] becomes All-Pro. When you look at that, it demonstrates you can coach offense. But defense you have to have the players."

30

Super Bowl XIX: Marino vs. Montana

PRAISE DRENCHED THE SAN FRANCISCO 49ERS' DEFENSE AS the 2022 team stormed toward the playoffs. Some called it the franchise's best-ever defense. They apparently did not recall the 1984 season. "We know the truth," quipped Keena Turner, a four-time champion linebacker on the 1980s dynasty and a special advisor to the 49ers general manager 40 years later.

All due credit to the 2022 defense for leading the NFL in fewest points allowed, but the 1984 team truly showed what makes for a legacy unit: the playoffs. The 49ers' 1984 defense did not yield a single point after halftime in any of its three postseason wins, including a 38–16 triumph against the Miami Dolphins in Super Bowl XIX at Stanford Stadium, located literally just down the street (El Camino Real) from the 49ers' then-training facility in Redwood City. In winning that Lombardi Trophy, the 49ers denied it from Dan Marino, that season's NFL MVP and a future Pro Football Hall of Fame quarterback.

Yes, it was Marino vs. Montana, two of the NFL's all-time best, two Western Pennsylvania products, leading the Nos. 1 and 2 offenses, respectively. Joe Montana stewed at the media framing this as a quarterback duel, asking him how he was going to stop Marino. "Fellows, you're talking to the wrong guy," Montana answered. "I don't have to stop Dan. Our defense does, and they've been having a great year. You agree with that, don't you?"

Indeed, the 49ers had the No. 1-ranked defense, surrendering just 14.2 points per game in the regular season. Of the franchise's five Super Bowl-winning defenses (from 1981 to 1994), this was the only one that led the NFL in scoring (or lack thereof). They also allowed 211.3 passing yards per game, which ranked them just 17th and potential prey for Marino, who'd thrown for 5,084 yards and an NFL-record 48 touchdown passes. The Dolphins scored 70 touchdowns in the regular season. That kind of production has been topped by only three teams (the 2013 Denver Broncos, 76; 2007 New England Patriots, 75; 2018 Kansas City Chiefs, 71) in NFL history. "In 1984 we set a standard for throwing the football that teams are still trying to match today," Marino said at his induction speech in Canton in 2005, part of a Hall of Fame class that included Steve Young.

It would be Marino's only Super Bowl appearance and it came two seasons into a 17-year career. How good was he? He retired as the NFL record holder in career passing yardage (61,361), completions (4,967), attempts (8,358), and touchdowns (420). Montana, in his 1986 autobiography *Audibles*, vividly described the vibe before kickoff. Specifically, he shared how Bill Walsh reclined on an equipment bag in the locker room and mused aloud: "All they can talk about is Miami's offense. What about our defense? All they can talk about is Marino, Marino, Marino. We have some guys who can play, too."

The 49ers held Marino and the Dolphins in check, at least after he threw his only touchdown pass and put Miami ahead 10–7 in the first quarter. (It was the only touchdown the 49ers' defense yielded all playoffs. One other touchdown came on an interception return in the divisional round.)

Montana and Roger Craig understandably stole the headlines. Craig, in his second year, showed his dynamic versatility as a rusher and receiver by scoring three touchdowns. Montana, in his second Super Bowl, showed his own play-making panache by accounting for three touchdowns (two passing, one rushing). "I finally felt vindicated. I was voted MVP of the game, but in reality I knew the 49ers played a perfect game," Montana wrote in his autobiography.

What about the defense? Well, in the 49ers' 2022 media guide, their Super Bowl recap only notes interceptions by safety Carlton Williamson and cornerback Eric Wright, as well as Turner's six tackles. Defensive coordinator George Seifert, Walsh's eventual successor, flummoxed the Dolphins by deploying a nickel defense. What made that defense so special was how well others stepped up at various times. Dwaine Board had two sacks in the Super Bowl, and one apiece came from Gary Johnson and Manu Tuiasosopo. Marino hadn't been sacked in the Dolphins' two playoff wins and he hadn't been sacked four times in a game that season until he met the 49ers.

In their NFC Championship Game 23–0 shutout win of the Chicago Bears, Johnson and Michael Carter each recorded two sacks, and Riki Ellison had eight tackles. The playoff run opened with Ronnie Lott intercepting Phil Simms to set up Montana's second touchdown pass for a 14–0 lead en route to a 21–10 divisional win against the New York Giants at Candlestick Park. Lott wasn't the only future Hall of Famer making plays, as Fred Dean also paved the way toward his second championship ring by notching two sacks.

What also made that 1984 crown fit so well is the defense's own vindication. The 49ers' previous season came to a cruel halt in Washington in the NFC Championship Game. Montana had engineered a game-tying comeback with three fourth-quarter touchdown passes, but after questionable penalties in pass coverage on Wright and Lott, the then-Redskins won on Mark Moseley's last-minute field goal. "We stayed mad [about that loss] until we redeemed ourselves against Miami in the Super Bowl," Randy Cross said.

The 1984 49ers were the NFL's first to win 15 games in the regular season. Their lone loss came in Week Seven when a penalty plagued their 20–17 home defeat to the Pittsburgh Steelers. Three more wins came in the playoffs. Add it up, and the 49ers allowed just 26 points in those three playoff wins to defeat Lawrence Taylor's Giants, Walter Payton's Bears, and Marino's Dolphins.

Their 1989 team matched that frugal total while complemented by a more explosive offense en route to a 55–10 blowout over Denver in that season's Super Bowl. The 1981 team allowed 72 postseason points, the 1988 squad caved for 28, and the '94 champs generously surrendered 69 points in a trio of double-digit wins. Inside the 49ers' museum at Levi's Stadium, where offense-oriented memorabilia is understandably prominent, the 1984 season's Super Bowl has a display with a three-ring binder open to the defensive coverages that worked so well. And it was viewed by a hometown crowd, sitting on white seat cushions printed with the Apple Computer, Inc. logo, which is in that museum display, too, right above the George Halas Trophy.

31

Super Bowl XXIII: The John Taylor Catch

SOME CALL IT "THE JOHN CANDY GAME" BECAUSE THAT LOVABLE actor was pointed out in the stands by Joe Montana to defuse the San Francisco 49ers' huddle before their pressure-packed, Super Bowl-winning drive. Some say Montana should have deserved more glory for engineering that last-minute drive and delivering a 357-yard, two-touchdown masterpiece. Some need a reminder that Jerry Rice won Super Bowl MVP honors with a 215-yard performance and a fourth-quarter touchdown that certainly validated his worth. But John Taylor, not John Candy, was the true hero of Super Bowl XXIII, a 20–16 win against the Cincinnati Bengals at Miami's Joe Robbie Stadium.

Nearly 35 years later, Taylor proudly reveled in that glory while attending a downtown San Jose fundraiser, the Dwight Clark Legacy Series, which benefitted 49ers alumni. Taylor and Rice stole the show on that California Theatre stage in June 2023. Taylor reminded everyone in the process how he made the Super Bowl show worthwhile. "I lived that dream a lot of us kids wanted when they're playing football in the street: if I make this catch, if I can make this throw, we win the Super Bowl," Taylor reminisced. "I can honestly say I did that. I caught the winning touchdown."

He did so with 34 seconds to spare. Montana found him on a 10-yard scoring strike. The Bengals were their prey, as was the case seven years earlier, when the 49ers won their first Super Bowl in Pontiac, Michigan. Taylor officially shared that Super Bowl stage with Rice's dominance, Montana's excellence, and a 49ers defense that got fourth-quarter sacks from Charles Haley (two) and Michael Carter.

The 49ers found themselves in a 16–13 hole once the Bengals got a third field goal from Jim Breech, a 5'6" native of Sacramento, California, and product of Cal-Berkeley. All of which set the stage for the 49ers' greatest finish among their five Super Bowl wins. As Taylor enjoyed his 2023 stroll down memory lane at that San Jose fundraiser, he was interrupted on stage by Rice, ever the crowd pleaser and glory hound. Rice had his own interpretation of the 1988 season's climactic finish. "You just brought something up. Final drive: three minutes, 10 seconds left in the ballgame, we have to go over 80 yards or more to win the Super Bowl," Rice began. "Joe Montana says something about John Candy in the stands. And I'm like, 'Joe, what are you talking about right now? We don't need to hear that right now.' So we're moving the ball down the field. I remember this one play over the middle—John, you know what I'm talking about, too, right?—I caught this deep-over and I was sprinting for six [points]. He missed his block. I would have scored."

Indeed, with 1:17 to go, Montana took a snap and hit Rice in stride, their third connection of that drive. Rice broke into the open field for 27 yards until Rickey Dixon shed Taylor's block and stopped Rice at the 18-yard line. Taylor frustratingly pounded his fist into the Miami sod. "I had my block, right. But he was slipping away from me," Taylor recalled. "I made the decision, 'Let him go.' It could have been worse. I could have held the block and actually held him, and that would have taken away more yardage, so I figured okay."

Rice interjected: "It happened for a reason. If we had scored early, [the Bengals] would have had more time on the clock to win that game. So things happen for a reason."

On the winning play, Taylor lined up next to left tackle Bubba Paris, Rice went in motion toward the left sideline, Montana took the snap under center on the left hashmarks, and *voila:* Montana retreated in three strides, Taylor got a clean release and faked an out route, and then the 10-yard scoring strike threaded past multiple Bengals, the last being Ray Horton, before it found Taylor racing through the end zone.

The Bengals took four more snaps and never made it past their 27-yard line courtesy of a Haley sack and two incompletions from Boomer Esiason intended for Cris Collinsworth.

Rice made 11 catches for 215 yards en route to his one and only Super Bowl MVP honors of an unparalleled career. Taylor's Super Bowl stats: one catch, 10 yards. "For him to make that catch, it was for me also. I feel I made that catch also," Rice said. "I'm happy he did it because once I came in motion everybody thought the ball was going to come to me. So it was my time to be Denzel Washington, it was my time to win that Oscar."

Rice knew the ball wasn't coming to him, that Montana-to-Taylor was "meant to happen" for the winning score. "The funny thing is: people never understand how much that can change your life," said Taylor, who was in only his second season and two months shy of turning 27. "I mean, prior to me making that catch, most people knew me for a play here, a play there."

In the ensuing 1989 season, Taylor made a 92-yard touchdown catch here, a 95-yard touchdown catch there, and he finished with a then-franchise record 286 yards (11 catches) in a 30–27 win against the Los Angeles Rams at Anaheim Stadium on December 11, 1989.

His younger brother, Keith, was a rookie Indianapolis Colts safety embarking on a nine-year NFL career in that 1988 season. Little brother had a question about the Super Bowl touchdown for his big bro: "How would you have felt if you dropped that?"

"I kind of looked at him. I was honest with him and said, 'I'd probably would have been the loneliest person in the world and unemployed,'" John Taylor recalled. "But fortunately I wound up catching it. So they kept me around for a little while."

Taylor indeed stayed through the 1995 season. He reached the 1,000-yard mark in the 1989 and '91 seasons. He made back-to-back Pro Bowls (1988 and 1989). His average of 16.1 yards per catch is second in franchise history to Gene Washington. Taylor also returned more punts (149) than any 49ers player, including a career-high 44 for an NFL-best 556 yards in that 1988 championship season. "I didn't care about individual stats," Taylor said. "People always said to me, 'If you'd have went to another team, you could have been the star of that team.' But why? I was happy with where I was at. We were winning Super Bowls, and that's what it was all about."

32

Super Bowl XXIV: The Big Easy

SCORING 55 POINTS AND THROWING FIVE TOUCHDOWN PASSES in any game is major. *Pulling that off in a Super Bowl?* That is the legacy set by the San Francisco 49ers of 1989 before the NFL took on a pass-happy identity via offensive-minded rules. A lot transpired at the Louisiana Superdome on January 28, 1990. A lot of points. A lot of greatness. A lot of Super Bowls over a lot of decades followed without anyone else reaching that 55-point threshold. "I feel like I'm in the twilight zone. That score is unreal," running back Roger Craig told the *San Jose Mercury News.*

Is that score the defining legacy of the 49ers' fourth world-championship team regardless of a 14–2 regular season? Three years later the rival Dallas Cowboys also breached the 50-point barrier, putting a 52–17 beatdown on the Buffalo

Bills (No. 3 in their Super Bowl-loss four-peat). Two years after that, the 49ers flirted with a 50 burger—a phrase coined or made popular by eventual 49ers coach Steve Mariucci—and walloped the then-San Diego Chargers 49–26 in Miami for their Lombardi Trophy 5.0.

Those scores are forever logged into the Internet. That Super Bowl XXIV rout is forever documented by the Bay Area's newspapers, which were still profiting and plentiful before print journalism's financial retreat three decades later. "The Big Easy," blared the *San Jose Mercury News'* banner headline, crowned atop nearly a full-page photo of Joe Montana high-fiving offensive lineman Guy McIntyre. "49ers Super Again," countered the *San Francisco Chronicle*'s special section edition. That front page offered a half-page photo of Jerry Rice celebrating one of his three—*three!*—touchdown catches with a black-and-white photo of the Super Bowl MVP anchoring the page's bottom left corner.

The 49ers already were coronated as "Team of the '80s!" a year earlier (the *San Francisco Examiner*'s headline for its Super Bowl XXIII souvenir edition). This 1989 team under rookie coach and former defensive coordinator George Seifert did more than just defend that championship. It eviscerated so many Super Bowl records in the process. How to explain scoring a then-record five touchdown passes against the NFL's toughest defense, which had allowed a league-low 14.1 points per game? "Every time we came off the field, we said, 'They can't stop us. They can't stop us,'" two-touchdown scorer Tom Rathman said.

Bud Bowl II proved a better game of the day (Budweiser 36, Bud Light 34).

The 49ers dominated in the trenches. Left tackle Bubba Paris vowed they would not sink to the Denver Broncos' level, so they just sank them. Or steamrolled them. "It's like a speeding locomotive. It has some finesse the way the wheels click, click,

click. But then it hits you. It explodes through you," Paris told the *Mercury News*' Dan Hruby. "And that's us: a runaway train roaring into the Super Bowl and making history as a champion that repeated."

The Niners defense yielded just 167 yards, made possible in part because Montana & Co. possessed the football for almost 40 of the 60 minutes. That triumph produced 18 individual records in a Super Bowl plus eight single-game team marks, including the obviously enduring one: most points. The previous record for that was set by the 1985 Chicago Bears, whose famous defense paved the way for a 46–10 rout of the New England Patriots also in the Superdome. Alas, those Bears neglected to get Walter Payton into the end zone in his lone Super Bowl of a legendary and Pro Football Hall of Fame career.

The 1989 Niners got Rice over the goal line three times. His first touchdown came on the game-opening and tone-setting drive when Rice caught a 20-yard pass from Montana and shook off a hit from Steve Atwater (Pro Football Hall of Fame's Class of 2020).

The 55-point, eight-touchdown parade:

Montana to Rice, 20 yards (Mike Cofer point-after kick), 7–0
Montana to Brent Jones, seven yards (Cofer kick failed), 13–3
Rathman run, one yard (Cofer kick), 20–3
Montana to Rice, 38 yards (Cofer kick), 27–3
Montana to Rice, 28 yards (Cofer kick), 34–3
Montana to John Taylor, 35 yards (Cofer kick), 41–3
Rathman run, three yards (Cofer kick), 48–10
Craig run, one yard (Cofer kick), 55–10

That final touchdown came with 13 minutes, 47 seconds to spare. The fourth quarter was like a Tour de France champion drinking champagne on his way down Paris' Champs-Élysées. The 49ers played ballhog for nearly the final seven minutes, ending with Steve Young's victorious kneel down at the Broncos' 32-yard line.

It was the fourth Super Bowl win in four tries for a quintet of 49ers: Montana, Ronnie Lott, linebacker Keena Turner, cornerback Eric Wright, and wide receiver Mike Wilson. "Three-peat!" the 49ers shouted in their locker room after Super Bowl XXIV rout. Alas, hearts would be broken in the next year's NFC Championship Game defeat.

But what a mismatch their second consecutive Super Bowl title was. John Elway, a Bay Area legend from his Stanford days, bombed by completing just 10-of-26 passes for 108 yards with two interceptions (but he ran for their lone touchdown). "Elway had the worst day of his life," Wright said. A decade later Elway retired after back-to-back Super Bowl wins (by seven and 15 points).

Not even Tom Brady could produce points so prodigiously as the 1989 49ers. Among Brady's seven Super Bowl rings, he maxed out at 34 points in the New England Patriots record-setting 34–28 comeback against the Atlanta Falcons in Super Bowl LI.

After losing 30–3 to the 49ers in the NFC Championship Game, then-Los Angeles Rams coach John Robinson wrote in a Super Bowl dispatch for the Associated Press two weeks later. "It was almost surreal to watch the 49ers. I don't know when I've seen a team like that. And I'm sick and tired of them," Robinson wrote. "The Broncos learned what those of us who played the 49ers know—the key thing with San Francisco is that they play the game with such great speed, such great quickness. They come at you so fast."

33

Super Bowl XXIX: The Monkey Off Young's Back

VISITORS TO STEVE AND BARB YOUNG'S HOME IN PALO ALTO, California, often are surprised by the décor. A replica of the Lombardi Trophy does not sit on the mantel. Oh, the Super Bowl MVP trophy is on display—just 800 miles away at BYU's Legacy Hall. "People have commented about our home: 'Steve, if I didn't know better, there's no sign that you ever played in the NFL.' That's kind of on purpose," Young said in a November 2023 interview.

Somewhere, in a storage unit or basement, Young has stashed his red jersey and white pants from Super Bowl XXIX, a legacy-securing win in which he and the San Francisco 49ers undressed the San Diego Chargers 49–26 for a memorable Miami night back on January 29, 1995. "I still have the uniform," No. 8 said. "And I have a ball that a few guys signed."

Memories, not memorabilia, are all Young needs to transport himself back to one of the finest performances in NFL history by one of its most star-laden teams. "I can close my eyes and feel the smoke still in the air from the fireworks. I can still smell it. It stays with you," Young said. "And Kathie Lee Gifford doing the national anthem with Brent Jones turning to me and saying: 'Kathie Lee Gifford?'"

There's no mistaking the 49ers were that night's headliners. They would produce the rout so many expected, seeing how they already passed their biggest postseason test with a 38–28 win against the Dallas Cowboys in the NFC Championship Game at Candlestick Park.

An All-Star cast was assembled precisely to secure the franchise's fifth Lombardi Trophy. They were the first franchise to five, and it came after a four-year wait from their last back-to-back titles. This wasn't like their four previous Super Bowl runs, when they flourished with talent, schemes, and chemistry grown in the 49ers' own garden. As stocked as they were with holdover stars, the 49ers christened the salary cap era by hiring an enormous array of talent. Joining their defense were Gary Plummer, Ken Norton Jr., Richard Dent, Rickey Jackson, Toi Cook, Charles Mann, and, best of all, Deion Sanders, who'd win 1994 NFL Defensive Player of the Year honors to further bolster his glaring fame and fortune.

Offensively, Young was reunited with his BYU center, Bart Oates, and that complemented a corps with Super Bowl veterans in Jerry Rice, John Taylor, Jones, Jesse Sapolu, Harris Barton, and Steve Wallace. Ricky Watters brought invaluable rushing and receiving skills, and fullback William Floyd panned out as one of their two first-round draft picks. The other was Bryant Young, a future Pro Football Hall of Fame defensive tackle. So many names. But so much of the pressure was on Steve Young. This was his eighth season since arriving as Joe Montana's successor, and this title bout came two years after Montana got traded to the Kansas City Chiefs.

Having arrived at their Joe Robbie Stadium locker room about four hours before kickoff, Young passed the time—"It took forever; it was insane"—by envisioning his record-setting passing performance. "The vivid memory I have is how upset Mike was and how much I appreciated that perspective," Young said, referring to Mike Shanahan, the 49ers' offensive coordinator.

Shanahan predicted—no, demanded—that Young shred the Chargers for eight touchdown passes, meaning Young underachieved. LOL. "My life was on the line, and I knew it," Young said. "So, before the game Mike could see the [extended wait], so he kept coming by and saying, 'Let's go over this, let's go over that.' Mike's ability to go through it again and again, then turn to me and say, 'You're going to throw eight touchdowns.' And I'm like, 'You're freakin' crazy. That's nuts.' But it was a relief."

Stoking the 49ers' flames was Chargers safety Stanley "The Sheriff" Richard. Three decades later Young recited Richard's Super Bowl hype, how the Chargers' safeties were impenetrable and would force the 49ers offense to redirect its path. The 49ers, mind you, won 38–15 in San Diego's venerable Jack Murphy Stadium on December 11 with Rice catching all 12 of Young's targets for 144 yards. Shy away from the Chargers' safeties with a championship at stake? Shanahan scoffed. "Mike's like, 'Oh, oh, no, that's not what we're doing,'" Young recalled. "All week long, you listen to it, then right out of the gate..."

Young connected with Rice over the middle for a 44-yard touchdown reception on the Super Bowl's third snap—only 84 seconds into the action. "Literally, the [pregame fireworks] smoke hadn't cleared, and—the thing you thought was the most sure thing you had going for you—we just broke you wide open," Young said.

Only three-and-a-half minutes later, the 49ers attacked again with Watters' 51-yard catch and run for a touchdown. "Same play, just a different way to do it," Young said. "Two touchdowns of the six were right where they said it couldn't be done."

That 14–0 lead surged to 28–7 after Young's touchdown passes to Floyd (five yards) and Watters again (eight yards). It took only two-and-a-half minutes after halftime to make it a 35–10 cushion. Watters' nine-yard scoring run gave him three touchdowns.

It would be Watters' goodbye game. After Watters spent just three seasons on the team, the 49ers let him escape in free agency to the Philadelphia Eagles, a move that Young cites as one of the franchise's two worst departures, behind only Charles Haley's 1992 trade to the Cowboys. "Ricky was uniquely qualified," Young said. "It wasn't like Ricky was the superstar we couldn't go without. But it was *the* piece. Everybody needs a lot of help. He allowed us to be really dynamic. That was a real bummer."

Young's final two touchdown passes went to Rice (15 and seven yards) to appropriately mark 49 points for the 49ers. Young was within two scores of the eight-touchdown goal Shanahan wanted. Alas, with a ballcap on the sideline, Young half-jokingly crowed: "Someone take the monkey off my back, please." Plummer obliged by yanking that imaginary weight off Young, who later would regret that plea because he felt it selfishly turned attention to him in a dominant team victory.

When it came to self-promotion on this team, however, there was no match to Sanders, who immediately won over Young upon arriving two games into the season after finishing his Cincinnati Reds duties. Young recalled Sanders' introduction: "Right away, he pulled me aside and said, 'I want you to understand a couple of things. One, I am lockdown on my preparation and in the locker room I will always be a great teammate. I'll be prepared, I'll be ready to play, and I'll play great. I just want you to know that. No. 2, I am a marketing genius. Everything I do from a marketing perspective is a whole other world that is essentially a parade. I want you to just enjoy it, grab some popcorn, and watch.' It played out exactly like he said."

So, even though Sanders drew the ire of Rice and others for curfew violations during Super Bowl week, Young claimed he had a different view: "Don't worry about him. I watched it that whole year. That dude, don't mess with him. He's fine."

Sanders had an interception in the NFC title game against his future Cowboys teammates, then he produced a fourth-quarter interception in the Super Bowl. Young came away with his own souvenir ball from that win, but he's not quite sure if it's from his first touchdown pass. "I can't remember if it's the first or the last one," Young said. "Jerry caught them both. So that's why I'm a little confused. Jerry took one, and I took one."

Maybe it's time put that one on display. "One day, we'll bring it all out when the kids are more grown," Young said of his Super Bowl mementos.

34

Super Bowl XLVII: The Har-Bowl

WIN A SUPER BOWL, AND YOUR PASSPORT IS GOOD FOREVER in San Francisco 49ers' lore. Lose one? That is what the 2012 team encountered. Excommunicated? Not quite. What a fascinating test case those runner-ups became after coming up short of an epic Super Bowl XLVII comeback and falling 34–31 to the Baltimore Ravens in New Orleans' Superdome. Fast forward to alumni weekend in October of 2022 at Levi's Stadium. "We must have been pretty good. They don't bring teams back unless they were pretty good," Jim Harbaugh said upon returning for the first time since a "mutual parting" as coach after the 2014 season.

Harbaugh's presence headlined that 2012 alumni weekend, in which that the franchise celebrated the 10th anniversary of that

NFC-winning season. Colin Kaepernick and Michael Crabtree were no-shows, a symbolic reminder of the Super Bowl's cruel ending. The 49ers' final three snaps inside the final two minutes saw Kaepernick fail to connect with Crabtree on three consecutive fade passes to the right side—only five yards from a potential winning touchdown and a Bourbon Street party.

Harbaugh, during that fleeting comeback and in the press conference afterward, insisted that two penalties, such as cornerback Jimmy Smith's hold preventing Crabtree's heroics on fourth-and-goal, should have been called against the Ravens on those final Kaepernick throws. "It was a lot of contact," Crabtree said. "Had the ball been a little lower and given me a chance to make a play, I'm sure it would have been called...It's frustrating. It was a game-winning touchdown. It makes you sad. It's the Super Bowl."

It was a wild Super Bowl to end a wild season. It was no fluke that the 49ers made it that far. They had one of their best defenses ever filled with All-Pros in Patrick Willis, NaVorro Bowman, Justin Smith, Aldon Smith, Ahmad Brooks, and Dashon Goldson. They had franchise rushing king Frank Gore lining up behind one of their greatest offensive lines ever with Kaepernick's dual-threat ability taking the NFL by storm.

And they had months of chaos, which in retrospect prepared them for the Super Bowl distractions. There was the "Har-Bowl" storyline of Jim Harbaugh coaching against his older brother, John, the Ravens' coach. The pair held a press conference together two days before the Super Bowl with John in a dapper suit delivering the opening remarks and paying respect to the family, including parents Jack and Jackie. Jim, meanwhile, wore his typical uniform (khaki pants, black sweatshirt, black cap) and avoided any sappy talk to focus on in his Michigan parlance, "the team, the team, the team."

Harbaugh, the 49ers' version, aptly summed up how they made it to that grand stage for the first time in 18 years. He started with their season-opening, 30–22 win in Lambeau Field and he immediately name-dropped Randy Moss, who fresh out of a one-year retirement scored their first touchdown on a pass from Alex Smith. Harbaugh, ever the historian, also noted David Akers' franchise-record, 63-yard field goal that provided a 16–7 halftime lead.

Harbaugh then mentioned the "terrific job" Kaepernick did in his victorious starting debut against the Chicago Bears on *Monday Night Football* while not mentioning the quarterback controversy that engulfed the team. Two games earlier Alex Smith completed 18-of-19 passes in a win at the Arizona Cardinals, then exited their next game with a first-half concussion. Doctors didn't clear Smith out of the concussion protocol, and Harbaugh stuck with Kaepnerick's hot hand (and legs).

Harbaugh's 2019 recap was not complete without a nod to a 31–21 win at the New Orleans Saints on November 25, when Brooks and Donte Whitner both scored off interceptions against Drew Brees. "The way our players have played, to me, that is why we're here, not because of any coaching decisions or anything we [Harbaugh brothers] did as kids," Jim Harbaugh said in that brotherly press conference.

Left unsaid were this era's off-field incidents: Aldon Smith getting arrested for alleged drunken driving in Miami in January 2012, then getting stabbed at his own house party in June; Ray McDonald getting arrested for an outstanding warrant from a 2010 DUI arrest; and another defensive lineman, Demarcus Dobbs, getting in an accident and arrested for suspicion for DUI.

All that previous drama paled in comparison to the Super Bowl stage. The Ravens raced to a 21–3 lead, and the 49ers couldn't keep pace as LaMichael James fumbled, and a Kaepernick pass to Moss got intercepted. The 49ers' deficit ballooned to 28–6 once they allowed a 108-yard return for a touchdown by Jacoby Jones on the second half's kickoff. Only one-and-a-half minutes later in the game, a boom echoed through the Superdome, and power was lost, resulting in a 34-minute delay in the near darkness.

An electrical malfunction? Yes, with a newly installed relay switch. But Ravens linebacker Ray Lewis later suggested it was no accident, to which 49ers CEO Jed York jokingly responded on Twitter: "There is no conspiracy. I pulled the plug."

It, though, was no laughing matter for some players. "My immediate first thought was, *I need to get off the field. This is a terrorist attack*," Joe Staley said. "I was scared shitless. I was waiting to hear explosions and guns going off. The whole week they have security meetings for players: 'This is a Class A security risk.' The eyes of the world are on you."

What ensued was an eye-catching comeback by the 49ers. Crabtree caught a 31-yard touchdown pass from Kaepernick, Gore scored on a six-yard run, Tarrell Brown forced and recovered a Ray Rice fumble, Akers booted a field goal, and the 49ers were within 28–23 entering the fourth quarter. The Ravens responded with a Justin Tucker field goal, and the 49ers' counterpunch was a 15-yard touchdown run from Kaepernick, whose two-point conversion attempt to Moss fell incomplete instead of tying the score.

Kaepernick completed only one of his remaining five passes, and after that 24-yard completion to Crabtree, Gore ripped off a 33-yard run to the Ravens' 7-yard line, cutting left behind the blocks of Staley, Mike Iupati, Bruce Miller, and Delanie Walker. Gore got steered out of bounds once Ed Reed and Dannell Ellerbe closed his sideline path. Reed got credited for the tackle, and it took Staley years to accept it wasn't Ellerbe, whom Staley initially blocked. "I honestly for two years had knots in my stomach about this one play. It affected the way I played the next two or three years," Staley said. "I did my job. I was able to make this play happen in my eyes, but I didn't finish it. If I were to actually finish it, I would make [Ellerbe] go underneath me. Instead, I carried him down and just shoved him."

Ellerbe stayed on his feet and pursued Gore. "I saved myself some lifetime agony because Frank, I saw, stepped out before he touched him," Staley said. "But for two-and-a-half years, I believed that I was the reason why [Gore didn't score]. And I probably still am. It's a good life lesson: always finish what you do."

Gore never touched the ball again, regrettably. James' two-yard squirt got the 49ers to the 5-yard line. Then came Kaepernick's first miss of Crabtree. On third down *Quarterback Power* was called, and the 49ers had it blocked so well that Kaepernick could have had a walk-in touchdown—if not for Harbaugh calling a timeout to scratch that play and the element of surprise. Because offensive coordinator Greg Roman's calls from the booth were relayed through Harbaugh to Kaepernick, the timing of communication wasn't always smooth, and this moment trumped all.

So, that made for a third-down redux, and Kaepernick failed to connect with Crabtree. Then, on fourth and goal, an all-out blitz prompted Kaepernick to give Crabtree "a chance." Crabtree, Harbaugh, and the 49ers Faithful demanded to no avail that Jimmy Smith be penalized for defensive holding.

Three months later Kaepernick reflected on what was just his 10th career start and said: "Most people don't realize the last few plays weren't the problem. We didn't execute the way we should have, so we wouldn't have been in that position."

A decade later Harbaugh reappeared at Levi's Stadium decked out in Michigan garb as coach of his up-and-coming alma mater. Draped around his neck was a 49ers lanyard with his all-access credential. "Just an attitude of gratitude for Jed and the York family for having us all back," said Harbaugh, who rattled off nearly 20 players and gave a nod to his coordinators (Roman on offense, Vic Fangio on defense, and Brad Seely on special teams). "I remember our defense would hit guys, and you could hear the air going out of who they were hitting's lungs: 'Huuuuuuh.' There's no better sound in football than to hear that from one of your defensive players."

A decade later the 49ers had caught their collective breath from that initial Super Bowl defeat. "It was a tremendous team," Harbaugh said. "We just worked really hard and had a fun time doing it. That's why it was the time of my life."

35

Super Bowl LIV: Stung by a Wasp

JOE STALEY HAD RIBS SMOKING ON HIS TRAEGER GRILL, AN iced highball in his hand, and painful Super Bowl memories to share during a 30-minute chat from his front yard in northern San Diego County. "I don't really want to remember it personally, knowing that was my last game and what I went through to play in it," Staley said of Super Bowl LIV—and the six sleepless nights that preceded it because of a painful neck condition that would spell his retirement.

Staley's 13-year career, its entirety spent on the San Francisco 49ers' roller coaster, was denied a fairy-tale ending. Seven seasons earlier he experienced another bummer: the 49ers' first Super Bowl loss in franchise history despite an electrifying comeback attempt in New Orleans.

Staley is the only 49ers player who participated in both Super Bowl heartbreaks in the 2012 and 2019 seasons. Don't dwell on that sad feat. His closing act embodies the sacrifices players make—both behind the scenes and in front of 102.1 million American television viewers—to achieve lifetime dreams and win a championship.

The red-and-yellow confetti that showered the field on February 2, 2020? That was in honor of the Kansas City Chiefs, who rallied from a 20–10, fourth-quarter deficit to stun the 49ers 31–20 at Hard Rock Stadium in Miami Gardens, Florida. That was the same venue the 49ers won their most recent Lombardi Trophy (in January 1995) behind Steve Young and the same field where Joe Montana threw a last-minute touchdown pass to John Taylor in the Super Bowl XXIII triumph against the Cincinnati Bengals.

Super Bowl LIV's heroic throw came not from the 49ers but rather the Chiefs' Patrick Mahomes on a third-and-15 heave to Tyreek Hill for a 44-yard gain to the 49ers' 21-yard line. That play call, *2-3 Jet Wasp Chip*, was the flashpoint to the Niners' demise. Instead of a Montana-to-Taylor redux for a grand finale, Jimmy Garoppolo overthrew an open Emmanuel Sanders on a potential winning touchdown pass, effectively sealing the 49ers' fate.

How could the 49ers blow a 10-point lead in the final seven minutes? Did third-year coach Kyle Shanahan not learn anything from the 2016 season's Super Bowl, when he was the offensive coordinator of the Atlanta Falcons as they squandered a 28–3 lead and fell to Tom Brady and the New England Patriots? Those were the main talking points—Mahomes' magic, Garoppolo's overthrow, Shanahan's fourth-quarter curse—in the wake of Super Bowl LIV.

Staley's potential retirement was not ignored, however. Once Staley reached the locker room at about 10:11 PM, the first person he saw was former teammate Frank Gore. "I bawled my eyes out. He didn't know the weight of that moment," recalled Staley, who last cried after a playoff loss ended his Rockford (Michigan) High School career. "To see him and the emotion I felt, it was therapeutic to have him there."

Obviously, all 49ers could use some comfort after the Lombardi Trophy slipped from their grasp. Garoppolo expressed condolences to his blind-side protector. "It sucks losing it for a guy like Joe and everything he's been through," Garoppolo said 50 minutes after the defeat while wearing a dapper black suit replete with a white pocket square.

Meanwhile, inside the 49ers' training room, team doctors were working on the eight stitches Staley required for his shredded right thumb. It had come out of its socket and forced him to miss a third-quarter series before he returned with a nerve block in his hand. "We're almost done, Joe. We're almost done," the medical staff promised.

"I'm not crying because of this bullshit thumb," Staley replied. "I'm crying because my career is done. I'm done playing football."

That was the first time he publicly uttered those dreadful words. They didn't fully believe him because, well, almost no one but Staley knew the extent of his neck condition, which got progressively worse through the postseason. Any time contact was made with his head or neck, his legs would go numb, his arms would tingle, a sensation of paralysis would take hold, then it would dissipate, and he'd play on with no strength. "I'm on the plane to go to Miami and I'm getting checked out by doctors because I'm worried I might be having a stroke," Staley said. "I'm having numbness on the right side of my face.

My heart was going like 150 beats per minute. I had no idea what was going on. I had numbness, weakness in my hands, arm, everything."

It subsided. Temporarily. Every night doctors checked his vitals, and every night Staley could not sleep. He did not want an MRI exam, knowing that an image would show "my neck was messed up," and that would keep him out of the Super Bowl. Cranial nerves, he later learned, were what threw his body out of whack, and he required two years of extensive physical therapy to recover. Entering his final game, however, he'd lost almost 10 pounds. Compound that with no sleep, and Staley was a zombie before kickoff. As he closed his eyes during the national anthem, he figuratively awoke to "the rockets' red glare" just as his body was shutting down. "It was a miracle I even played. I don't remember much from the game honestly," Staley said. "I was out there just on muscle memory, trying to do everything I could to not cost us the Super Bowl. I was proud of myself I was out there."

Win or lose after all, it's how you play the game, and the 49ers were playing it quite well, especially on defense. Tied 10–10 at halftime, the 49ers retook the lead on Robbie Gould's second field goal of the game. Fred Warner and Tarvarius Moore intercepted Mahomes on back-to-back series, and in between those momentum-rolling plays was a 49ers touchdown drive as Garoppolo delivered completions to Deebo Samuel (16 yards), Kendrick Bourne (16 yards), and Kyle Juszczyk (10 yards) before Raheem Mostert's one-yard score gave them a 20–10 cushion two-and-a-half minutes before the fourth quarter.

And then...avert your eyes, 49ers Faithful.

On Mahomes' third-and-15, 44-yard, game-changing completion to Hill, DeForest Buckner was a step away from hitting Mahomes. Nick Bosa was in hot pursuit, too, only to get held by Eric Fisher, a penalty that officials overlooked. "Was I held? It's pretty...it comes down to the opinion of a human being, and that's what refs are," Bosa said six months later at training camp. "I'm not going to say that's the reason we lost the game."

Staley, in his 2023 retirement, noted that neither Fisher nor any Chiefs drew a holding call all night, as Mahomes uncorked 42 passes (completing 26 of them for 286 yards) and got sacked four times. "[Bosa] beat him inside. He was held completely across his chest in the blatant view in front of the ref and zero flag," Staley said.

A few snaps later, officials called a pass-interference penalty on Moore, and Mahomes promptly threw a one-yard touchdown pass to Travis Kelce, cutting the 49ers' lead to 20–17 with 6:13 to go. The 49ers' ensuing possession is what irks them—Staley, Shanahan, others—more than their next one in which Garoppolo missed Sanders deep. The 49ers, after Kelce's score, went three-and-out in just 64 seconds, when a first down could have killed more time and preserved the lead. Their most regretful play was a second-and-5 pass to an open George Kittle, which Chiefs defensive tackle Chris Jones batted down. A third-down incompletion to Bourne set up a punt, and the Chiefs followed with their go-ahead touchdown drive. Mahomes hit Sammy Watkins for a 38-yard pass to the 10-yard line and then found Damien Williams for a five-yard score and a 24–20 lead.

Richie James' kick return to just the 15-yard line meant Garoppolo had to move the 49ers 85 yards in two minutes, 44 seconds for the Lombardi. Hey, Montana pulled off a 92-yard drive in under three minutes before his winning touchdown to Taylor in Miami in January 1989.

Garoppolo's 16-yard completion to Bourne got them to the Chiefs' 49-yard line out of the two-minute warning. Incompletions followed to Samuel and Bourne before the deep shot toward Sanders, who split two defensive backs to break free. The pass, sailing in the direction toward wide-eyed reporters in the press box, simply was too long for Sanders to even make a diving attempt. Could Samuel have had the speed to catch up to that ball? It's a moot point. "We had so many opportunities to put points on the board to put more pressure on them earlier," Staley said.

When Staley wiped away his tears and entered the post-game press conference tent, he composed himself, explained how tough of a loss it was, and expressed confidence in how "this football team is built for the long haul." It wasn't until the end of the ensuing draft on April 25 that he announced his retirement; the 49ers traded the same day for his replacement, Trent Williams. "I love Joe Staley. He is incredible," tight end George Kittle said after the Super Bowl. "To see him get back to this stage, how happy he was, and how locked in he was, he has been a leader for us all year...There is nothing more than I want than to give him a win and give him a ring. So that one hurts."

36

Super Bowl LVIII: Not-So-Sudden Death

JUST UP LAS VEGAS' STRIP, A FEW MILES FROM ALLEGIANT Stadium, rises the sparkling new Fontainebleau hotel. The morning after Super Bowl LVIII, three middle-aged couples shared a booth inside the serenely quiet sportsbook. As plates of food arrived, their eyes and smiles stayed trained on a giant videoboard to their left. "There's no game-changing, bullshit call they can pin anything on," one Kansas City Chiefs fan boastfully said while watching the Super Bowl LVIII replay.

Indeed, the San Francisco 49ers had no shortage of reasons why they lost 25–22 in overtime. It was a four-hour, six-minute march into more Super Bowl misery. Four years before, the

49ers blew a fourth-quarter lead and lost to the Chiefs, whose comeback started with a 44-yard, third-and-15 conversion in which officials failed to call a holding penalty that kept Nick Bosa from reaching Patrick Mahomes.

While those Chiefs fans enjoyed their celebratory brunch—to the victors go the spoils—the 49ers boarded a flight home to the Bay Area still without the sixth Lombardi Trophy that's eluded the franchise for 29 years. The next morning, that empty feeling reverberated through the 49ers' locker room at Levi's Stadium after they met a final time and packed their belongings into supersized cardboard boxes. Anguish, second-guessing, heartbreak, and uncharacteristic finger pointing raged around their ring of lockers.

Grieving a Super Bowl loss was new to most of them, including wide receiver Brandon Aiyuk, whose sunglasses covered his teary eyes as he struggled to tell reporters how this team reported to work daily to become champions. Only eight 49ers also participated in the Super Bowl LIV collapse to the Chiefs. This game also saw the 49ers squander a 10-point lead, though that was a 10–0 margin in Super Bowl LVIII's first half, not the 20–10 lead with seven minutes remaining against a trophy-less Mahomes four years ago.

This game, too, wasn't all bad. For example:

- Brock Purdy did not commit a turnover despite being the Super Bowl's third-youngest starting quarterback (age 24). A year earlier Purdy's elbow ligament was still awaiting surgery to repair it, and his ensuing comeback saw him set the 49ers' single-season passing record with 4,280 yards.
- Jauan Jennings not only caught Purdy's lone touchdown pass, but also threw one himself on a cross-field shot

to Christian McCaffrey, who raced through a perfectly blocked lane via his linemen.

- Rookie Jake Moody, after missing a kick in three straight games, made a 55-yard field goal to temporarily set a Super Bowl record until Chiefs counterpart Harrison Butker made good from 57 in the second half. Another special-teams standout was Chris Conley in punt coverage to pin the Chiefs at their 11-, 2-, and 14-yard lines.
- The 49ers' defense forced two turnovers. Deommodore Lenoir forced a fumble that Javon Hargrave recovered at the 49ers' 8-yard line in the second quarter, and rookie safety Ji'Ayir Brown intercepted a Mahomes toss three snaps after halftime. Alas, neither turnover was converted into 49ers points, typifying the missed opportunities that will haunt them from Super Bowl LVIII.

It took four hours, six minutes for the 49ers to succumb to the defending champions. And it took 10 flashpoints for that result to surface, cascading in the following order:

1. McCaffrey Fumbles

Christian McCaffrey, after going wire-to-wire for his first NFL rushing title, found work quickly in his Super Bowl debut. The 49ers' opening drive went like this: McCaffrey six-yard run, Kyle Juszczyk 18-yard catch, McCaffrey 11-yard catch-and-run, McCaffrey 11-yard run, and then, surprise, a McCaffrey fumble at the Chiefs' 27-yard line when stripped by linebacker Leo Chenal. "I can't put the ball on the ground on the first drive," McCaffrey said. "It's going to sting. Put that on me."

It was shocking, but it wasn't. On the 49ers' opening series in a Week Seven loss in Minnesota, McCaffrey lost a fumble at the Vikings' 13-yard line. His other two fumbles in 2023: on his first catch in the season opener at the Pittsburgh Steelers (he recovered the ball) and on the first snap of the second quarter of their Week Five win against the Dallas Cowboys. Offsetting this fumble, however, was the one Lenoir created by stripping Isiah Pacheco of the ball early in the second quarter right after Mahomes' 52-yard lightning bolt to Mecole Hardman at the 9-yard line. Not long after, the 49ers went up 10–0 on Jennings' trick-play toss to McCaffrey for a touchdown, and the Chiefs could only answer with a field goal (courtesy of Arik Armstead's belly-rubbing, third-down sack). That left the 49ers a 10–3 halftime lead to protect. Neither that nor three other leads proved safe.

2. Greenlaw Exits

No injury was more shocking this season than linebacker Dre Greenlaw rupturing his left Achilles tendon while sprinting off the 49ers' sideline for a second-quarter series. True, Greenlaw was scratched from the regular-season finale with "Achilles tendinitis," but his sudden exit made fellow linebacker Fred Warner wail "NO!" upon seeing his fallen comrade on this Vegas felt. "We've got to snap out of it for him. I'm sorry, dude," Nick Bosa later said while consoling a teary-eyed Warner on the 49ers' bench, as caught by NFL Films' microphones.

Two months earlier Greenlaw got ejected from the 49ers' NFC-shifting win at Philadelphia, where he got in a sideline scuffle with the Eagles' security czar, "Big Dom" DiSandro. The 49ers briefly staggered upon his exit there, then recovered to win 42–19. In the Super Bowl, Oren Burks filled in well early for Greenlaw, but Burks finished with the defense's second-worst rating (35.3) by Pro Football Focus.

3. Three-and-Outs

Scoring only 19 points in regulation was no way to beat Mahomes and the Chiefs. The 49ers' offense struggled as the Chiefs switched to man coverage. Even after Brown intercepted Mahomes shortly after Usher's halftime show, the 49ers couldn't capitalize with points. Not only did the 49ers go three-and-out on three straight possessions in the third quarter, but they also failed to gain positive yardage before punting each series. "I just keep thinking about those three-and-outs we had," Purdy said two days after the game, "and what an opportunity we had to go take control of the game."

The Chiefs' offense couldn't muster much to that point either. (Note: the Chiefs were not called for an offensive holding penalty in any of their Super Bowl wins to cap the 2019, 2022, and '23 seasons. They drew four such penalties in the 2020 team's Super Bowl loss to the Tampa Bay Buccaneers.)

4. Muffed Punt

Capping off a perilous season by the punt-return unit, disaster struck late in the third quarter when a punt ricocheted off the foot of 49ers rookie Darrell Luter Jr., and rather than pounce on the loose ball, return specialist Ray-Ray McCloud tried in vain to scoop it up. The Chiefs recovered, and then on their ensuing snap, Mahomes threw a 16-yard, go-ahead touchdown pass over Burks to Marquez Valdes-Scantling. Just like that, the 49ers trailed 13–10.

McCloud had rushed back from a broken wrist in August and broken ribs in November just so the 49ers could have a reliable punt catcher, something that rookie Ronnie Bell proved he wasn't during McCloud's absence. It turns out the most critical punt to retrieve was one that glanced off an unsuspecting rookie even as McCloud warned him to abandon the area.

5. Another Special Teams Gaffe

Their best collection of offensive personnel in 25 years allowed the 49ers to finally fight fire (Mahomes' touchdown) with fire (Purdy's touchdown to Jennings after a fourth-down conversion on George Kittle's full-effort catch). Instead of taking a 17–13 lead, Moody's point-after kick got blocked. That single point proved critical. Making it could have denied the Chiefs a chance to tie the score in the ensuing flurry of field goals (two by the Chiefs, one by the 49ers). Moody made the first 60 point-after kicks of his career until he missed his final try of the regular-season finale. He also missed a field-goal attempt in each of the three games preceding the Super Bowl. Alas, he would not win a Lombardi Trophy as a rookie like Doug Brien (a third-round draft pick like Moody) did as the 1994 team's kicker.

6. Third-Down Completion

Tied at 16 with two minutes left in regulation, the 49ers faced third and 5 from the Chiefs' 35-yard line. If they got the first down, they could take precious seconds off the clock before delivering go-ahead points, presumably on a field goal like the one Moody did make from 53 yards, though that ended up leaving 1:53 for Mahomes. What went wrong on third down is what some will blame for this defeat. The Chiefs sent cornerback Trent McDuffie on a blitz, and he raced untouched from Purdy's left. Kittle was in the backfield to Purdy's right. A mic'd up Shanahan wanted Purdy to throw to his right to McCaffrey. Purdy, in retrospect, wishes he threw for Brandon Aiyuk, who had just three catches in all three playoff games after posting his second straight 1,000-yard regular season. Instead, Purdy slung that third-down pass at Jennings, and McDuffie leaped to slightly deflect it. Incomplete. "In practice I've hit the outside slant a million times in that coverage—cover zero—and having our receiver winning outside," Purdy said. "I trusted J.J. to win a contested ball like it was going to be."

7. Overtime Flip

Gifted nearly two minutes to save the Chiefs' reign, Mahomes sure enough produced a game-tying drive. They got into field-goal range with him converting a third-down pass to ex-49ers running back Jerick McKinnon. They got even closer on a 22-yard, third-down connection to a wide-open Travis Kelce, who sprinted across the middle past Fred Warner at 19.68 mph, Kelce's fastest speed in seven seasons (to the delight of his onlooking girlfriend, Taylor Swift). Warner's tighter coverage on the ensuing snap prevented a Kelce touchdown catch at the front-left pylon. So the Chiefs settled for an overtime-forcing field goal.

What happened next sparked a debate that reverberated from morning talk shows to analytics' computers. The 49ers won the overtime coin flip, and rather than defer the ball as usual, Shanahan wanted it—to the surprise of the Chiefs and many others. Shanahan based his call off the 49ers' analytical staff advice, factoring in it being a "field-goal game" not to mention the staggered state of his defense after the Chiefs' 11-play, game-tying drive. So Shanahan told Warner to take the ball first in overtime. The motive: to get the ball third, assuming the Chiefs' first possession would match the 49ers, thus giving Purdy and his All-Star crew the first shot at a sudden-death score on the overtime's third possession. Some 49ers acknowledged afterward they weren't aware the NFL changed overtime rules in 2022, assuring each team a possession. Purdy knew the scenario, as did Shanahan. The true lesson was about to be delivered by Mahomes.

8. Third-Down Bust

Seven years after Shanahan was the Atlanta Falcons' offensive coordinator when they lost the Super Bowl's first overtime game—after blowing a 28–3 lead against Tom Brady and the New England Patriots—this second edition started off in his favor. Buoyed by a defensive holding penalty on McDuffie and a third-down conversion catch by Aiyuk near midfield, the 49ers got into scoring position, so to speak, on McCaffrey's 24-yard catch and run to the Chiefs' 26. An improvised, 13-yard sideline snag by Juszczyk moved them to the 15. Back-to-back McCaffrey runs set up a fateful, third-and-4 snap from the 9-yard line midway through the extra 15-minute session.

Purdy's final snap of a sensational season took a sudden turn for the worse. Right guard Spencer Burford, having replaced an injured Jon Feliciano, followed what he called "instincts" rather than "rules" and shifted left for a double-team block. Chiefs defensive star Chris Jones was left unblocked—aside from a feigned swipe by right tackle Colton McKivitz. Jones jetted toward Purdy, who didn't have time to see Aiyuk break open from the left toward the post. Instead, Purdy committed to throwing right and overthrew Jennings, who beat his defender. The 2012 49ers saw their Super Bowl dreams dashed with three incompletions to the right from Colin Kaepernick to Michael Crabtree. These 49ers still got go-ahead points, however, via a 27-yard field goal from Moody.

9. Fourth and Run

Mahomes said that 49ers field goal inspired the Chiefs to "go win the game right here." But the 49ers were only one snap from winning. Their defense just needed to stop the Chiefs on fourth and 1 from the Chiefs' 34-yard line. Mahomes suggested a play (*Slide Keys*) to coach Andy Reid, noting that if Kelce was covered, Mahomes would run the ball. "All right," a mic'd-up Shanahan said on the sideline. "We stop them, we're world champs, right?"

An onlooking Trent Williams hollered: "Alert the quarterback keep!"

That is exactly what transpired. Once Bosa bit on a play-action dive inside, Mahomes kept the ball and raced into an open pasture past the defense's unmanned left flank for an eight-yard, season-extending gain. Bosa openly complained how the 49ers were not prepared for Mahomes' runs. Three days after the Super Bowl, defensive coordinator Steve Wilks was fired but not necessarily as this game's scapegoat. That move was foreshadowed at midseason once he got ordered down from the coaches' booth to the sideline to help cure a three-game losing streak.

10. Game-Ending Play

As the Lombardi Trophy slipped from their grasp, the 49ers let the Chiefs' once-butterfingered receivers catch Mahomes' next five passes. When Mahomes blazed 19 yards up the middle past Warner and others on a third-and-1 run, the Chiefs were 13 yards from the goal line. Three snaps later, Mahomes called for their "Tom and Jerry" play, a version of last Super Bowl's "Corndog" special that produced victory. Bosa, again from left defensive end, cut off a potential inside handoff, so Mahomes looked to his right and found Hardman open for a three-yard, championship-winning touchdown catch. As Warner stepped forward to chase Mahomes, so did nickel back Logan Ryan, who then was late sliding to his left to cover Hardman. Two months earlier, Ryan was on a Disney cruise with his family, when Talanoa Hufanga's knee injury prompted the 49ers to summon Ryan. By midnight Ryan was in Disneyland's commercial replaying the winning pass from Mahomes, the three-time Super Bowl MVP.

"I couldn't really look anybody in the eye, especially all my teammates," Bosa said of the locker-room scene after. "I could have done more. Everybody could have done more. And there's really not much to say at this point. It's going to hurt and it's going to hit in waves, but that's life."

So ended a season that began with five wins, then three straight losses. The bye week gave them time to reboot—and for Purdy to rest his arm while driving a tractor on his fiancee's family's Iowa farm. Six straight wins followed, including a victorious sweep of the so-called gauntlet that took them from Seattle on Thanksgiving to a NFC Championship Game rematch in Philadelphia before a home win against the Seahawks, then the NFC West-clinching road win against the Arizona Cardinals. Humbled in a Christmas night rout by the Baltimore Ravens—pitting each conference's top team—the 49ers rebounded to not only win in Washington on New Year's Eve, but a wild celebration ensued in the locker room once the No. 1 seed was secured by virtue of Philadelphia's upset loss to Arizona.

The 49ers, in that instant, had what they sought for 10 months: the NFC's home-field advantage and a wild-card bye to pave an easier path to the Super Bowl. Once there, in Las Vegas, the 49ers instantly condemned their practice field as too soft (grass was improperly laid atop UNLV's artificial surface). NFL commissioner Roger Goodell dismissively countered that the fields were "playable," a term to which the NFL Players Association took great exception in regards to player safety.

Meanwhile, both the 49ers and the Chiefs were sequestered 45 minutes away from The Strip's trappings. If the 49ers needed more of an inferiority complex, their press conferences were held Tuesday through Thursday in the dank basement of the abandoned Casino Monte Lago adjacent to their Lake Las Vegas hotel. Sportsbooks pegged the 49ers as two-point favorites over the reigning champs, over Mahomes' magic, over a 29-yard drought since their last Super Bowl triumph. Once the Chiefs rolled into the end zone, this game was done. Craps indeed. "We have the team obviously to do it, to win the whole thing," Purdy said. "And to come up short like that the way things have been the last couple of years here, everyone wanted it so bad."

Perhaps no one wanted it more than Shanahan, who was reminded he'd lost three Super Bowls (one as the Falcons' coordinator, two as the 49ers' coach) in which his teams blew double-digit leads. "You guys can have any narrative you want, but the success or the failure, it comes down to one game, and I hope that I can be a part of a team that wins a game at the end of the year," Shanahan said two days later in his concluding press conference. "But to say that the Niners can't win a big game would be an extremely inaccurate statement."

PART 5

DISCOVERING GOLD

37

Trades

Fred Dean

Trading for Fred Dean during the 1981 season figured to key a run at the Lombardi Trophy. It is what the San Francisco 49ers had in mind and the nearby Oakland Raiders, too. Yes, Al Davis had designs on acquiring Dean to help them repeat as world champs. Hey, when your motto is "Just Win, Baby," that means going after anyone who'll help even if he plays for your rival, which in Dean's case was the San Diego Chargers. "Bill [Walsh] was catching hell," Davis recalled in a 2006 interview. "So he makes a trade for a guy we wanted."

When it comes to trades that panned out for the 49ers, that history starts with Dean's acquisition—with all due respect to Steve Young's 1987 arrival and the annual shopping sprees that enhanced playoff runs under coach Kyle Shanahan. In 1981 Walsh and the 49ers were quietly building their Super Bowl-winning dynasty. They went 2–14 and 6–10 in Walsh's first two seasons out of Stanford, and 1981 got off to a 1–2 start after a seven-point opening loss at the Detroit Lions and a 17-point defeat two weeks later at the Atlanta Falcons. "He saved Bill's career, this guy...It made the 49ers," Davis said of the Dean trade. "They couldn't have won without him."

Dean already was an accomplished, pass-rushing demon. Only the Chargers weren't willing to pay him as such. So they were willing to trade him. Ironically, the Raiders traded for pass-rushing prowess a year earlier by poaching Cedrick Hardman from the 49ers for a fifth-round draft pick. Hardman had spent a decade accumulating a 49ers-record 108 ½ sacks (unofficially because sacks did not become an NFL stat until 1982). Upon joining the Raiders, Hardman delivered a team-high nine-and-a-half sacks on a Silver and Black defense that included Ted Hendricks, John Matuszak, Matt Millen, and Lester Hayes.

When it came to adding Dean the following year in 1981, left tackle Art Shell certainly did not object, telling Davis to "get him." So, according to Davis, the Chargers wanted offensive tackle Bruce Davis, Shell's eventual successor, and at least one other player. The Raiders' counteroffer: offensive tackle Lindsey Mason and a second-round pick. "We go back and forth. Two geniuses," Davis recalled with sarcastic wit about his talks with the Chargers. "They want to make the deal, and I'm real smart and don't make the deal."

Instead, the 49ers swooped in for a future Pro Football Hall of Famer and franchise flipper. "That was the pot of gold," Dean said. "It was a different lifestyle for me altogether. I felt free to perform once I got there."

He reeled off three sacks in his debut, playing far more than the 10 to 12 snaps prescribed by Walsh in the 49ers' long-sought win against the Dallas Cowboys. It was a 45–14 rout in Week

Six (on October 11, 1981) and marked the 49ers' third straight win. Even better was a five-sack game by Dean two weeks later against the Los Angeles Rams. He'd finish with 12 sacks in 11 games for a 49ers team that went 15–1 after its 1–2 start. Dean repeated as an All-Pro and Pro Bowler.

If Hardman was the NFL's first pass-rush specialist, then Dean was its second, and his 49ers presence certainly made NFL life easier for the 1981 rookie contingent of safeties Ronnie Lott and Carlton Williamson and cornerback Eric Wright. Three years later Dean and the 49ers won their second Lombardi Trophy. But after the 1985 season, Dean was done with the 49ers and the NFL. "We wouldn't have won five Super Bowls if we hadn't won the first two," said ex-49ers owner Eddie DeBartolo, Dean's presenter to Canton's hallowed Hall of Fame. "We would not have won the first two if it weren't for Fred Dean."

All Dean initially cost them was a 1983 second-round pick and the swapping of 1983 first-round spots with the Chargers. Once that draft day came, so did another 49ers–Chargers trade. The 49ers dealt their first-round pick for two second-round selections (one used on Roger Craig and the other part of a package that brought in Wendell Tyler).

Another odd connection to all that era's wheeling and dealing: the Raiders did find a taker for Mason, and it was the 49ers in 1982 in exchange for the fifth-round pick in the 1980 Hardman deal. The Raiders did take one more look at Dean, too. He auditioned for them in Oxnard, California, in July 1986 after which coach Tom Flores said: "He has shown a great interest in coming to play for us."

Though Dean didn't end up coming out of retirement in 1986, the interest was mutual only a half-decade earlier. Dean played only 57 games for the 49ers after 84 with the Chargers. In his 18th year of eligibility, he was the Pro Football Hall of Fame's Class of 2008. Two months later he went into the Chargers' Hall of Fame for his exploits with them even if he went down as their worst trade ever and arguably the 49ers' best.

Steve Young

On April 24, 1987, Bill Walsh released a statement insisting that the San Francisco 49ers' trade for left-hander Steve Young was "not a reflection on Joe Montana. We fully expect Joe to continue as the leader and mainstay of our team."

And yet Montana's back injury in the 1986 season left Walsh and quarterbacks coach Mike Holmgren with the NFL's ultimate contingency plan: Young, who'd gone from eighth string at BYU (where Holmgren coached) to a professional career in the United States Football League with the Los Angeles Express and then the NFL's dungeon known as the Tampa Bay Buccaneers. "Everyone was concerned about Joe's back since he had the surgery, and I believe Bill had a sense Joe was not coming back," Young said in retrospect 20 years later. "Then the first day I come out to practice, I see Joe and I say, 'Hey, he looks pretty good.'"

Indeed, the 49ers' succession plan would be far from immediate. What ensued was the NFL's ultimate quarterback controversy, and it ultimately yielded back-to-back Pro Football Hall of Famers. "Oh, it was fine between the two," Walsh said, "but right under the surface...Steve wanted to play, and Joe didn't want him to play. Other than that, everybody got along fine and worked together."

Young cost the 49ers 1987 second- and fourth-round draft picks after he reportedly balked at a trade to the St. Louis Cardinals for a first rounder. He'd gone 3–16 as the Bucs' starter, completing just 53.3 percent of his passes and throwing 21 interceptions in 19 games.

"Tampa taught me a lesson," Young said. "I knew I found a really special place in San Francisco. Why did I know it? Not because I was in San Francisco. Because I had been in Tampa Bay."

Young would complete 65.8 percent of his 3,648 passes with the 49ers, earn two NFL MVP awards, make seven straight Pro Bowls, and set a Super Bowl record with six touchdown passes for their 1994 team's championship win against the San Diego Chargers. "He had to do a lot of work. He had to learn our system of football, and there's so much to it that it takes time," Walsh said. "He did fine with it, but it took a full year. He was very intelligent and learned quickly and he had habits we didn't want to break but had to alter."

Young's first four years with the 49ers saw him play in 35 games and start 10. Montana's career-threatening elbow injury saw Young turn his opportunity into the first of his six passing titles followed by a 1992 MVP run. In 1993 Montana got traded to the Kansas City Chiefs. "They were competitors, and therefore their personal relationship wasn't the best," Young's father, LeGrande, said. "But he was able to learn a lot about the quarterback position from him, and it helped immensely."

As imposing as it was to arrive in Montana's shadow, Young cherished how Ronnie Lott approached him to say he'd have his back like the ultimate teammate he was. In 2017 Young related that "I've Got Your Back" message to the new-age 49ers under Kyle Shanahan, whose father, Mike, was offensive coordinator of Young's Super Bowl masterpiece. "Steve's like, 'Guys, you might not win a lot of games this first year, but you're going to be a hard out and you have to improve that culture,'" CEO

Jed York said. "That has kind of built its way into what we have now."

Christian McCaffrey

Looking ever comfortable in a red suit with a white shirt and black boots, Christian McCaffrey sat on a barstool on stage at the California Theatre to address San Francisco 49ers fans at an alumni fundraiser in May 2023. Only seven months earlier, the former Stanford star arrived back in the Bay Area via an initially bittersweet trade from the Carolina Panthers. "In hindsight I firmly believe it's the best thing that ever happened to me," McCaffrey said.

It was the best thing, too, for the 49ers, who initially feared they overpaid by coughing up four draft picks (2023 second, third, and fourth rounders plus a 2024 fifth rounder) to outbid the rival Los Angeles Rams. McCaffrey learned of his new employer at 11:30 PM on October 20, 2022, then boarded a cross-country flight the next morning, passed a physical, and squeezed in a cameo in the 49ers' October 23 home loss to the Kansas City Chiefs.

After that McCaffrey entered the starting lineup, and the 49ers would go on one of the longest regular-season win streaks (12 games) in their history. He showed his scoring prowess by accounting for touchdowns a trio of ways—a 34-yard pass to Brandon Aiyuk, a nine-yard catch of a Jimmy Garoppolo throw, and a one-yard run—to key a 31–14 comeback at the Rams' SoFi Stadium.

McCaffrey kept scoring, and the 49ers kept winning. He earned only his second career Pro Bowl nod, produced 1,210 rushing and receiving yards combined in his 11 regular-season games, and then gained 299 yards more in three playoff games.

When McCaffrey racked up four touchdowns (and nearly a franchise-record tying five) in an October 1, 2023 win against the Arizona Cardinals, it marked his 13th straight game with a touchdown (playoffs included), and that passed Jerry Rice's 1987 record. Staked with a 4–0 record and the NFL's rushing leader at that point of the 2023 season, coach Kyle Shanahan was asked if he could imagine not having traded for McCaffrey 346 days earlier. "No, don't ever say that," Shanahan said with a wry smile, then noting how "there's always a huge risk" and a "huge debate" on whether to up the ante in a trade. "There's always a gamble to it. But, no, life has been much better."

McCaffrey would agree, noting that he felt comfortable from Day One. "The cool part from my perspective is how these guys took me in a year ago, and none of that has changed," he said after his four-touchdown masterpiece on October 1, 2023. "I got the call [from Panthers general manager Scott Fitterer] that I was traded, John Lynch called me right after that, and then I got a call from George Kittle. He was the third person that called me and he represents the whole team and how they took me in. I'm just really honored and blessed to be a part of this team."

Jimmy Garoppolo

It was before dawn on Halloween 2018, and Jimmy Garoppolo feared for his life. He was in a limousine en route to Rhode Island's T.F. Green International Airport. Suddenly, he saw headlights come his way from a car that careened off the exit ramp and barreled toward him.

Garoppolo's driver zoomed into a ditch and out of harm's way, and Garoppolo gasped at his near-death adventure. His exhilarated driver proclaimed how awesome that was, and the San Francisco 49ers-bound quarterback retorted: "That was *not* awesome, but that was crazy. Great job."

What an appropriate start to Garoppolo's first day as a 49er, which saw him arrive later that afternoon at 49ers headquarters—safely exiting from the front passenger side of a black Chevrolet Suburban. "We brought him here because we want him to be the quarterback of the future," said Kyle Shanahan in the first year of a six-year contract.

Shanahan first studied and recommended Garoppolo ahead of the 2014 draft when Shanahan was the Cleveland Browns' offensive coordinator. Shanahan praised Garoppolo's toughness, visual discipline, quick release, and intelligence. "From the first time I met Kyle, there was a connection there," Garoppolo said.

The 49ers opened 0–9 in Shanahan's first season as 49ers coach in 2017. Garoppolo was given a month runway to learn the scheme, then produced a 5–0 mark while given freedom to adapt in his December starting debut. By the time he left town after the 2022 season, he compiled a 42–19 overall record, including the 2019 season's NFC Championship Game win and the ensuing Super Bowl collapse to the Kansas City Chiefs.

Trent Williams

General manager John Lynch and coach Kyle Shanahan opened their tenure with big trades for Garoppolo (2017), Laken Tomlinson (2017), Dee Ford (2019), and Emmanuel Sanders (2019). Perhaps their most stunning move through three years, though, came when they sprang Trent Williams from Washington, a troubled franchise whose then-owner, Daniel Snyder, held a grudge against Shanahan from when he and his father, Mike, coached there in 2010–13.

Williams was more than an ideal replacement for left tackle Joe Staley, who retired after their Super Bowl loss to cap his 13-year tenure (six Pro Bowls, three second-team All-Pros).

Williams entered the NFL in 2010 under the Shanahans and took two years to become a perennial Pro Bowler. Then after missing 2019 due to cancer surgery, Williams came to the 49ers for 2021 third- and 2020 fifth-round picks. He promptly recaptured Pro Bowl form, took the San Francisco 49ers' offer in 2021 free agency over the Kansas City Chiefs' to become the NFL's highest-paid offensive lineman, then captured the first of multiple All-Pro honors as an athletic, powerful dynamo in a dynamic offense. "Trent's passion for the game could be felt from Day One, and this fits exactly with our vision of the 49er Way and a championship culture," Lynch said upon Williams' 2021 deal.

From Day One, Lynch and Shanahan emphasized a desire to build through the trenches. That is a common emphasis in draft strategy, but trading for a lineman certainly worked out with Williams. The 49ers tried replicating that magic trick with ensuing, in-season deals for defensive linemen, including Jordan Willis (2020, playoff hero for blocking a punt in 2022 divisional playoff win in Green Bay), Charles Omenihu (2021), Randy Gregory (2023), and Chase Young (2023). Like Williams, Young was culled out of Washington for a minimal rental price (2024 third-round pick), even though he was a No. 2 overall draft pick in 2020 and won NFL Defensive Rookie of the Year honors. Young didn't exactly pan out for the 49ers, however, as he delivered just three-and-a-half sacks in 12 games, and his lack of hustle in the NFC Championship Game was alarming, though he did rebound with a sack in the Super Bowl before exiting in free agency for New Orleans.

Gary "Big Hands" Johnson

Like Fred Dean three years earlier, the San Francisco 49ers traded for a defensive-line menace from the San Diego Chargers to help complete a Super Bowl run. Johnson arrived in 1984 for the final 12 regular-season games and then did more than his share to earn his first and only Super Bowl ring with five sacks, three fumble recoveries, a safety. He had two sacks in the NFC Championship Game win against the Chicago Bears, then had one while further pestering the Miami Dolphins' Dan Marino throughout the 49ers' Super Bowl win at Stanford. He retired after the 1985 season and eventually was enshrined in the Chargers' Hall of Fame for his nine-plus years there.

Anquan Boldin

Barely a month after Anquan Boldin helped the Baltimore Ravens beat the San Francisco 49ers in the Super Bowl, the 49ers acquired him for a 2013 sixth-round draft pick. Colin Kaepernick promptly declared it "a great trade," and he was right.

Boldin led the 49ers in receiving each of the next three seasons—under two different head coaches—in the twilight of a Pro Football Hall of Fame-caliber career. After Boldin's back-to-back, 1,000-yard seasons in 2013 and 2014, the 49ers did not have a wide receiver reach that threshold until Deebo Samuel in 2021. Boldin's final season in 2015 saw him still lead the 49ers with 789 yards on 69 receptions with just four touchdowns as they toggled between quarterbacks Kaepernick and Blaine Gabbert, to which Boldin simply said: "As a team you have to be behind whoever it is the coach puts out there. It doesn't change your job or what you have to do."

John Henry Johnson

It's not every day a Pro Football Hall of Famer saunters into the locker room some 50 years since his time with the San Francisco 49ers. That's what John Henry Johnson did in

2002, when he stopped by the Santa Clara facility and joked that he wouldn't mind playing again to make "a little more bread."

Ironically, Johnson was part of what was famously called the "Million Dollar Backfield" from 1954 to 1956, when he was part of a fearsome foursome with Joe "The Jet" Perry, Hugh "The King" McElhenny, and quarterback Y.A. Tittle. Johnson joined the 49ers by way of a 1954 trade from the Pittsburgh Steelers (for Ed Pullerton). The Steelers drafted him in the second round of 1953 after a college career at St. Mary's and Arizona State, but Johnson opted to start his pro career in Canada. The 49ers dealt him to the Detroit Lions, who promptly won the 1957 NFL championship, then he returned to the Steelers for six seasons before a 1966 finale with the Houston Oilers. He passed away in 2011 in Tracy, California, some 65 miles east of Kezar Stadium.

Freddie Solomon

Freddie Solomon had the crowd all aflutter...when he showed up at a Monta Vista High School football game in Cupertino, California, in the late 1980s. As the San Francisco 49ers built their dynasty, Solomon served as one of their building blocks once they traded for him from the Miami Dolphins in 1978 (along with safety Vern Roberson in exchange for running back Delvin Williams). Solomon became beloved not only by the fanbase, but also by franchise owner Eddie DeBartolo Jr. When Solomon passed away in 2012 from colon and liver cancer, DeBartolo said at his memorial service: "People scratched their heads about our friendship. They just couldn't figure it out. But Freddie was simply the finest human being I'd ever encountered in my life."

Solomon was part of the 49ers' first two Super Bowl-winning teams. Of his eight playoff games, he had a touchdown catch in six of them with the exceptions being those Super Bowl wins with the 1981 and 1984 teams. Although his overall reception statistics have been dwarfed by the NFL's pass-happy progress in the decades since he retired, he scored a career-high 10 touchdown receptions on that 1984 team.

Ray Rhodes

Before he won Super Bowls on Bill Walsh's 1981 and 1984 coaching staffs, Rhodes first joined the organization in 1980 as a cornerback via a trade from the New York Giants with wide receiver Jimmy Robinson in exchange for safety Tony Dungy and fullback Mike Hogan. It would be Rhodes' one and only season as a San Francisco 49ers player before he became a defensive backs coach and ultimately their 1994 defensive coordinator, which served as his stepping stone to head coaching stints with the Philadelphia Eagles and Green Bay Packers.

Russ Francis

The free-spirited tight end had retired from the New England Patriots and begun a broadcasting career when he interviewed Joe Montana and Bill Walsh at the 1981 season's Pro Bowl. Walsh enticed him to unretire, and the San Francisco 49ers sent 1982 first-, second-, and fourth-round picks to the Patriots. He appeared in 75 games (196 catches, 12 touchdowns) before being released in 1987. The Hawaiian native had five catches for 60 yards in the 1984 team's Super Bowl win. Francis was 70 when he died in a plane crash October 1, 2023.

The Ugly Trades

Gambling in the trade market doesn't always pay dividends. There are also some notorious trades that did not go the San Francisco 49ers' way.

Seeking a quarterback whose rookie contract would help them afford high-priced veteran stars, the 49ers made a regrettable move on March 26, 2021. To climb from the No. 12 to No. 3 spot in the draft, they sent the Miami Dolphins first-round picks in 2021 (No. 12), 2022 (No. 29), and 2023 (No. 29), plus a 2022 third-round pick (No. 102). Draft day arrived a month later, and quarterbacks went with the first three picks: Trevor Lawrence (Jacksonville Jaguars), Zach Wilson (New York Jets), and **Trey Lance**, whom the 49ers fell for despite him playing just one full season at North Dakota State and totaling only 318 passes from 2018 to 2020. Injuries piled up, and playing opportunities were scare for Lance. He went 2–2 as their starter, attempted just 102 passes (56 completions, five touchdowns), and lost out to Sam Darnold as Brock Purdy's backup in 2023. The 49ers, before their preseason finale, unloaded him to the Dallas Cowboys for a fourth-round pick, prompting Steve Young to declare: "Trade nothing to Dallas ever."

A San Jose native and Heisman Trophy winner at Stanford, **Jim Plunkett** came back to the Bay Area at a price comparable to the 2021 Lance deal. The 49ers sent two 1976 first-round picks and 1977 first- and second-round picks to the New England Patriots, who drafted him first overall in 1971. Plunkett got off to a 6–1 start with the 1976 49ers, but he lost his final five starts that season and his first five in 1977. Rather than improve on his 11–15 record through two seasons, Plunkett was released and merely became a two-time Super Bowl winner in eight years on the Raiders.

A San Francisco native and a Heisman Trophy winner himself at USC, **O.J. Simpson** returned to the Bay Area in 1978 as part of a five-pick package: 1978 second and third rounders and 1979 first, second, and fourth rounders. His body ravaged from nine previous seasons and 2,123 carries with the Buffalo Bills, Simpson ran for just four touchdowns and 1,053 yards in two seasons with the 49ers, who went 2–14 in both 1978 and 1979.

After **Y.A. Tittle**'s decade of service, the 49ers turned to John Brodie to run Red Hickey's inventive formation known as the "shotgun." After the 1961 preseason opener, Tittle was dealt to the New York Giants for guard Lou Cordileone, and the quarterback went on to lead the Giants to the NFL Championship Game in three straight seasons (losing each time) before retiring after the 1964 season and heading to the Pro Football Hall of Fame in 1971.

Yes, the 49ers traded away two Hall of Fame quarterbacks in Tittle and Montana. Those weren't the only quarterbacks wanted elsewhere. Not to say these trades bombed or succeeded, but these other quarterbacks were exported by trade: Earl Morrall (1957, Pittsburgh Steelers), Tom Owen (1976, Patriots), Steve DeBerg (1981, Denver Broncos), Steve Bono (1994, Kansas City Chiefs), Ty Detmer (1999, Cleveland Browns), Jim Druckenmiller (1999, Miami Dolphins), Tim Rattay (2005, Tampa Bay Buccaneers), Ken Dorsey (2006, Browns), Cody Pickett (2006, Houston Texans), Shaun Hill (2010, Detroit Lions), and Alex Smith (2013, Chiefs).

38

Feeling a Draft

RATING THE SAN FRANCISCO 49ERS' BEST DRAFT PICKS IS an easy exercise. Just look who made the Pro Football Hall of Fame and won the Super Bowl. Thus, it's all too obvious to celebrate Joe Montana (1979, third round), Ronnie Lott (1981, first round), Jerry Rice (1985, first round), Charles Haley (1986, fourth round), and Bryant Young (1994, first round). Each has a special story, a gold jacket, and a ring or two (or three or four).

Haley's story is unique beyond that he was the first NFL player to five rings—with the final three coming on the Dallas Cowboys after the 49ers infamously traded him to their archrival in 1992. What makes Haley even more compelling is his draft class is one of, if not, the NFL's greatest ever. Of that 13-player haul in 1986, eight went on to play at least 80 games in their respective careers, and more critical to the 49ers' cause, seven started in the 1988 season's Super Bowl victory as third-year veterans.

Starting in that Super Bowl XXIII win against the Cincinnati Bengals were fullback Tom Rathman (third round), wide receiver John Taylor (third round), left tackle Steve Wallace (fourth round), cornerbacks Tim McKyer (third round) and Don Griffin (sixth round), and defensive linemen Larry Roberts (second round), Kevin Fagan (fourth round), and Haley. Rathman, Taylor, Fagan, Haley, and Griffin also started—and won—on the next year's championship defense.

Haley was discovered out of James Madison in his native Virginia. He paid immediate dividends with 12 sacks as a rookie, then aided Super Bowl runs in 1988 under Bill Walsh and in 1989 with George Seifert. "I had two of the best coaches there. I played with some of the best teammates ever," recalled Haley, who totaled 100 ½ career sacks and made five Pro Bowls. "They were the hardest-working men that I've ever been around in my life. "

Haley's strategy was simple. "I wanted to whoop that guy's ass that I had to play," he said. "You want to earn the respect of your teammates? If you earn the respect of the guy you have to play against, your teammates see that."

One such teammate was Young, who won the Super Bowl as a 1994 rookie and eventually would play next to Haley once the latter came out of retirement for a 1998–99 swan song. Fast forward to 2022, and it was Haley who knocked on the door of Young's Charlotte-area home to tell him he made the Pro Football Hall of Fame.

The 49ers were compelled to trade Haley in his prime because of his insubordination, mood swings, and temperament, much of which was explained later by his diagnosis of bipolar disorder. "I was a 22-year-old athlete that had an 11-year-old kid inside of me crying for help, but I refused to ask for it," Haley said. "People saw me, knew I needed help. I was too dumb or weak to ask for it."

As Haley entered the Hall of Fame in 2015, he made sure to give thanks to the late Bill Walsh, who had the "shoulder I cried on a lot" and who partnered with John McVay to craft that famed 1986 draft class. "Bill Walsh, when I was there, that door was wide open, and all these great players kept coming back," Haley said. "That's how we learn. Bill never got up there and told us how to be a champion. He let other guys do that."

Haley is the first (and only) player from the 1986 draft to get enshrined into the Pro Football Hall of Fame. The first player drafted that year was Bo Jackson, but he refused to sign with the Tampa Bay Buccaneers (and potentially team with Steve Young). Considering the massive attention cast on NFL draft's first rounds, it's even more significant to note the 49ers did not have a first-round pick in that 1986 haul.

Was that draft class the NFL's best? It depends on the valuation either from the team standpoint (see: Lombardi Trophy case) or Pro Football Hall of Fame entrants. The Pittsburgh Steelers' 1974 draft class sent four players (Lynn Swann, Jack Lambert, John Stallworth, Mike Webster) to Canton, Ohio; the 1957 Cleveland Browns, 1958 Green Bay Packers, and 1964 Cowboys each spawned a trio of Hall of Famers from those respective draft years.

Every year another class arrives with visions of stardom and championships. Here are the best of the best with a nod to the worst in a round-by-round review:

First Round

Jerry Rice (1985, No. 16 overall pick): Bill Walsh traded up for him thanks to the New England Patriots accepting the San Francisco 49ers' picks at the end of the first, second, and third rounds. That dowry was just enough to leapfrog the Dallas Cowboys, who picked at No. 17. That's how Jerry Rice took the stage. Funny sidebar: when Rice was summoned off a San Jose stage at a 49ers alumni fundraiser in 2022, he reminded the audience of his NFL records (22,895 receiving yards, 208 touchdowns), then added: "Joe Montana, Steve Young—I put both of those guys in the Hall of Fame!" He was joking. Maybe.

Leo Nomellini (1950, No. 11 overall pick): Leo "The Lion" Nomellini was the 49ers' first player taken in an NFL draft and he never missed any of the 49ers' 174 games between 1950 and 1963. Displayed in the 49ers' museum are his game jersey, jacket, 1951 contract ($7,000 salary) alongside *West Coast Wrestling News* promoting Nomellini's title defense on a Tuesday night against Gene Kiniski. Also on display is a plaque the Minnesota Vikings bestowed upon his 158th consecutive game with the 49ers for how he "enriched the reputation" as a University of Minnesota product. He made first-team All-Pro six times, second only in 49ers history to Rice's 10.

Ronnie Lott (1981, No. 8 overall pick): A five-time All-Pro and nine-time Pro Bowler in his 1981–90 tenure, Ronnie Lott remained a hard-hitting leader decades later albeit it as a guest speaker. When he addressed 49ers rookies at a 2022 minicamp, he asked them their goals, their aspirations. "A lot of Ronnie's message—he's so intense—but it's about having your teammate's back, it's about knowing everyone's job on the defense, and what it takes to be special and to win championships," 49ers general manager John Lynch shared. Lott, originally a cornerback out of USC, was the second defensive back drafted in 1981, going four spots after Kenny Easley from rival UCLA. Lott was a first-ballot Hall of Famer in 2000, and Easley joined him 17 years later in Canton, Ohio.

Jimmy Johnson (1961, No. 6 overall pick): This Pro Football Hall of Famer played in the second-most games in 49ers history (213) and produced their second most interceptions (47) while playing his entire 16-year career with them, most noticeably as a five-time Pro Bowler between 1969 and 1974.

Hugh McElhenny (1952, No. 9 overall pick): If black-and-white film highlights don't royally show off "The King," then take a trip into the 49ers' museum, which displays his autographed, red helmet with a clear, plastic facemask and enough rough spots to remind all of his style. No. 39 rambled for 4,288 yards and 35 touchdowns in nine seasons plus 2,666 receiving yards and 15 more scores as a Hall of Fame-bound member of the Niners' "Million Dollar Backfield."

Nick Bosa (2019, No. 2 overall pick): No addition flipped the 49ers' fortunes more than Nick Bosa's arrival as the No. 2 pick after the NFC West rival Arizona Cardinals gambled on quarterback Kyler Murray at No. 1. Bosa immediately proved a maniacal technician with precise pass-rushing moves, super-sized quadriceps, and a soft-spoken swagger. He reached heights—NFL's Defensive Rookie of the Year (2019), NFL Defensive Player of the Year (2022)—and overcame lows of 2020 reconstructive knee surgery and brutal playoff heartbreaks in four of his first five seasons. Once his 2023 camp holdout paid off with the NFL's largest contract ever for a non-quarterback (five years, $170 million), Bosa said: "It's going to be a weight off my shoulders, and I'll be able to not think of the negative thoughts that come with playing this game. I can play free and play for one reason: to win games."

Patrick Willis (2007, No. 11 overall pick): A San Francisco hotel ballroom saw Patrick Willis lean into a microphone at his 2023 Bay Area Sports Hall of Fame induction and offer this defining quote of his 49ers career: "When you buckle the chin strap, there are no friends. It's straight business. It's game time." Foot injuries ended a run that began with NFL Rookie of the Year honors in 2007 and then drew seven straight Pro Bowl invitations and six All-Pro selections.

Y.A. Tittle (1951, No. 3 overall pick): The 49ers' 2001 training camp was in Stockton, California, when a 74-year-old Y. A. Tittle paid them a visit. "The coaches are treating me like a king," said Tittle, whose Pro Football Hall of Fame career began with the 49ers from 1951 to 1960. He got traded to the New York Giants (for guard Lou Cordileone) and led them to the league championship three straight years (and earned 1963 MVP honors). Tittle was the first football player on a *Sports Illustrated* cover (1954), the first recipient of the 49ers' Len Eshmont Award (1957), and one of four Hall of Famers who comprised the "Million Dollar Backfield," joining Joe Perry, Hugh McElhenny, and John Henry Johnson. The 49ers were actually the third franchise to use a first-round pick on Tittle, who initially got drafted in 1948 by both the Cleveland Browns (All-America Football Conference) and the Detroit Lions (NFL). He played three years for the Baltimore Colts before they folded and he got nabbed by the 49ers, where he'd return after his playing days to serve as an offensive consultant from 1965 to 1969.

Bryant Young (1994, No. 7 overall pick): Winning a Super Bowl as a rookie was only the start of a 14-year career that landed Bryant Young in the Pro Football Hall of Fame in 2022, 15 years after his career ended. "B.Y., he was a selfless leader," Steve Young said. "And it fit us to a T." That was reflected when teammates honored Bryant Young with the Len Eshmont

Award a record eight times, and it was punctuated when he got carried off on teammates' shoulders after his December 23, 2007 finale at Candlestick Park. The soft-spoken Young basked in that spotlight, wearing his red, No. 97 jersey with a red, 49ers ballcap turned backward. He left as the 49ers' all-time sack leader with 89 ½ over his 14-year career. Not to be overlooked: he played with a 16-inch titanium rod in his right leg, which he broke in 1998 against the Giants before winning NFL Comeback Player of the Year honors in 1999.

Joe Staley (2007, No. 28 overall pick): The 49ers landed more than just a 13-year anchor at left tackle from Central Michigan. Joe Staley mentored linemen and acted as the franchise's perfect front man, invoking a serious tone when needed but also a joy of football and humanity during high times. One of the greatest blocks in franchise history came when he sprinted down field to clear Alex Smith's touchdown path in an epic, January 2012 playoff win against the New Orleans Saints. He reached two Super Bowls and he retired on 2020 draft weekend after a final season in which he played through a broken leg, a mangled knuckle, and ultimately a career-ending neck condition. "It's not about accolades, it's not about doing stuff to get noticed," Staley said. "Whatever you're doing, you're trying to give your best at. You're trying to win and be the best you can be. The Super Bowl is the best thing you can do, to win a Super Bowl. It sucks. It really does, to not be able to win that."

Harris Barton (1987, No. 22 overall pick): A three-time champion at right tackle, Harris Barton's nerves were calmed in the Super Bowl XXIII huddle before the 49ers' Lombardi Trophy-winning drive, when Montana pointed out to him that actor John Candy was in the end-zone stands. Barton made first-team All-Pro in back-to-back years before the 1994 championship run. He played through the 1996 season to earn a spot on the 49ers' coveted 10-Year Club. Decades later he remains a visible ambassador from the 49ers' Super Bowl-winning seasons by attending games or playing in Pebble Beach golf tournaments. No 49ers offensive tackle made the Pro Bowl between Barton in 1993 and Staley in 2011.

Dana Stubblefield (1993, No. 26 overall): His first stint (1993–97) produced NFL Defensive Rookie of the Year honors in 1993, a Super Bowl the next year, and NFL Defensive Player of the Year in 1997 (15 sacks). He made an encore from 2001 to 2002, then finished his career across the bay in Oakland in 2003. In 2020 he was sentenced to 15 years in prison after a jury found him guilty of rape.

Vernon Davis (2006, No. 6 overall pick): His 55 touchdown catches were the most by a 49ers tight end, including an NFL best 13 scores in 2009, before he got traded in his 10th season to the Lombardi Trophy-bound Denver Broncos. The one touchdown that most resonates: the Vernon Post, also known as The Catch III, in which Vernon Davis caught a 14-yard touchdown pass from Alex Smith to beat the Saints in January 2012 for the Niners' first playoff win in nine years.

John Brodie (1957, No. 3 overall pick): From Oakland Tech to Stanford, John Brodie stayed in the Bay Area and spent a franchise-record 17 seasons with the 49ers, which turned out to be 15 years longer than another quarterback drafted No. 3 overall (Trey Lance in 2021). Drafted two spots after Brodie was arguably the NFL's greatest player ever in Jim Brown (No. 6, Browns). Preceding Brodie's selection were Paul Hornung (Green Bay Packers) and Jon Arnett (Los Angeles Rams), and among the other quarterbacks taken were Hall of Famers Len Dawson (No. 5 overall by the Pittsburgh Steelers) and Sonny Jurgensen (fourth round by the Philadelphia Eagles).

Forrest Blue (1968, No. 15 overall pick): He served as a 6'6" center as the 49ers won three straight NFC West titles from 1970 to 1972, hiking the ball to Brodie in the process. Forrest Blue was a three-time, first-team All Pro and four-time Pro Bowl lineman. Sadly, he died in 2011 at the age of 65. He was found to have suffered from Chronic Traumatic Encephalopathy after his brain was studied by Boston University researchers, and Blue's case was part of a class-action lawsuit leading to the NFL's concussion settlement with former players.

Gene Washington (1969, No. 16 overall pick): Local boy made good, specifically in that Gene Washington made the Pro Bowl his first four years out of Stanford. He led the NFL with 1,100 receiving yards in 1970 and 12 touchdown catches in 1972—his All-Pro seasons when he paired so well with Brodie, a fellow Stanford man. Washington worked some 15 seasons in the NFL office and, when it came to announcing tricky names at the draft, he once said he pulled it off by simply using a confident voice.

Charlie Krueger (1958, No. 9 overall pick): An oversized picture of Charlie Krueger in his No. 70 jersey adorns a Levi's Stadium hallway outside their east-side luxury club. No one wears No. 70 on the field because the 49ers retired it to honor their Hall of Fame member. Krueger devoted his 15-year career to the 49ers and twice earned All-Pro and Pro Bowl honors. He was 84 when he passed away in 2021 in the East Bay enclave of Clayton.

Second Round

Roger Craig (1983, No. 49 overall pick): What do you do as an encore after scoring three touchdowns in a Super Bowl win, only two years into your NFL career? You become a pioneer. Roger Craig's 1985 season was the NFL's first in which a player produced 1,000 yards rushing (1,050) and receiving (1,016). Marshall Faulk became the next 1K/1K player for the 1999 Super Bowl-champion St. Louis Rams, and when Christian McCaffrey joined that fraternity in 2019 in also his third season, Craig celebrated. He messaged McCaffrey, and the current 49ers running back appreciated it. "He didn't have to do that," McCaffrey said. Craig also didn't have to show anyone "The Hill" he famously trained on in San Carlos, but he shared it with Jerry Rice. Craig's legacy extends beyond The Hill and the 1K/1K feat. He won Offensive Player of the Year honors in 1988 with his NFL-best 2,036 yards. Then came a Super Bowl win that season and the following one, but not in 1990, when the San Francisco 49ers' playoff run infamously ended with a 15–13 NFC Championship Game loss to the New York Giants, who parlayed a Craig fumble into their winning field goal.

Ricky Watters (1991, No. 45 overall pick): Ricky Watters' 49ers career lasted only three seasons before he bailed (with a Super Bowl ring in tow) and headed to the Philadelphia Eagles. Steve Young called it the 49ers' worst free-agency mistake, saying: "I wanted to take a fork and stick it in my eye. Who does stupid stuff like that?" Watters' rushing and receiving skills perfectly complemented the Young-led offensive machine with more than 1,250 yards and 11 touchdowns in each of his three years. He ran for a franchise-record five touchdowns—in only three quarters—of a January 1994 divisional playoff rout of the Giants. His grand 49ers finale came in Super Bowl XXIX, where he had a 51-yard touchdown catch and a nine-yard scoring run in the 49–26 win against the San Diego Chargers.

Colin Kaepernick (2011, No. 36 overall pick): Four hours after getting drafted, Colin Kaepernick drove with his parents west from their Turlock, California, home en route to the 49ers' headquarters, where they offered his "perfect situation." Five other quarterbacks were off the board before the 49ers traded up nine spots to take Kaepernick, who'd passed for more than 10,000 yards and run for more than 4,000 yards at Nevada. His pre-draft process included a private throwing competition with 49ers coach Jim Harbaugh, who wowed at Kap's "arm strength to power a ball through a defense." That arm would toss a touchdown pass in 18 straight games to tie Young's franchise record. Harbaugh remained an ally long after the quarterback opted out of his 49ers contract in March 2017, following a farewell season during which he led a national anthem protest against racial inequality and police misconduct.

Eric Wright (1981, No. 40 overall pick): Before winning four Super Bowl rings, Eric Wright and the 49ers needed their first championship, and they may not have done that without his heroics in the 1981 NFC Championship Game victory against the Dallas Cowboys. Just after Dwight Clark made "The Catch" to put the 49ers ahead, Wright chased down Drew Pearson to make a touchdown-saving tackle at the 44-yard line with 39 seconds remaining to preserve the win and ensure his spot in 49ers lore. When the 49ers launched the Kyle Shanahan and John Lynch regime 35 years later, Lynch peered to the back of Levi's Stadium's auditorium and recognized Wright with other alumni, then noted how "those guys created the standard we're striving for."

Deebo Samuel (2019, No. 36 overall pick): His physical nature turned him into an NFL prototype for teams desperate to duplicate Deebo Samuel's ability to gain yards after the catch and as a rusher out of the backfield. He dubbed himself a "wide back" in a breakout 2021 campaign that rose to the occasion in playoff wins at Dallas and Green Bay.

Randy Cross (1976, No. 42 overall pick): As the 49ers built their 1980s dynasty, Randy Cross was entrenched on the offensive line's interior, working at guard then center and emerging with wins on their first three Super Bowl teams. But back in 1980, they trailed 35–7 to the New Orleans Saints when they received halftime inspiration from Bill Walsh to spur Joe Montana's first of many comebacks to win. "He had two nuggets for us," Cross recalled of Walsh. "One, he reinforced to those of us who hadn't been playing what complete fools we were making of ourselves. Second was to not worry about anything other than scoring a touchdown, then worry about the next touchdown, and then the next one." Cross played 185 games in 13 seasons, and the 49ers scored many touchdowns.

Abe Woodson (1957, No. 15 overall pick): The most enduring franchise records—with all due respect to Rice—might just belong to Abe Woodson. He had 166 kick returns for 4,873 yards and five touchdowns over seven seasons. The five-time Pro Bowler and two-time All-Pro also racked up 19 interceptions as a cornerback and ranks among the 49ers' top punt returners.

Third Round

Joe Montana (1979, No. 82 overall pick): The San Francisco 49ers took covert measures to land the scrawny kid from Notre Dame and Western Pennsylvania with the last pick of the third round. That meant discreet workouts in Southern California and misleading phone calls to other NFL teams. Years later, Montana returned to the 49ers' headquarters for his first visit since his 1993 trade to the Kansas City Chiefs. "Bill [Walsh] wanted to get some things down [on tape] before he said, 'I got too fat and old and couldn't throw anymore,'" Montana said.

Walsh, then a 49ers consultant, escorted Montana to the practice field with the greatest intention for the NFL Films' instructional video: "This is something we should have for history of Joe's fundamentals and mechanics for playing the position because Joe Montana was clearly the greatest quarterback and maybe the greatest player of all time. His mechanics were the best in the history of the game, and so we want that on tape."

Bob St. Clair (1953, No. 32 overall pick): Rather than just lump Bob St. Clair in with the other Pro Football Hall of Fame members from the 49ers, the franchise's museum pays homage to his San Francisco roots and his eventual delving into local politics as a San Mateo County supervisor and Daly City mayor. Football-wise, St. Clair's 6'9", 265-pound frame was an intimidating force on the field from 1953 to 1963. A five-time Pro Bowler and three-time captain, he called Kezar Stadium home—while also playing there for Polytechnic High and University of San Francisco—for all but one year of his playing days. (After the USF program collapsed, he then detoured to Tulsa for a year.) Other go-to stories: he blocked 10 field goals in 1956, he once lost sixth teeth blocking a punt, he ate raw meat, and his No. 79 jersey is among the dozen retired by the 49ers.

Dave Wilcox (1964, No. 29 overall pick): To capture what "The Intimidator" meant to the 49ers beyond being a hard-hitting linebacker from 1964 to 1974, consider what teammate Mike Giddings said in presenting Dave Wilcox at his 2000 Pro Football Hall of Fame enshrinement: "The heart and soul of the first NFC West 49er champions." Wilcox was drafted by the 49ers only two days after the Houston Oilers selected him in the American Football League's draft. He missed only one game due to injury and otherwise played 153 en route to seven Pro Bowl honors.

Terrell Owens (1996, No. 89 overall pick): Terrell Owens came to the 49ers out of Tennessee-Chattanooga and by the time his polarizing and notorious NFL career came to an end, he ranked behind only Jerry Rice in terms of receiving yards (15,934) and touchdown catches (153), though those marks were since surpassed by Larry Fitzgerald and Randy Moss, respectively. Of his 81 touchdown receptions wearing No. 81 with the 49ers, Owens' most historic grab—The Catch II—came in traffic on a 25-yard pass from Steve Young to beat the Green Bay Packers 30–27. When it came to volume, Owens set an NFL record (since broken) with 20 receptions in 2000 against the Chicago Bears to overshadow Rice's final 49ers home game. When it came to celebrations, there were the 2000 trips to Dallas' midfield star that incited the Cowboys, the Sharpie-in-a-sock to autograph a football at Seattle, the popcorn, the pom-poms, and so much more. In 2018 Owens was enshrined into the Pro Football Hall of Fame, a spotlight he refused to enter because he had to wait three years for that installation.

Owens reflected on his 49ers career in 2019. "I've always loved the 49ers. That's where I started my career," he said. "I remember driving to the stadium at Candlestick. I had my routine where I'd get my car washed and drive to the stadium. Those are very vivid moments I remember: driving to the stadium, seeing the fans, seeing the 81s. It was mutual [affection] because I couldn't wait to get on that field to really represent that scarlet and gold every Sunday, Monday, whenever we played. The tradition is very, very rich there with the championships they have in place. That's why I played as hard as I did."

Frank Gore (2005, No. 65 overall pick): Armed with the top pick of the 2005 draft, the 49ers opted for Alex Smith over

Aaron Rodgers. Armed with the top pick of the third round, they took an injury-battered running back from Miami who'd already torn the anterior cruciate ligament in both knees. Once the 49ers traded Kevan Barlow to the New York Jets in the 2006 preseason, Frank Gore was the full-time back. He became the 49ers' all-time leading rusher during a decade of service with those 11,073 yards counting toward his career mark of 16,000 that ranked No. 3 in NFL history when he retired after the 2020 season. Come 2023, he was back with the 49ers. This time he canvassed the country to scout potential draft picks and uncover potential hidden gems like himself.

NaVorro Bowman (2010, No. 91 overall pick): Arguably no defender was playing better in the NFL in 2013 than NaVorro Bowman—up until his knee buckled in a friendly-fire hit from safety Eric Reid during their NFC Championship Game loss to the Seattle Seahawks. "That one play, I used to always say, 'Should I have just let him score and then maybe I'd be playing 12 to 13 years, six-time All-Pro?' I don't know," Bowman recalled in 2019 upon retiring as a 49er. "But I was giving everything for my teammates." Bowman rebounded from that knee injury in 2014 to lead the league in tackles and reclaim All-Pro status. He earned three Pro Bowl nods—all after his snub in 2011, a season in which All-Pro voters recognized him as a dynamic partner with Patrick Willis. The 49ers were going to deal him to the New Orleans Saints during the 2017 season, but instead he was released and joined the cross-bay Oakland Raiders to finish off his career that year.

Fred Warner (2018, No. 70 overall pick): Those who doubted how his 6'3" frame would adapt as an NFL linebacker never saw this coming: Fred Warner's instincts, speed, and intelligence turned him into the league's All-Pro prototype. "He has been the quarterback of our building really since halfway through his rookie year and his second year he owned it," coach Kyle Shanahan said. A mic'd up Rodgers told Warner midway through 2020 he was the NFL's best linebacker, an endorsement that rang true with his first of multiple All-Pro honors.

The 49ers' perennial leading tackler also served as their hype man in pre-practice, pregame huddles. When he pulled off a Sunday night hat trick (sack, interception, forced fumble) to defensively key a 42–10 rout of the Cowboys in October 2023, Warner was the first 49ers player with those single-game stats since Bowman a decade earlier. "I know the caliber player I am," Warner said after that win. "And I don't need anyone else's recognition or people to tell me how great I am."

Tom Rathman (1986, No. 56 overall pick): Some recall old No. 44 as a two-time Super Bowl champion who excelled at fullback as a lead blocker for fellow Nebraska Cornhusker Roger Craig. Some can recite how he led all NFL running backs with 73 receptions for the 1989 champion 49ers. Tom Rathman meant so much more to the 49ers than just playing for them from 1986 to 1993. He coached their running backs for 14 years. During his first stint, he mentored Garrison Hearst and Charlie Garner, and then a 2009–16 term escorted Gore to the franchise's all-time rushing mark. Through it all Rathman emphasized pass protection, ball security ("Squeeze It!"), and top-tier professionalism.

Guy McIntyre (1984, No. 73 overall pick): Winning three Super Bowls reserves you a key to the 49ers' loyalty. But it's not as if Guy McIntyre was a bystander. He was a Pro Bowl left guard five straight seasons (1989–93). He is one of 36 players who can claim to have caught a touchdown pass from Montana. One of the cooler sights was seeing McIntyre's 6'3", 260-pound frame act as a lead blocker to move the Bears' famed front in a 23–0 shutout win for the NFC Championship Game en route to a Lombardi Trophy his rookie season. (The vengeful Bears mimicked the 49ers' methods the next regular season and inserted lineman William "The Refrigerator" Perry into their backfield.)

Greg Clark (1997, No. 77 overall pick): Greg Clark's enduring legacy is not defined by him catching two touchdown passes from Young in the 1998 49ers' wild-card win against the Packers. Sadly, Clark is among the legion of NFL players who waged a secret battled with Chronic Traumatic Encephalopathy. He was only 49 when he died by a self-inflicted gunshot wound in his family's Danville, California, home in July 2021. Boston University researchers found signs of severe, Stage Three CTE in Clark's brain, prompting Clark's widow, Carie, and his brother, Jon, to encourage others to seek help and proper medical treatment rather than suffer in silence.

Fourth Round

Charles Haley (1986, No. 96 overall pick): On his way into the Pro Football Hall of Fame in 2015, Charles Haley racked up the most tackles in James Madison University's history, became their highest drafted player in school history, and was the signature piece of the San Francisco 49ers' epic 1986 class. He joined the franchise's dynasty as a 12-sack rookie and would become the first NFL player to win five Super Bowl rings, the first two of which came on the 49ers' 1988 and 1989 teams. He wasn't the first homegrown Hall of Famer traded away—see: John Henry Johnson, Y.A. Tittle, Joe Montana—but he haunted the 49ers more than any other by winning three more rings with the rival Dallas Cowboys before ultimately emerging from retirement to rejoin the 49ers in 1998–99.

Fifth Round

Merton Hanks (1991, No. 122 overall pick): Merton Hanks broke out in 1994 as a Pro Bowler and All-Pro and in 1995 he returned a Dallas Cowboys fumble for a touchdown and a way to debut his celebratory, head-bobbing "Chicken Dance," which was inspired by *Sesame Street* character Bert. Through eight seasons on the San Francisco 49ers, Hanks produced the fourth-most interceptions in team history (31 in 125 games, including two returned for touchdowns).

George Kittle (2017, No. 146 overall pick): A scrawny, blocking tight end from Iowa didn't take long to transform into a superstar as measured by All-Pro and Pro Bowl nods, NFL records, multiple appointments as a captain, and infectious joy as both a trusted receiver and maniacal blocker. In his NFL debut, he caught 5-of-6 targets, including a 13-yard catch and run that foreshadowed the physical, determined nature ahead in his career. "We didn't know how special he'd be, but we knew we got a steal right away," coach Kyle Shanahan said. "It's funny. You go back and watch his film from the first year and he had no ponytails, socks were pulled up perfect, no wristbands. Now you watch him, and he is a WWE rockstar. So it's been fun to be with him this whole time." George Kittle set the NFL's single-season record among tight ends with 1,377 yards in 2018 highlighted by a franchise-record 210-yard effort against the Denver Broncos.

Michael Carter (1984, No. 121 overall pick): Bill Walsh ranked Michael Carter among his all-time best draft picks, and he certainly was one of the most unique. He became the first man to win an Olympic medal (silver in the shot put) and a Super Bowl (rookie nose tackle) in the same year (1984). He was a four-time All-Pro and three-time Pro Bowler while playing all nine of his NFL seasons for the 49ers.

Sixth Round

Andy Lee (2004, No. 188 overall pick): Who was the greatest punter in San Francisco 49ers history? No one played more games than Andy Lee's 176 between 2004 and 2014, using that term to set team records for punts (941), yards (43,468), and an even 300 punts inside opponents' 20-yard line. Before getting traded to the Cleveland Browns in 2015 for a seventh-round pick, Lee was in prime form as the 49ers returned to playoff action in 2011 (44.0-yard net average, second best in NFL history at the time). Lee once had a better passer rating (39.6) than Eli Manning (36.6) in a 2014 49ers win against the New York Giants. Lee threw an incompletion on a botched field-goal attempt, while Manning got intercepted five times.

Seventh Round

Brock Purdy (2022, No. 262 overall pick): No quarterback in the Super Bowl era won his first five starts in each of his first two seasons. That is until Brock Purdy entered the picture and proved to be anything but "Mr. Irrelevant" as the 2022 draft's final pick. Purdy replaced an injured Jimmy Garoppolo to lead a December 4 rout of the blitz-happy Miami Dolphins. Then he became the first rookie to win his debut start against Tom Brady, doing so with a 134 passer rating (fourth best in NFL history for a rookie opener). Purdy delivered eight wins—including playoff triumphs at home against the Seattle Seahawks and the Dallas Cowboys—before sustaining a torn elbow ligament on the opening series of the NFC Championship Game loss at the Philadelphia Eagles. He recovered in time for the 2023 opener and, by winning that season's first five games, Purdy was officially 10–0 in his career (second best start in NFL history) with a 121.1 passer rating that was the NFL's all-time best through

10 games. He reset the San Francisco 49ers' single-game record for completion-percentage (95.2 percent on 20-of-21 passes) in a Week Four win against the Arizona Cardinals, then followed that with a career-high four touchdown passes in a rout of the Cowboys. He became the 49ers' first Pro Bowl quarterback in 21 years, plus he took fourth in NFL MVP voting, won the 49ers' Len Eshmont Award, set a franchise record with 4,280 yards, and delivered comeback wins in the playoffs against Green Bay and Detroit before playing turnover-free in the Super Bowl loss to Kansas City. General manager John Lynch refused to take full credit for picking Purdy, instead lauding the efforts of scout Steve Slowik and quarterbacks coach Brian Griese. "Obviously, I'm a big believer that it doesn't matter where you're drafted," Purdy said. "It's what you do when you get there with that opportunity."

Fred Quillan (1978, No. 175 overall pick): It was a seventh-round pick from Oregon who would hike the ball to Joe Montana—and make critical assignments at the line—on those initial Super Bowl teams. Fred Quillan, a two-time Super Bowl winner, appeared in 143 games during 10 seasons. Quillan made the Pro Bowl in the 1984 and 1985 seasons. He passed away in 2016.

10th Round

Dwight Clark (1979, No. 249 overall pick): Before 506 catches in nine regular seasons for the San Francisco 49ers and before "The Catch" against the Dallas Cowboys immortalized him in NFL lore, Dwight Clark caught the eye of Bill Walsh's pre-draft visit to scout Clemson quarterback Steve Fuller. Clark passed away in June 2018 at age 61 after battling ALS.

11th Round

Jesse Sapolu (1983, No. 289 overall pick): He became the sixth player to win four Super Bowl titles with the San Francisco 49ers, but he is the only one to capture that final ring on their 1994 team. Jesse Sapolu was born in Samoa and raised in Hawaii, where he played collegiately before his NFL career with the 49ers (1983–97) as a center and guard. He did all this despite a heart condition stemming from rheumatic fever as a child. Less than six months after requiring surgery to repair a heart valve, Sapolu rejoined the 49ers for his 1997 final season to fill in for injured center Chris Dalman. Sapolu remained a vibrant presence decades later as a 49ers alumni coordinator.

39

Free Agents

DEION SANDERS REFLECTED ON HIS ONE AND ONLY SAN Francisco 49ers season in just the way you'd expect: with swagger, confidence, bravado, and Prime's honest to goodness truth. "Honestly, when I went to San Francisco, they were like inferior to the Cowboys," Sanders recalled on *Inside the NFL* in October 2023. "The Cowboys had the upper hand, and they didn't truly believe at that point in time that they could overtake the physical, flamboyant, flashy, winning Dallas Cowboys. And I'm thankful that I was able to ignite them and enlighten them."

Sanders said this amid his meteoric rise as the University of Colorado's first-year coach when his flamboyance and flash turned that program into college football's most captivating watch. Sanders proved such an instant success with the 1994 49ers that he ranks as the franchise's best free-agent signing of all time and one of the NFL's greatest. "He was ahead of his time and did things and said things nobody thought about or did, and it didn't affect his play or work ethic," Steve Young said in November 2023. "He could separate the two. He explained it to me upfront."

Sanders joined a collection of All-Stars—holdovers such as Young and Jerry Rice but also a slew of other free agents such as Ken Norton Jr., Rickey Jackson, Gary Plummer, Richard Dent, and Bart Oates—to snap the 49ers' four-year championship drought and interrupt Dallas' dynasty. It was Sanders who emerged as the NFL's Defensive Player of the Year, and 16 years later, he was a first-ballot entrant to the Pro Football Hall of Fame.

Not that the 49ers pay much homage to Sanders' super season with Levi's Stadium's signage or in their museum. Maybe that's because he is so associated with the rival Cowboys, where he defected in 1995 for another ring plus more fame and fortune, including via endorsement deals with Nike and Pepsi. "Deion was a great player," former 49ers executive John McVay said in a 2006 interview. "But we only had Deion for a year. Then he went on to Dallas."

Because Kyle Shanahan's father, Mike, was the 49ers' offensive coordinator on that Super Bowl-winning team, Kyle was a ballboy on that 1994 49ers team and he was thrilled to get Sanders' No. 21 throwback jersey as a Christmas present. Decades later it still pains him that someone stole it from his closet. "I remember people making fun of me because I got a Deion Sanders throwback jersey for Christmas and I didn't take it off until the day after the Super Bowl, when my dad became the Broncos head coach," Kyle Shanahan recalled before leading the 2019 49ers into their playoff opener. "So I wore it for a month and 10 days. I changed my undershirt though, I promise. I was dedicated. I was so 100 percent the Niners and the playoffs at that time."

Sanders came to the 49ers in a bidding war, one the 49ers initially bowed out of as market prices soared. Sanders just had his third straight season earning Pro Bowl and All-Pro honors with the Atlanta Falcons, who drafted him No. 5 overall in 1989 out of Florida State. In his penultimate home game with the Falcons, he had two interceptions in a 27–24 win against the 49ers. Then Sanders bet on himself, accepted the 49ers' offer (one year, $1.2 million), and proved himself as a championship-caliber cornerback beyond the Prime Time and Neon Deion aura.

When Sanders returned to Atlanta's Georgia Dome with the 49ers, he high-stepped his way to the end zone on a 93-yard interception return, famously crowing, "This is my house!" after the 49ers' 42–3 rout. That was the second of his three interception returns for touchdowns that season. Sanders didn't debut with the 49ers until Week Three once he finished his commitments with the Cincinnati Reds in his sixth Major League Baseball season as a rare two-sport star.

He would call the 49ers the most talented team he ever played on and he contributed more than swagger and lockdown ability. He totaled six interceptions in the regular season, one in the NFC Championship Game breakthrough against the Cowboys, and one on football's grandest stage in the fourth quarter of a 49–26 Super Bowl rout of the San Diego Chargers at Joe Robbie Stadium, two hours east of his Fort Myers, Florida, hometown. "Deion Sanders changed the scope of the game in that he took a side (of the field) away and made a team a lot better," former NFL executive Ron Wolf said in 2006, "no matter who he played for, whether it was San Francisco or Dallas."

Wolf was the Green Bay Packers' general manager when in 1993 they beat out the 49ers for the NFL's prized free agent in defensive lineman Reggie White. A year later Sanders made the right call joining the 49ers, using them as a championship-winning stepping stone, something that would not have happened if he had stayed with the Falcons or taken offers from the New Orleans Saints, Miami Dolphins, or Detroit Lions. He's a 49ers legend, and they got Prime in the prime of his career.

Here are some other great free-agent signings:

Justin Smith

The San Francisco 49ers courted Justin Smith with a helicopter tour of the Bay Area and a beer-guzzling session into the night. What he did on the field, however, is what made him "one of the 49ers' all-time greats," as CEO Jed York lauded upon Smith's May 2015 retirement.

For all Smith's greatness on the defensive line, perhaps his most impactful play came down field in a Week Four win in 2011 at Philadelphia, when he chased down speedy Eagles wide receiver Jeremy Maclin to force a fumble and preserve the 49ers' second-straight win in an eight-game heater. "The thing about that was we got a big win on the road, and we just got on a roll; we kind of went on a three-year roll," Smith said. "We had a hell of a team and we had a hell of a lot of fun playing together."

Smith was known as "The Cowboy," willing to wrangle any offensive lineman in his way. In 2011 that meant lining up at defensive tackle (first-team All-Pro) to clear a lane for an Aldon Smith sack or at defensive end (second-team All-Pro) in a January 2012 playoff classic to bullrush New Orleans Saints left tackle Jermon Bushrod into Drew Brees on a third-down incompletion. His impact was measured beyond his 43 ½ sacks in both of his seven-year stints with the 49ers and the Cincinnati Bengals. He made 185 consecutive starts before sustaining a torn triceps in December 2012, an injury that should have but did not keep him out of a playoff run culminating in his one and only Super Bowl.

Ken Norton Jr.

Defecting from the Dallas Cowboys as a reigning champion, Ken Norton Jr. wasn't just a one-year wonder for the San Francisco 49ers. He did not miss a start in his seven seasons as the 49ers' marquee linebacker and defensive ringleader. "Kenny has done a marvelous job here," Bill Walsh, then the 49ers' general manager, said leading up to Norton's 2000 home finale. "He's a great campaigner, an outstanding player. He could be a Hall of Fame football player."

When that December 17, 2000 farewell came at 3Com Park, Norton was the 49ers' only defensive player announced during pregame introductions, followed by their offensive starters, including Jerry Rice, the day's guest of honor in his home farewell. "I am truly thankful for the opportunity to come here in 1994 and contribute in the fashion that I did," Norton, 34, said in leaving the 49ers. "I really enjoyed my time here. I was greeted with open arms when I arrived and I'll never forget that."

Tim McDonald

The advent of free agency saw the San Francisco 49ers pursue two All-Pros in Reggie White and Tim McDonald. Although White headed for the Green Bay Packers, the 49ers made McDonald the NFL's highest-paid defensive back (five years, $12.75 million). The Arizona Cardinals tried to keep him, but the 49ers' winning tradition helped give them the nod over all suitors, including the Kansas City Chiefs and the Philadelphia Eagles. The Cardinals were 32–63 in his six seasons, then the

49ers went 75–37 plus perennial playoff runs his first six seasons with them.

Two weeks before Joe Montana got traded to the Chiefs, McDonald arrived as a three-time Pro Bowler and he'd repeat those honors the next three seasons while pairing with Merton Hanks as a dynamic safety tandem. McDonald, a Fresno, California, native and USC product, had an interception in his playoff debut with the 1993 49ers. He had a team-high nine tackles in the 1994 team's Super Bowl rout of the San Diego Chargers, then returned an interception for a touchdown in his first two games as a reigning champion in 1995. He was a hitter, a leader, a mentor, and a free-agency pioneer.

Jack "Hacksaw" Reynolds

Released by the Los Angeles Rams after an 11-year tenure, "Hacksaw" came up the coast to help transform a San Francisco 49ers defense with the additions of Fred Dean (trade) and rookie defensive backs Ronnie Lott, Eric Wright, and Carlton Williamson. One of Jack Reynolds' greatest contributions came in the 49ers' meeting room. When Lott took a seat next to him and asked to borrow one of Reynolds' 100 pencils, Reynolds refused and implored Lott to come better prepared if he wanted to become a champion alongside him. Lott took that message to heart—and to Canton, Ohio.

Garrison Hearst

Some will recall Garrison Hearst's franchise-record 96-yard touchdown run for an overtime win in the 1998 opener against the New York Jets. Some will recall how he set the San Francisco 49ers' single-season record with 1,570 yards that season. And everyone forever will cringe at the 1998 finale, when his left foot twisted in Atlanta's unforgiving artificial turf to dash the 49ers' playoff hopes. Hearst's 49ers tenure might be best defined, however, by his 2001 comeback after missing two seasons because of that left-ankle injury against the Falcons and its ensuing complications with blood flow and talus-bone decay. "We literally tore up the entire ankle to come back and fix it," Dr. Pierce Scranton said of a May 6, 2000 surgery, one of four procedures Hearst would require.

Scranton called it "history in the making" when Hearst returned to action as the 49ers' starter in 2001. "I've come a long way to get back on the field," Hearst said before that 2001 debut. "I just always thought I'd be back. I never thought it was over for me." He won NFL Comeback Player of the Year honors in 2001, starting every game, rushing for 1,206 yards, and winning the 49ers' prestigious Len Eshmont Award.

Jeff Garcia

The hometown San Francisco 49ers made for a logical starting spot to an NFL career for Jeff Garcia, a Gilroy, California, native and San Jose State star. But first came a four-year stint in Canada and a Grey Cup championship with the Calgary Stampeders. Even then Bill Walsh had to convince the coaching staff to take a flyer on Garcia. But once Steve Young retired, Garcia became the full-time starter in 2000. He then got benched for Rick Mirer in a Week Two blowout loss to the Carolina Panthers. Garcia kept his job, became the first-ever 49ers quarterback to throw 30 touchdowns in back-to-back seasons, and made three straight Pro Bowls in his first seasons as a full-time starter. On January 5, 2003, Garcia delivered what was then the NFL's second-greatest comeback in playoff history. He threw two touchdown passes—finding Tai Streets for the game-winner with a minute to spare—and ran for a score to erase a 24-point deficit in the final 20 minutes. A year later

Garcia was released amid the 49ers' 2004 salary-cap crunch and ensuing rebuild.

Joe Perry

Joe Perry was the San Francisco 49ers' first African American player and spent more than 66 seasons as their all-time leading rusher. How did they find his speedy, all-around talent? Right tackle John Woudenberg and 49ers founder Tony Morabito discovered Perry as he finished U.S. Navy commitments while playing with the Alameda Naval Air Station Hellcats. Perry took five years to pass Johnny Strzykalski atop the 49ers' rushing list, doing so in 1953 with the first of back-to-back 1,000-yard, All-Pro seasons. He was 84 when he died in 2011; seven months later Frank Gore passed Perry's record (8,689 yards) atop the 49ers' all-time rushing list, but Gore would finish four scores shy of Perry's team-record 68 touchdown runs.

Robbie Gould

"Man of the hour," Jimmy Garoppolo said to Robbie Gould as they crossed paths outside Lambeau Field's visiting locker room in the wake of Gould's 45-yard game-winning field goal as time expired in a snow-dusted, divisional playoff win on January 22, 2022. It wasn't Gould's only game-winner since joining the San Francisco 49ers' 2017 makeover, but it was the most clutch amid storybook scenery. Gould was automatic in the 49ers' playoff runs, making all 21 field-goal and 19 point-after attempts in their 2019, 2021, and 2022 appearances. He hit the second-most field goals (161) in 49ers history behind Ray Wersching (190) and ranked fourth in scoring (704 points). "You love the team, the guys you play with, but at the end of the day, it's all about dollars and cents," said Gould, whose job was bequeathed to 2023 third-round draft pick Jake Moody.

Raheem Mostert

Clocked at 21.87 mph on the first of his four touchdown runs, Raheem Mostert finished with a single-game franchise record 220 yards in the San Francisco 49ers' first NFC Championship Game victory at Levi's Stadium, a 37–20 win against the Green Bay Packers on January 19, 2020. Cut from six teams before joining the 49ers' 2016 practice squad, Mostert took the post-game media podium in an NFC Championship Game T-Shirt and said: "I never gave up on my dream. I never gave up on the opportunities when it presented itself. And I always worked hard no matter what. And it's crazy that I've been on seven different teams. I actually still have the cut dates. And I look at that before every game. The journey's been crazy." The 49ers had a different leading rusher in each of Kyle Shanahan's first six seasons as coach, and Mostert led the way that 2019 season (772 yards). A meniscus injury cut short his tenure just four snaps into the 2021 season, and his 2022 comeback would come with the Miami Dolphins. In 2023 the Dolphins speedster led the NFL with 18 rushing touchdowns.

Kyle Juszczyk

Introduced with six others in the San Francisco 49ers' initial free-agency class under Kyle Shanahan, Kyle Juszczyk outlasted all from that group and earned perennial Pro Bowl honors along the way. He wasn't just a lead blocker for a run-oriented offense that competed for championships. His athleticism and Harvard-educated know-how provided versatility in an ever-evolving scheme that seizes on mismatches. Asked in 2023 camp how that offense evolved since his arrival, Juszczyk said: "There's some Shanahan staples like when we've got to move the ball, you don't know what you're getting. You're getting any play in the playbook."

Richard Sherman

The San Francisco 49ers' arch nemesis during his Seattle Seahawks days, Richard Sherman brought with him instant credibility, leadership, and savvy coverage skills. His pick-six in the 2019 opener set the tone for the 49ers' march to Super Bowl LIV. Injuries, though, shelved him 11 games his last season with the team. Sherman captured the fifth and final Pro Bowl berth of his career in the 2019 season and he made second-team All-Pro. While his young, impressionable teammates learned under "Uncle Sherm," he drew constant praise and admiration from coach Kyle Shanahan and general manager John Lynch (a fellow Stanford man) throughout a three-year term. What makes Sherman's free agency arrival even more unique: he shrewdly acted as his own agent, meaning he could both charm Shanahan over dinner in Los Gatos and then hammer out a three-year, $30-plus million contract with the 49ers' notoriously tough cap specialists in their boardroom.

Gary Plummer

After winning just one playoff game in eight seasons on the San Diego Chargers, Gary Plummer came home to the Bay Area. The Cal product, who played in the infamous band-on-the-field, Stanford–Cal game, and Mission San Jose High (Fremont) product made the playoffs in each of his four seasons with the San Francisco 49ers, and he started every game upon his arrival en route to the Lombardi Trophy. Plummer served as the 49ers' radio color commentator for 12 seasons. In the wake of ex-Chargers teammate Junior Seau's 2012 suicide, Plummer became an outspoken advocate for mental health, estimating he himself sustained more than a thousand concussions while playing football. Plummer became an inspiration to others with his holistic approach to battling depression by using meditation, gardening, and music therapy.

Bart Oates

It should be no surprise that Steve Young, a former BYU teammate, vouches for the impact of Bart Oates from that 1994 free-agency haul. Oates left the New York Giants to secure his third Super Bowl ring. Jesse Sapolu moved from center to guard to make room for Oates, who made the Pro Bowl in both his seasons with the San Francisco 49ers before retiring.

PART 6

HOME, SWEET HOME

40

Kezar Stadium

HIGH SCHOOL FOOTBALL PLAYERS TASTE IT ON FRIDAY nights. The weekend warriors feel it jogging the quarter-mile loop or playing rec league soccer on the green grass. Even San Francisco's tourists do a double take at the ancient archway when passing by Golden Gate Park's southeast corner. Kezar Stadium, the San Francisco 49ers' first-ever stadium, remains alive like a nearby Victorian home that's still vibrant with its rent-controlled occupants.

Mind you, the stadium is literally a shell of what it was during the 49ers' 1946–70 tenancy. Yet it still gives off an intoxicating vibe with communal gatherings offering a chance to watch or partake in athletic feats of strength. The city calls it "Little Kezar" as a nod to its 1991 remodel two years after the Loma Prieta earthquake devastated so much of this picturesque city. Instead of 59,942 seats, Kezar's reduced capacity allows for 10,000 to either brave the coastal fog and chill, bask in a cherished clear sky, or soak in the city's aura five blocks down from another famous corner at Haight and Ashbury Streets.

Don't look at Kezar's two-story archway as a gravestone on its west flank, and same goes for the columns at the Frederick Street entrance gate. Instead, imagine all the history that unfolded here as the 49ers' birthplace. That's what the 49ers themselves did in 2016, when they held an open practice during training camp at Kezar. They hoped it would bring positive mojo for their 70th season. Instead, that team went 2–14 in Chip Kelly's lone season as coach and Colin Kaepernick's last as their quarterback/social justice crusader. The 49ers had last practiced at Kezar in August 2004, and that team also went 2–14 en route to the No. 1 overall draft pick. Moral of this abbreviated story: don't practice at Kezar unless you're staging a 2–14 season.

Like Kezar's original days, the modern-era players reached the field via a tunnel after suiting up in the nearby gym, Kezar Pavilion. Unlike the 1946–70 teams, the players did not have beer cans or trash hurled onto them when it was time to exit, something that required Kezar to install a protective chain-link screen back in the day. "The tunnel is awesome. That's like old-school gladiator stuff," left tackle Joe Staley said.

"The bathrooms in there were from like the 1940s, and I thought that was cool," fellow offensive lineman Anthony Davis said. "Some greats played in here and set the foundation for our organization. So I think that's cool."

Those greats included Pro Football Hall of Famers like running backs Hugh "The King" McElhenny and Joe "The Jet" Perry, cornerback Jimmy Johnson, fullback John Henry Johnson, lineman Bob St. Clair, defensive tackle Leo Nomellini, linebacker Dave Wilcox, and quarterback Y.A. Tittle. Then there were those inducted into the Edward. J. DeBartolo Sr. 49ers Hall of Fame: quarterback John Brodie, wide receiver R.C. Owens, defensive tackle Charlie Krueger, and wide receiver Gordy Soltau. "We had great fan support. Kezar Stadium was maybe not the most comfortable stadium from a spectator point of view, but it was a good place to play," Soltau said upon his 2012 induction to the 49ers' Hall of Fame. "The playing field was usually a wreck by the time we played on it because all the high schools had played there. The field got all torn up between the hashmarks, and you were playing in the dirt, but you didn't mind it."

Back then the north-side stands climbed high like the Golden Gate Bridge towers just four miles in the distance. Beyond Kezar's south stands, fans would peer down from Frederick Street's third-story rooftops. Only a third of the stadium's 59,000 seats were between the goal lines—an area now laden with red, plastic seats that were rescued from Candlestick Park, the 49ers' second home from 1971 to 2013.

Kezar Stadium may have opened in 1925, but the 49ers did not show up until 1946, playing their first four seasons in the All-America Football Conference (AAFC) before joining the NFL. Season tickets cost just $22.50 from 1950–57 amid the bring-your-own-booze, sit-on-a-pillow days. Picking up those seat cushions, selling peanuts, and working as an usher was a wide-eyed teenager from Polytechnic High School. "My high school was right across the street from Kezar Stadium, and we played our games there in high school," said George Seifert, who'd go on to win five Super Bowl rings with the 49ers as a defensive assistant (1980–88) and then as Bill Walsh's successor as coach (1989–96).

Seifert was among the 60,118 who witnessed and mourned the 49ers' collapse in a 31–27 loss to the Detroit Lions in their 1957 NFL playoff debut. That same year, Seifert and Polytechnic lost in the city championship at Kezar, too. Another Polytechnic product was St. Clair, the strapping, 6' 9" lineman who also called Kezar home for his college games with the University of San Francisco and his entire NFL career (1953–63).

But Seifert also remembers more glamorous times: watching the "Million Dollar Backfield" of McElhenny, Perry, Johnson, and Tittle; witnessing Brodie's "alley-oop" touchdown pass to Owens; and marveling at fellow linebacker Matt Hazeltine, who has an annual award named after him for the 49ers' most courageous and inspirational defender. This being San Francisco, Kezar had its share of quirky moments, too, like the Minnesota Vikings' Jim Marshall returning a fumble recovery to the wrong end zone in 1964. Heck, even the Oakland Raiders called it home for their first four games in 1960.

Quarterback Mike Holmgren led Lincoln to its first city championship there in 1966. Dan Fouts went from 49ers ballboy (his father, Bob, was the 49ers' play-by-play man in the 1950s and 1960s) to starring at St. Ignatius the next two years in the West Catholic Athletic League championship.

Nearly 30,000 fans saw the 49ers lose their NFL debut 21–17 in 1950 to the New York Yanks, four years after the 49ers dropped their AAFC entrance to the Yankees in 1946. The 49ers' first NFL touchdown at Kezar came on a two-yard pass from Frankie Albert to Paul Salata, the latter of whom did more than also score their last AAFC touchdown the previous season. Some 30 years later, Salata created Irrelevant Week, where the last pick in the NFL draft would be honored annually in Newport Beach, California. Salata passed away in October 2021 just ahead of the 49ers selecting quarterback Brock Purdy as the 2022 "Mr. Irrelevant" who would become quite relevant to their playoff quests.

Kezar was where team owner Tony Morabito passed away of a heart attack during a 1957 win against the Chicago Bears. Three years later Kezar was where the shotgun formation debuted under coach Red Hickey, leading to Tittle's trade to the New York Giants. It wasn't until the Niners' 1970 swan song at Kezar that they delivered a championship, their first NFC West title. Spoiling that grand exit, however, was a 17–10 loss to the Dallas Cowboys in the NFC Championship Game. Of the 59,364 fans, some took out their frustrations on each other in fights, and some simply took part of Kezar with them as mementos. Yet to this day, Kezar lives on, and so do the 49ers' memories there.

41
Candlestick Park

JOE MONTANA, IN HIS NO. 16 JERSEY, ROLLED 16 STEPS TO his right, threw a high-arching pass, and the San Francisco 49ers' fate—that day and perhaps forever—hung in the air. Once Dwight Clark's fingertips secured "The Catch" in Candlestick Park's north end zone, the 49ers' dynasty was underway. "It's a madhouse at Candlestick!" Vin Scully exclaimed on the 49ers' television broadcast of their 1981 season's NFC Championship Game comeback against the rival Dallas Cowboys.

The 'Stick was the ugliest house on the block but also a launching pad for the best of times. It could be called a "pigsty" by 49ers owner Eddie DeBartolo to get then-mayor Dianne Feinstein to promise upgrades. It could be called a "fortress" by 49ers coach Jim Harbaugh to celebrate a long-awaited playoff victory. Both depictions were equally valid. The majority of 49ers lore evolved there for 43 years from 1971 to 2013 between their Kezar Stadium starter home in the city's vast

Golden Gate Park to their Levi's Stadium relocation 39 miles south amid Silicon Valley's office space. Steve Young, in a 2005 halftime ceremony for his Pro Football Hall of Fame ring, told the Candlestick crowd: "This is where I was born. This is where I was raised. This is where I became a man."

Those words rang true for generations of Bay Area sports fans, who learned how to hunker down amid windy and chilly elements. Some of the harshest tests came during baseball season to watch The Stick's original tenants, the San Francisco Giants, who moved out in 2000.

A decade after the 49ers' closed up shop there, a chain-link fence cordoned off the historic, abandoned site abutting the Candlestick Point State Recreation Area and the bay's shoreline. It's an unmarked graveyard with scattered mounds of demolition debris, which is best viewed from the left-window seats on planes ascending out of San Francisco International Airport. Someday, the soil will be tilled, and humanity will return to reside, shop, work, or continue to fish for halibut and striped bass. But there will not be a red sign spanning the four-lane access road that states: "The San Francisco 49ers Welcome You to Candlestick Park."

Eight Super Bowl berths were decided there—with half those NFC championships going to the 49ers (1981, 1984, 1989, 1994 seasons) and half not (1990, 1992, 1997, 2011). None was more iconic than "The Catch" game on January 10, 1982, a finish witnessed in the upper deck by a four-year-old Tom Brady. That long-range view still was better than DeBartolo's after he scurried down to the field (through the locker-room tunnel and out to the visitor's dugout). "I was trying to see what was happening, but I was behind the biggest horse that you could ever imagine with the police officer on him about 12 feet above me," DeBartolo recalled during his Pro Football Hall of Fame speech in 2016. "Then I heard the screams of the crowd and looked up to the officer. He put his thumb up and winked and said, 'Clark, touchdown.' That's how I found out. At our moment of glory, I was literally blocked by a horse's ass."

There would be other receptions worth seeing like The Catch II (Terrell Owens' last-second touchdown to beat the Green Bay Packers in a January 1999 wild-card game) and The Catch III (Vernon Davis' last-second touchdown to beat the New Orleans Saints in a January 2012 divisional-round thriller). In that latter win, pandemonium engulfed Candlestick as the 49ers and Saints each scored two touchdowns in the final four minutes, including a 28-yard bootleg from Alex Smith and then Smith's 14-yard scoring strike to Davis with nine seconds left.

"Our fans turned that stadium into a fortress. That's as good as it's going to get," Harbaugh said the following day. "We got 70,000 in a city behind us. It felt good. It felt like an advantage."

Bigger fourth-quarter comebacks preceded that one, as riveting as it was. Montana's first was the 49ers' biggest: December 7, 1980, when they erased a 35–7 halftime deficit behind Montana's three second-half touchdowns (two passing, one rushing) and an overtime field goal from the head-down, no-look Ray Wersching. Of Montana's 31 career fourth-quarter comeback wins, only eight were at Candlestick, including the 1981 NFC Championship Game win and a 1983 divisional round defeat of the Detroit Lions.

Their best playoff comeback at Candlestick went down on January 5, 2003. Trailing 38–14, the 49ers scored 25 unanswered points in a wild-card victory against the New York Giants. Jeff Garcia's go-ahead touchdown pass to Tai Streets came with a minute to spare, but victory wasn't assured until a botched field-goal attempt by the Giants.

Big wins. Big throws. And big catches, including an NFL-record 20 by Owens in the 2000 home finale against the Chicago Bears to overshadow Jerry Rice's going-away party.

Candlestick had its share of big runs. Young made a 49-yard mad dash through the Minnesota Vikings before staggering across the goal line on October 30, 1988. Garrison Hearst sprinted a franchise-record 96 yards down the right sideline (with the help of an Owens block) for an overtime touchdown that toppled the New York Jets in the 1998 opener. Frank Gore accrued 6,148 yards of his franchise-record 11,073 yards at The 'Stick.

The 49ers weren't short on defensive heroics at Candlestick either. Eric Wright's touchdown-saving, last-minute, horse-collar tackle of Drew Pearson preserved their 1981 NFC Championship Game win. Eric Davis' 44-yard interception return for a touchdown gave the 49ers a sudden 7–0 lead three snaps into their 1994 season's NFC Championship Game breakthrough also against the Cowboys. One last defensive feat—"The Pick at The 'Stick"—delivered Candlestick's final touchdown on December 23, 2013. NaVorro Bowman intercepted a Matt Ryan pass and returned it 89 yards for a close-up-shop score with one minute, 10 seconds left in the 49ers' 34–24 win. Bowman said he honored the 49ers' forefathers: "[They] put the work in and won those championships. This game is for them. We want to leave on a good note." Mission accomplished, as they headed for a third straight NFC Championship Game appearance.

There were other special sendoffs. Victory laps were enjoyed by Steve Young (after the 1994 NFC title win) and Rice (after his final home game in 2000). Bryant Young, upon concluding his Hall of Fame career with a December 23, 2007 win against the Tampa Bay Buccaneers, rode off on the shoulders of teammates Jeff Ulbrich, Marques Douglas, Derek Smith, and Isaac

Sopoaga. Last but certainly not least, thousands gathered to mourn Bill Walsh in an August 10, 2007 memorial service on what was that day renamed Bill Walsh Field.

The stadium gods didn't always rule in the 49ers' favor. Roger Craig's infamous fumble set up the 1990 Giants' NFC Championship thievery. Anthony Carter's 227 receiving yards keyed the 1987 Vikings' divisional-round upset. Kyle Williams' second muffed punt return set up the Giants' overtime field goal to claim the 2011 season's NFC crown. That was the 49ers' last shot at winning a Super Bowl berth at The 'Stick, a ticket also obtained by the 1972 Cowboys, 1992 Cowboys, and 1997 Packers.

Candlestick opened in 1960 for the San Francisco Giants, and the first NFL hosts were actually the Raiders, who went 2–8 there in late 1960 and 1961 before moving to Oakland. The 49ers' first touchdown at Candlestick came October 10, 1971 on a nine-yard pass from John Brodie to Ted Kwalick in a 20–13 loss to the Los Angeles Rams.

Over the decades the field conditions were notorious. Artificial turf got pulled up after the 1978 season, the San Francisco Giants' infield dirt shredded elbows through 1999, and muddy fields generated below-sea-level myths. Corporate naming rights tried to claim that turf—3Com Park (1995–2002), Monster Park (2004–08)—but Candlestick's version of luxury suites consisted of a small ribbon between the upper and lower decks. Fine dining? Try the Hofbrau on that suite level, where an unreliable elevator would make a lone stop en route to the press box.

That didn't generate enough revenue to keep the 49ers from falling behind in the NFL's fiscal boom, at least not after DeBartolo was forced to sell his majority share of the team to his sister, Denise DeBartolo York, a transition that finally took hold in 2000.

No matter what or where they built their next home, nothing would match Candlestick's charms and concrete warts. There were swirling winds, bathroom troughs, bright orange and dark red plastic seats, plus east-side stands that retracted like a Murphy bed. Peaceful views glistened off the bay when driving in from the backside on Jamestown Avenue and on the way past the St. Francis of Assisi statue that stood guard near Gate B. Just imagine the double doors fans would have to pass through to the lower-level seats after wasting the first quarter in line at concession stands. The north-side scoreboard stretched wide to display ads for Marlboro cigarettes, Chevron gas, and Lucky Lager beer. The overhead lights went out twice in a 2011 *Monday Night Football* win against the Pittsburgh Steelers.

One of Candlestick's most storied moments saw The Beatles play their final public concert there in 1966. Not a bad opening act for the 49ers' legacy that would follow. Yes, Candlestick mirrored the city it resided in with an eclectic blend of majestic moments, stunning sights, and for-the-love-of-humanity heartbreaks. Montana had this to say at Walsh's 2007 memorial service there: "Knowing Bill, as soon as he heard it's Bill Walsh Field, I can envision him looking down on us, holding a white Styrofoam cup with margaritas in it, saying, 'Bill Walsh Field. It's got a nice ring.'"

42

Levi's Stadium

Cop cars zoomed through hairpin turns, and tires screeched. This was not a high-speed pursuit but an ordinary scene across the street from the San Francisco 49ers' headquarters. It is where local police occasionally trained on an overflow parking lot at California's Great America park. Then a $1.2 billion stadium rose from that asphalt and opened in 2014 for the 49ers to protect myriad quarterbacks and serve Super Bowl dreams.

It took just over two years (819 days) to build and it took just two seasons until a Lombardi Trophy was awarded in the heart of Silicon Valley—albeit to Peyton Manning and the Denver Broncos in Super Bowl 50 for their defeat of the Carolina Panthers. Not until Year 10 did a home-field advantage truly emanate inside Levi's Stadium. Yes, there had been back-to-back playoff wins there to send the 2019 team into a Super Bowl ambush in Miami. But a victory drought and COVID pandemic ensued, as the 49ers went more than a calendar year (393 days) between the video boards blaring "NINERS WIN!" When the 49ers lost their first four home games of 2021, Levi's Stadium ranked 73rd out of 76 stadiums in terms of a home-field advantage since 1970. Levi's Stadium seemed cursed, and fans sounded off with potential cures: bring back Eddie DeBartolo as owner, track down the St. Francis of Assisi statue that watched over Candlestick Park, bury a lucky charm under the midfield logo, incorporate Levi's jeans into their uniform, move the stadium back to San Francisco, and paint the exterior scarlet red instead.

Instead, Levi's Stadium kept its stick-figure look with white steel beams on full display from its exterior. What counted most is how the 49ers played inside on two-and-a-half acres of Bermuda grass. Sure enough, that grass sure looked greener during a 2022–23 stretch of success. "That's how we expect to play here," coach Kyle Shanahan said, "and it's been long overdue."

Starting with their 2021 team's Monday night win against the same-old-sorry-bleeping Los Angeles Rams in mid-October, the 49ers won 17 of 18 on their home field. "The Faithful has stayed faithful through ups and downs, and I'm happy that we got this one," linebacker Fred Warner said amid that breakthrough.

Winning their final four home games of the 2021 season yielded a playoff run ultimately ending in the NFC Championship Game in Los Angeles, where the same-old-Shanahan blew a fourth-quarter lead. (Sorry, Kyle.) Then came the great 2022 quarterback revolution. Trey Lance (ankle) got carted off in the home opener, Jimmy Garoppolo (foot) got carted off 11 weeks later, and, *voila*, Purdy went from the draft's Mr. Irrelevant to the 49ers' Mr. Incredible. The 49ers won their final eight at

Levi's Stadium in the 2022 season, including playoff wins against the Seattle Seahawks and Dallas Cowboys. Defensive end Nick Bosa credited vocal fans for helping. "Whenever you have a fanbase that shows up as good as we do home and away," he said, "it makes the offense on the other team a little bit behind on some of their cadences. It gives us an edge, and that goes a long way."

Doom awaited outside those friendly confines. The next and final stop for that 2022 season was Philadelphia's hostile territory for the NFC Championship Game. "I love Levi's. I think it's a fantastic atmosphere," tight end George Kittle said ahead of that showdown. "But if I'm not going to be biased, besides Kansas City, the Eagles' [stadium], man, they're pretty top tier. I know how much the fans love the opposing team."

The 49ers came away heartbroken from that 31–7 loss in Philadelphia after Purdy wrecked his elbow on the opening snap. Purdy made a speedy recovery, however, and after the 49ers opened the 2023 season with road wins at the Pittsburgh Steelers and the Rams, they swept a three-game homestand. All in all, the 49ers strung together 11 consecutive wins between 2022–23, a heater topped off by pummeling the rival Cowboys 42–10 and improving the Niners to 5-0 on the 2023 season. That home streak ended with a 31–17 flop against the Cincinnati Bengals on October 29, but it matched the longest in franchise history (1996–97, 1998–99) when factoring in home playoff games. All that winning made everything so much brighter at 4900 Marie P DeBartolo Way (the stadium's formal address, named after the wife of former 49ers owner Edward J. DeBartolo Sr.).

Levi's Stadium's housewarming party bombed. The grass was too slick, the seats too empty at kickoff, the sun too hot, the sports bars too far away, and the traffic too congested like any other day on Highways 237 and 101. What else could go wrong?

Oh yes, internal discord between the coach (Jim Harbaugh), the general manager (Trent Baalke), and the CEO (Jed York) made that inaugural season at Levi's their only one together.

But for years the stadium's signature moment was a postgame scene from Thanksgiving Night 2014, when the rival Seahawks Russell Wilson and Richard Sherman celebrated a victory by eating turkey legs on NBC's postgame set on the 49ers' midfield logo. Meanwhile, York sent out a viral apology on social media, thanking fans for showing up but panning a "performance that wasn't acceptable."

Home-field advantage would come. Cheers of victory would ring out and, as promised, bounce off the west-side, eight-story suite tower that was decorated with art and photos tugging on the 49ers' historical heartstrings. The first championship celebration arrived at 6:43 PM on January 19, 2020. Red-and-gold confetti was sprayed into the air, and "NFC CHAMPIONS" adorned the stadium's electronic billboards. The 49ers had won a Super Bowl berth at home for the first time since the 1994 season at Candlestick Park, and fittingly Shanahan received the NFC's Halas Trophy from his father, Mike, who was the 49ers' offensive coordinator on that 1994 Super Bowl-winning team.

Ten months later the 49ers weren't allowed to play or practice at home, the result of Santa Clara County's ban on contact sports during the COVID pandemic. That news broke as the 49ers headed to Los Angeles for a November 29 game, after which they relocated to Glendale, Arizona, and played their final three home games at the Cardinals' State Farm Stadium. Home, sweet home? Not during that 2020 season. They went 1–4 at Levi's Stadium with no fans allowed in because of COVID precautions, then 0–3 in an Arizona hostel that drove them stir crazy. "I'm not going to lie. I've had some harsh feelings that have gone through my mind about our county because they put us in a tough position," general manager John Lynch said of their Arizona exile. "They had people they have to answer to as well. So, we understand that. But I was looking forward to coming home last night. I wanted to get home, and when you land and you see the beauty of this place and driving in—it's a rainy morning, but it was a beautiful morning. All the opportunities aside from playing for the San Francisco 49ers and walking by Lombardi Trophies every day you walk in the building...Some love the fact that the water is all over, and you have a tremendous city right down the road. So, doing a little recruiting pitch, this still remains a great place, great destination, and we've got high hopes."

How the 49ers ended up playing games there, an hour south of their San Francisco roots, had more to do about business than pleasure. In a July 2006 press conference in a posh San Francisco hotel, the 49ers unveiled architecture firm HNTB's design for a $600 million-$800 million stadium that would replace Candlestick Park on the same bayfront site. If that 68,000-seat venue wouldn't come to fruition, "our best backup is Santa Clara," then-49ers spokesperson Lisa Lang said. "But we're absolutely focused, absolutely committed to make this happen in San Francisco."

Teasing about a revived Candlestick wasn't anything new. The NFL planned to hold Super Bowl XXXIII there, but with stadium upgrades in doubt, that 1998 showcase got moved to Miami. A decade later there were ballyhooed plans for a stadium and mall project at Candlestick with a $100 million bond measure in tow. Alas, bureaucratic red tape and financial costs prompted the 49ers to shift their stadium focus to Santa Clara, where they moved their offices and practice fields in 1988 from Redwood City. The 2006 redesign for Candlestick simply shifted south with more suites but similar concepts such as an in-stadium museum and restaurant. Gold shovels hit the ground on April 19, 2012 for Levi's Stadium's groundbreaking ceremony. "I hate that 49ers won't be playing on that field where all the Super Bowls were won, but I totally understand it," 49ers legend Dwight Clark said during Candlestick's final days in 2013 about five years before he died. "The new place is going to be awesome, and they'll be able to make great new historic moments there."

Indeed, extra events have funneled in gobs of revenue with concerts (Taylor Swift made three tour stops between 2015–23), pro soccer, NHL hockey, college football (2019 national championship), and much more, including corporate holiday parties in the stadium's various clubs. All that extra business also spurred feuds and lawsuits with Santa Clara City officials over bookkeeping, curfews, and, of course, profit sharing.

Across the street from the 49ers' headquarters on the old Santa Clara Golf and Tennis Club, a 240-acre project was slow to develop over the decade since Levi's Stadium opened for business. If homes, hotels, offices, restaurants, bars, and parks eventually do sprout up, the 49ers will still be the greatest show in town—except for the 2026 double whammy of World Cup soccer and Super Bowl 60. "Being able to bring a Super Bowl and World Cup in the same year, no one will ever do it, and we will," 49ers president Al Guido said in May 2023 upon news of the Super Bowl's return. "We know it's a tall task putting this on."

That innovative spirit embodied Silicon Valley, where amid the office buildings of high-tech companies is a football franchise's home just a mile or so down from the San Francisco Bay's southernmost slough and marshes. It's where the 49ers will keep digging for gold—and a silver Lombardi Trophy.

43

Road Warriors

A "Let's Go Niners!" chant rang out from the crowd in the final minutes of a 2023 season-opening win. Home-field fervor? No, this was on the road amid Pittsburgh's Terrible Towel-twirling fans. It could have been anywhere the way the San Francisco 49ers Faithful follow this franchise. "It's great. I think we have the best traveling fanbase overall," defensive end Nick Bosa said after that 2023 debut. "Pittsburgh was impressive, and I think we'll take over L.A."

Los Angeles is where the largest 49ers Takeover takes place annually, so much so that the host Rams must resort to silent snap counts when on offense. "It's one of the coolest things I've seen in sports," 49ers coach Kyle Shanahan said ahead of a 2022 visit to the Rams' SoFi Stadium (or "Levi's South" as fans call it). "And home-field advantage is a big deal in the NFL because of crowd noise, and when you don't have to worry about that as much on the road, it's huge."

It's become a phenomenon for fans who want to (a) support their team and (b) get away from the Bay Area for a football trip or two or three or more. "To have Levi's Stadium go wherever we go," linebacker Dre Greenlaw said, "you can't beat that."

Greenlaw came aboard in 2019, which is when the 49ers' bandwagon really picked up steam from road win to road win. That Super Bowl-bound season opened with victories at Tampa Bay and Cincinnati. Those wins against the Buccaneers and Bengals set up a defining moment in the franchise's turnaround: an October 13 win vs. the reigning NFC champion Rams at the Los Angeles Memorial Coliseum, where the crowd of 75,695 seemed 50/50 between 49ers/Rams fans. The most raucous support came December 8 in New Orleans from a 48–46 shootout victory inside the Superdome and then afterward, as the 49ers Faithful took over Bourbon Street in their red jerseys and throwback, satin gold jackets. Similar celebrations played out after the 2021 season's playoff wins in Dallas and snowy Green Bay before the Rams pulled out an NFC Championship Game comeback en route to the Lombardi Trophy.

It's not like the 49ers are unbeatable on the road with their caravan of fans, though they set an NFL record by winning 18 consecutive away games between late in the 1988 season through the '89 and '90 campaigns. You don't win the Super Bowl five times in a 14-year span—and go to the playoffs 16 times in 18 years between 1981 and 1998—without fans catching on and showing up on the road. In their luggage was a stereotype: they were wine-and-cheese snobs. Known as the "49ers Faithful," there were some lean years after that championship dynasty, and a few incidents by unruly fans toughened up that Niners image. Then again, the franchise's original logo depicts a pistol-shooting gold miner in black boots, checkered pants, and a red shirt.

The Niners went 13 years without an NFC Championship Game appearance before returning to that stage in 2011 under first-year coach Jim Harbaugh. When the 49ers won a Super Bowl berth the following season, they did so against the Falcons in Atlanta, where fans raised signs with Harbaugh's credo: "Who's got it better than us? Noooo-body!" During that 2011–13 stretch of three straight NFC title games, the 49ers went 6–2, 5–3, and 6–2 on the road in the regular season, which surely helped attract fans to come along for the ride after posting losing records on the road the previous eight seasons.

That 2013 season included a win in London against the Jacksonville Jaguars with 49ers fans swarming Wembley Stadium. Another regular-season game required a passport in 2022, when the 49ers beat the Arizona Cardinals in a rematch in Mexico, where those same teams played the NFL's first international game in 2005 before 103,467 fans. A reduced stadium capacity for the 2022 game allowed for a crowd of 78,427, and the overwhelming majority cheered the 49ers on to a 38–10 victory. The 49ers were key to expanding the NFL's global reach decades earlier when the American Bowl exhibition first took them to London (1988, 1992), then Tokyo (1989, 1995), Berlin (1991), Barcelona (1993), Vancouver (1998), and Osaka, Japan (2002).

The international fanfare goes both ways. "The road is special," safety Talanoa Hufanga said. "When I look at the fanbase personally, there is a big Tongan community, so I get to see a bunch of big Tongan flags. That hits home for me not only as a family thing but the culture as a whole. In Atlanta I looked all the way up high in the nose bleeds and saw a Tongan flag high at the top. That's what is so meaningful to me about this game: the fans."

Do the 49ers have the NFL's hugest caravan traveling to away games? Arguments will come from the Packers' Cheeseheads,

Raider Nation, Bills Mafia, Chiefs Kingdom, and those stubborn fools who insist the Cowboys are...ahem...America's Team. "We have the best fanbase in the NFL right now," wide receiver Deebo Samuel said. "They travel everywhere we go. So it's not something I'm not used to. We're used to seeing red everywhere."

Acknowledgments

THE MOST BIZARRE PRESS CONFERENCE IN BAY AREA SPORTS history—at least in my 25 years attending them—was about to get even weirder. Reporters would preface questions by announcing their name and affiliation, and before my question could tumble from my "Cam Inman, Bay Area News Group" lips, Al Davis interrupted:

"Oh, how's your mother?"

"She's fine, thank you," I replied before powering through to ask the Raiders' iconic owner about yet another coaching change amid his franchise's freefall.

At "halftime" of that press conference—between the announced firing of Lane Kiffin and the default hiring of Tom Cable—fellow reporters quizzed me on why the reclusive Davis wanted to know about Irene Inman. This might be my lasting legacy in Bay Area sports journalism: my mom. And I love that. It's a fitting connection.

This was the dream job I became dead set on achieving, while my mom raised me and my two sisters in Cupertino, a South Bay suburb known best for Apple Computer's birthplace. I grew up rooting for whatever team was winning and on our television via a roof antenna. We Bay Area kids could be frontrunners up until the San Francisco 49ers, Oakland Raiders, San Francisco Giants, and Oakland A's started winning championships. I liked the Dallas Cowboys, Pittsburgh Steelers, the Raiders, the 49ers (see: those teams' Super Bowl progression). And I donned caps of the Cincinnati Reds, San Diego Padres, the A's, the Giants.

Irene read a book at my first Giants game as we sat in Candlestick Park's left-field bleachers for hours until Mike Ivie's game-winning, extra-inning hit. My mom was not a sports fan. Nor was my father, not that I can recall; he died when I was 12. My mom was a medical researcher at Stanford for over 20 years. She loved to read and stored hundreds of her books in my childhood bedroom. She grew up in Buffalo ("worst climate in the world"), made high school valedictorian, went to Syracuse (Davis' alma mater) on a full scholarship but hated it there after a year. So she then earned degrees at the University at Buffalo (chemistry), Cal-Berkeley (teaching credential), and San Jose State (molecular biology). Maybe I got my writing gene from my mother because, oh boy, if you saw the Letters to the Editor section in newspapers of my youth, you'd know that Irene Inman had opinions to share/educate.

Maybe that's why I wasn't totally shocked when Davis stopped me in my tracks in the Raiders' locker room after a loss at the Oakland Coliseum. His impromptu interview with a gaggle of scribes had ended, and as I parted for the exit doors, he muttered: "I heard from your mother." What? "She wrote me a nice letter for meeting with you."

At this embarrassing moment, I wondered if my mom had written thank you notes to the thousands of athletes, coaches, team execs, and others who lent me their time. In between my stints as a 49ers beat writer (2000–2004 and 2011–present),

I was a sports columnist covering various events around the Bay Area and beyond. One of my first tasks was to cover John Madden's long-awaited induction to the Pro Football Hall of Fame. That began one of my life's most treasured relationships.

It was not because of Madden's ginormous stature in the NFL and American sports. We had a true kinship and common-sense outlook on life—perhaps through similar backgrounds as Bay Area natives who graduated from Cal Poly-San Luis Obispo, found post-grad jobs in Santa Maria, then returned to the Bay Area to raise fabulous families and never "work" a day in our lives. All I need now is to develop a revolutionary video game, win a bunch of Emmy Awards, become America's favorite pitchman, and chuckle away at life, as just one of the guys.

Madden's trust in me surely convinced Al Davis to grant the one-on-one interview I'd pursued for years. Sick as a dog, I got a call from the Raiders asking if I wanted to talk to Davis over the phone or in person primarily about him presenting Madden at the 2006 Pro Football Hall of Fame enshrinement. Without hesitation, I wanted to meet Davis in person, and to make this long story shorter, what ensued was my most memorable interview of all time. Davis and I spoke for nearly three hours in the windowless, black-and-white conference room just past his side-room office. Our official interview covered two-and-a-half hours. Then we talked off the record another 30 minutes. At some point I shared how my mother was also a native New Yorker (she from Buffalo, Davis from Brooklyn) and also attended Syracuse. He delved further.

Davis: "I haven't asked you too many questions."

Me: "Go ahead."

Davis: "Nah, I'm not too smart. What do you want to do?"

Me: "This is what I've always wanted to do."

Davis: "Do what?"

Me: "Cover professional football in the Bay Area."

Davis: "Is that what you wanted to do?"

Me: "Yeah."

Davis: "How long do you think that's going to last?"

About 15 years later, the Raiders left for Las Vegas, Davis had passed away, and, well, I'm still covering professional football.

As for my mom, she unexpectedly passed away the morning of the 49ers' divisional playoff win against the Green Bay Packers on January 20, 2024. It was a tough day, but we all got through it, including the 49ers as they used a fourth-quarter comeback to advance to a third straight NFC Championship Game and eventually the Super Bowl. Everything I have I owe to her. There are others who've helped me and deserve acknowledgment, however, in case they did not receive thank you notes from Irene Inman.

First and foremost: my angelic wife for 25 years, Jennifer Branchini, and our inspiring children—Kate, Brooke, and Grant.

My oldest sister Susan preceded me as Monta Vista High School's editor in chief. ("Don't write the X's and O's but find the human element.") My other sister, Allison, forged my fascination for competitive athletes (an enforcer on the soccer field, an A+ teacher for decades in elementary-school classrooms).

So many other family members and friends are in on this secret, too, of how I've bamboozled my way through a sports-writing career for decades. It's more than a hobby, though. My passion for journalism runs deep, and the California Scholastic Press Association workshop resets my compass each summer.

The 49ers' beat reporters are, no doubt, the nation's best collective group, balancing competitive reporting with congenial spirit with this latest crew: Matt Maiocco, Matt Barrows,

Jennifer Lee Chan, Eric Branch, Nick Wagoner, Mike Silver, Tracy Sandler, Josh Dubow, Kate Rooney, and more.

My teammates at the Bay Area News Group, present and past: Jerry McDonald, Dieter Kurtenbach, Bud Geracie, Mike Nowels, Laurence Miedema, Steve Corkran, Dan Brown, Tim Kawakami, Ann Killion, Marcus Thompson II, Dennis Georgatos, Mark Purdy, Gary Peterson, Monte Poole, Mike Lefkow, Eric Gilmore, Jimmy Durkin, Kerry Crowley, Dave Belli, Curtis Pashelka, Jon Becker, Sarah Dussault, Tom Barnidge, and the incomparable Mitch Stephens and John Cardinale.

The Bay Area honor roll also includes Ira Miller, Art Spander, Scott Ostler, Ray Ratto, and Janie McCauley, plus broadcasting buddies Vern Glenn, Greg Papa, Tim Ryan, Joe Fonzi, Brian Murphy, Matt Steinmetz, Daryle "The Guru" Johnson, Mark Willard, Dan Dibley, Bonta Hill, Damon Bruce, Tom Tolbert, Raj Mathai, Brian Dea, Dennis O'Donnell, Chris Alvarez, Mike Shumann, Kirsten Moran, and Chris Biderman.

Never forget those who gave you a chance, and my unforgettable mentors since turning pro as a 16-year-old: Terry Cress, Mike Betz, Jim Hayes, Eric Burdick, Rich Guiremand, Dan Wood, Jerry Micco, Larry Welborn, and my fellow CSPA alumni.

Photographers never get enough credit, and I have a huge appreciation for Jose Fajardo, Karl Mondon, Nhat Meyers, Terrell (and Robert) Lloyd, Michael Zagaris, Kym Fortino, Brad Mangin, and so many more.

Inheriting the 49ers beat in 2000 came with valuable mentors in waiting: Steve "Mooch" Mariucci, Greg Knapp, Jim Mora, Marty Mornhinweg, Dan Quinn, Bruce DeHaven, Richard Smith, Jason Tarver, Ted Tollner, Dr. Harry Edwards, and team chaplain Earl Smith.

Steve Young, Keena Turner, Tom Rathman, Guy McIntyre, Greg Clark, Brent Jones, Randy Cross, Joe Staley, Frank Gore, and other ex-players became valuable resources and cherished friends. Same goes for the 49ers' communications staff: Kirk Reynolds, Rodney Knox, Jason Jenkins, Chad Steele, Ryan Moore, Bob Lange, Dan Beckler, Mike Chasanoff, Corry Rush, Peter Volmut, and the current crew.

Through fair and professional reporting, mutual respect is built, and hopefully that's been the case with the 49ers' front office past and present: Eddie DeBartolo, Carmen Policy, Dr. John York, Denise DeBartolo York, Jed York, Al Guido, Paraag Marathe, as well as the personnel wizards: Bill Walsh, Terry Donahue, Scot McCloughan, Trent Baalke, John Lynch, and Adam Peters. Thanks to others in the NFL's vast landscape, including a "hi" to Amy Trask, who walked out of Davis' office as I walked in for that epic interview in 2006.

If there's one life lesson I can share through all this, make sure you know how your mother is doing and, while you're at it, ask how others' are. It's that human connection that makes sports so intentionally invigorating (I.I., like my mother's initials). Thanks, Mom.

Sources

Newspapers

San Jose Mercury News
Contra Costa Times
San Francisco Chronicle
San Francisco Examiner

Books

Maiocco, Matt. *San Francisco 49ers: The Complete Illustrated History*. MVP Books. 2013

Georgatos, Dennis. *Stadium Stories: San Francisco 49ers*. The Globe Pequot Press. 2005

Newhouse, Dave. *The Million Dollar Backfield: The San Francisco 49ers in the 1950s*. Frog, Ltd. 2000

Websites

NFL.com
NFLGSIS.com
ProFootballReference.com
TheAthletic.com
NBCSportsBayArea.com

Museums

Edward J. DeBartolo Sr. Hall of Fame, Levi's Stadium, Santa Clara, California

Pro Football Hall of Fame, Canton, Ohio

About the Author

Cam Inman started covering the 49ers and the NFL in 2000, doing so as a beat writer and columnist for the Bay Area News Group and *San Jose Mercury News*. His first book, *The Best Bay Area Sports Arguments*, was released in 2008. Born in Santa Clara and raised in Cupertino, California, he lives in Pleasanton with his family, plus his running shoes, golf clubs, and laptop.